GOING PUBLIC

Schooling for a Diverse Democracy

GOING PUBLIC

Schooling for a Diverse Democracy

JUDITH RÉNYI

The New Press
New York

Published in the United States by The New Press, New York
Distributed by W. W. Norton & Company, Inc.,
500 Fifth Avenue, New York, NY 10110

LIBRARY OF CONGRESS CATALOGING-IN-PUBLICATION DATA

Rényi, Judith.
    Going public : schooling for a diverse democracy /
Judith Rényi.—1st ed.
        p.   cm.
    ISBN 1–56584–083–6
    1. Education—United States—Aims and objectives.
2. Intercultural education—United States. 3. Educational equalization—United States. 4. Educational
change—United States. 5. Education—Social aspects—
United States. I. Title.
LA210.R46 1993
370'.973—dc2   92–56918

Book design by Laura Lindgren

Established in 1990 as a major alternative to the large, commercial publishing houses,
The New Press is the first full-scale nonprofit American book publisher outside of
the university presses. The Press is operated editorially in the public interest, rather
than for private gain; it is committed to publishing in innovative ways works of educational, cultural, and community value that, despite their intellectual merits, might
not normally be "commercially" viable. The New Press's editorial offices are located
at the City University of New York.

Printed in the United States of America.
93 94 95 96   9 8 7 6 5 4 3 2 1

This book is dedicated to my favorite English teacher, who once said, "Teachers must have three attributes: they must know the subjects they teach and must continue to learn more than they will ever teach all their lives long; they must know the tricks of the trade, which they will learn from other teachers; and they must have a good heart."

CONTENTS

ACKNOWLEDGMENTS

A major report on *The Humanities in American Life* commissioned by the Rockefeller Foundation in 1980 urged significant improvements in public education to prepare young people for a vigorous and engaged participation in our society. The report called for a vision of language, literature, and history in the formation of citizens very different from what until then had prevailed in our schools. Under the inspired leadership of Dr. Alberta B. Arthurs, the foundation began working with thousands of urban and rural teachers in schools all over the country to develop new ways of approaching these subjects. Over the past decade I have been privileged to learn from these teachers and their students about the complexities of teaching and learning in difficult circumstances, the cultivation of the mind in settings destructive of individual dignity, and the persistence of noble causes in the midst of social turmoil. Despite the difficulties, the teachers and students have triumphed in demonstrating their desire to learn and to contribute new understandings to the humanities in the United States.

This book is dedicated to all those who took part in the continuing effort to understand what it might mean to "educate a diverse America"—indeed, what any one of those words might mean. The teachers and students in American schools taught me that ultimately it is they who will construct meaning for us all through the work they do in school.

My thanks are due, therefore, to the great teachers I was privileged to have in public school, especially Mr. Hamsher, Miss Reed, and Mr. Young, and to the great teachers I have worked with over the past decade, especially Jeanette Jimenez.

The work of the teachers and students and my own learning about educating a diverse America are immensely indebted to Alberta B. Arthurs, Mary Patterson McPherson, and Constance E. Clayton, who have dedicated themselves to the support of great teachers and students. Richard H. de Lone breathed sanity, honesty, and great good humor into tireless work to make school make sense. In our last meeting before his untimely death he advised me once again on the art of the possible and the imperative to keep working to achieve the impossible.

I am very grateful to the many readers of drafts of this book; their wise guidance is responsible for any felicities it may contain but none of its many faults, which I reserve as my own responsibility. Paul LeMahieu, friend and mentor, and my colleagues Dennis Lubeck, Molefi Kete Asante, Denise McKeon, and especially Joseph Featherstone and Tanya Hamilton—all suffered through early manuscript drafts. I owe extra thanks to Richard Sterling and a very special acknowledgment to Erich Martell.

Librarians and archivists have been exceedingly helpful at Bryn Mawr College, the University of Pennsylvania, Rutgers University in Camden, Central High School in Philadelphia, and the U.S. Department of Education's Office of Educational Research Initiatives' archive of textbooks and children's literature.

I am most grateful to the Rockefeller Foundation for its enlightened and sustained support since 1983 of Collaboratives for Humanities and Arts Teaching, which has enabled me to work toward understanding multicultural education in our public schools.

My greatest debt and admiration is due to Lucy Beard, without whom the book could not have been written, and to Carol S. McGuire and Dolores M. Spena, who tirelessly corrected my mistakes and made the manuscript real. Finally, my greatest thanks are owed to Jessica and Quentin for indulging me in my work of the past decade while they brought themselves up superbly well.

A NOTE ON USAGE

As various ethnic groups continue to define themselves, preferred usages to describe them change. If I have erred in designating "Native Americans" or any other group, I apologize. I have no wish to offend or irritate; if I have done so, it is neither out of malice nor arrogance, but the result of simple ignorance.

I use "he" and "she" alternately, whenever possible, when singular third-person pronouns are required by the syntax. I prefer this to "s/he" or "they" in singular contexts, since Miss O'Day, my third-grade teacher, would never have approved.

I

AMERICAN REVOLUTION

Introduction

In the fall of 1989, as 2.3 million teachers and nearly 50 million students trudged off to public school, the president of the United States convened all of the country's governors in an unprecedented education summit at the University of Virginia in Charlottesville. This was the university Thomas Jefferson had founded in his belief that a democratic society required an educated populace. The governors pledged to work together with the president to do something new and strong and important about public education. Among the goals they shared was a belief that every American should not only go to school, but stay there long enough to graduate from high school. This belief, shared widely by Americans today, represents a revolutionary idea about who needs schooling and how many of our children should earn high-school diplomas. Less than forty years ago it would never have occurred to most Americans that we should all spend so much time in school; today, a diploma for every single one of us seems both right and fitting.

This new idea about the place of schooling in the lives of all Americans has caused us to wring our hands over high drop-out rates, which continue to prevail in many school districts, especially those serving the poor and minorities. In some big-city and rural districts where poor and minority students constitute the majority, students drop out before graduation at rates of 20 to 40 percent. Americans seem generally agreed that this is a tragedy both for the students and for the society, whose capacity to find useful work for dropouts has vastly diminished. Salaries for dropouts between the ages of 18 and 24 average no more than $6,000 a year.[1] The United States economy is no longer primarily an agricultural or a manufacturing one, each of which once required large numbers of unskilled laborers for whom schooling beyond the three Rs was unnecessary, but who could expect to support a family decently on the basis of unschooled labor alone. Today, fully one child in five is poor,[2] and the places where the unskilled poor are to be found offer few jobs of any kind. Success for a young person growing up in our failing cities or rural areas means leaving home, getting out, finding one's way to other places where jobs are available, housing is decent, and schools show promise of helping later generations to become comfortably successful Americans in their turn.

America believes that the schools in places where poverty abounds are the transforming institutions that can turn around a child's chances of economic success. This belief, sometimes called "the civic religion," says that to get an education, get out, find a job, and do well in life is the American way out of poverty and hopelessness. When the poor become productive members of our society, America as a whole succeeds, because success is defined primarily in economic terms. We need all of our children to graduate from high school because we need their productivity to keep America strong, wealthy, and constantly growing and developing.

But too many of the poor and minority communities in our country continue to attend school erratically, learn little of use to them or to the rest of us, and end up as a drag on our economy. A number of remedies for the drop-out problem have been offered. One group, spearheaded by politicians and business leaders, wants us to design our schools with an eye to student success on tests that will allow us to measure our scholastic productivity against that of other industrialized nations and not find our students wanting. Advocates of international competitiveness want a more rigorous curriculum that stresses science and mathematics, English, history, and geography at its core, that sees these subjects as the basic or common curriculum for all students, and through that common knowledge forges a strong, unified nation. Advocates of such an education enlist the help of corporate executives to sponsor experiments in every congressional district that will take the lead in demonstrating model ways of changing schools to produce this educated populace. And they want schools to imitate the marketplace, competing for corporate money to redesign themselves and competing for students in a system where parents choose schools not only on the basis of residence, but on the basis of excellence and productivity as well.

All of these are laudable goals, witnessing a profound concern among our nation's elected and business leaders that all of our children and schools take part in the economic success of the nation and further its economic ends. These reform measures come at a time when schools nationwide have already begun to reexamine themselves to better serve their students. The belief, prevalent throughout the history of public schooling in America, that the fault or problem in educating the poor is the fault or problem of the poor themselves has yielded to a belief that it is just possible that some fault might lie with the system trying to educate them. That change, very recent and new to the complex bureaucracies, politics, and big business of education in our country, has barely begun to make itself felt in schools and among teachers and the public, but it represents an unprecedented transformation of thinking. It has led to a movement in many school districts to "restructure," meaning to invite teachers, administrators, and community members to assist in joint decision-making, and to alter dramatically the organization of work in schools. Like the education summit's push for change, however, school restructuring efforts tend to focus primarily on economic and management issues; how much the teachers are paid and for what kind of work figures largely in discussions and meetings as a school sets about its effort to change.

The revolutionary idea that all students should graduate from high school has also opened up the possibility of reconceiving what and how we teach. Quietly, here and there, with stimulus from foundation and government grants, teachers have begun to change their thinking about what children know, how they learn, and therefore what the school needs to provide. This new work seeks to bring the content of America's schools into closer alignment with America's populace. Changing what and how we teach in order to educate all of our children is the subject of this book.

Until the early 1980s, the children of the poor and children of minorities were the problem. They suffered "deprivations," "lacked" things necessary for school success, and came from "deviant" backgrounds. Those deprivations and deviations from the school norm needed, in the past, to be corrected or replaced with the healthier, more normal, more moral ways of knowing and behaving that school taught. In the past, the typical attitude toward the children of the poor was to look at them as bringing to the school either nothing of value or the wrong values, which needed to be remedied. But as ethnic pride among many Americans grew during the 1970s, new ideas about the values of different ethnic groups began to surface. Teachers began to see their students as offering much deserving of respect—knowledge, culture, language, and the capacity to learn. Teachers saw that when they accorded these attributes a place in school curricula instead of dismissing them as unworthy, children discovered connections between themselves and the world of learning.

Respecting the cultures of students of all kinds has profound implications for curriculum and instruction. Unlike the structural changes advocated by politicians, business leaders, managers, and bureaucrats, however, the revolution in school curricula has little to do with economic goals and purposes. This revolution has to do with the actual daily purposes and content of school—with what Americans know and what they ought to know, with what Americans bring to school with them and what they ought to take with them when they leave at the age of seventeen. When we tamper with curriculum, we are touching on the very idea of America: what it has been, what it is, and what it ought to be. Curriculum embodies knowledge and values, morality, and the purposes of education, and the new ideas about curriculum go well beyond school as a place primarily of interest to the economic well-being of America. These ideas look at school as a place that defines us as Americans and suggests what we might become through our cultural and intellectual development. The new curriculum changes have caused a national uproar. Not everyone agrees that they have laudable goals.

The problem of what to teach in American public schools is the focus of this book. Many observers of education see no problem: they believe that we already know what to teach schoolchildren, and that we simply need to stiffen up accountability, which usually means some form of testing, to ensure that larger numbers of children will in fact learn the existing curriculum. A growing number of others, however, believe that many American children are ill-served by what is taught in school. Testing more often or changing the management of school buildings is not enough. The content of instruction must change if we are to succeed in educating everyone.

These two positions on the content of school have exploded into heated debates among educators, academics, and political figures. Since national media have given the debate some play over the last few years, the general public has also taken sides on the issue. It is not the case that much change has yet actually occurred in public-school classrooms. Our education system is a monolith not subject to easy adoption of new ideas. The challenge to traditional curricula in our public schools remains largely just a set of ideas about what children ought to learn that is not currently being taught very widely. Yet some states and locales have adopted legislative mandates that curricula become "multicultural," and many teachers and schools have begun to look about them to see what that might mean for their own settings.

This book seeks to probe the question of what we teach and what we ought to teach by providing a background for further discussion and development of the curriculum question. Many false assumptions about what has been taught in the past are made on both sides of the conflict. Many facile or merely ideological responses have been made to the challenges being brought to traditional curricula. I believe it is important to know as precisely as possible what actually has been taught in public schools and whether such teachings have been effective for children's intellectual development, before we can either review the current controversy about content or consider recommendations for the future.

The plan of this book enables us to look at the content of school history, literature, and language as these subjects developed from the beginnings of public schools in America 150 years ago to the present. With this history as background, we will be able to evaluate the curriculum wars being conducted in the name of American schoolchildren and then move on to a consideration of where we might go from here.

The revolutionary idea that we ought to educate all Americans gives rise to questions concerning how and what we offer all children in the name of education. Those questions, however, are being raised amidst salvos of attack and counterattack. I hope in the pages of this book to lead us to a quieter way of considering the issues, preparing for the future, and assisting all American children to do well in school and thereby to do well for themselves and for America.

The Making of a Revolution

❦

We want all of our children to graduate from high school. We want our schools to consider the possibility that they are poorly organized to achieve this aim. But the question of who decides what is taught in school and the basis on which school values are determined is widely disputed. Many Americans believe that we already basically know what we want our children to know, we just have to devise better methods and structures for making sure all our children learn those things. New voices have been raised, however, that say some of the things worth knowing have never been taught in school. These are things relating to what children know already, and especially children of minorities and the poor, who have been less successfully schooled in the past than the middle class. These voices say that we will never achieve the goal of school success for everyone until and unless the knowledge the children bring with them is respected, and indeed taught to develop, in school. These voices have joined a national debate that has angered and even outraged many Americans of all colors and classes.

The anger and outrage, audible on all sides of the arguments about what to teach in our schools, comes from a recognition that the determination to help all children graduate from high school has crept up on us without having caused any major changes in what we teach. Many Americans believe that what we teach should not change, but simply be offered more strongly and cohesively so that more Americans can learn to participate in what makes us great as a nation. But many Americans, and particularly Americans of color who are distressed at their children's continuing school failure, believe that that failure has to do in part with school teachings that leave them out or despise them. These critics say that schools will never reduce the drop-out rate until they teach a curriculum more inclusive of all Americans. In order to achieve the goal of school completion for all, a curriculum revolution must take place that respects the children and their knowledge and includes that knowledge in the content of school. Yes, the multicultural-education advocates say, school needs to teach a stronger, more cohesive curriculum, but that should not mean just more of the same. They say it should mean a transformed curriculum that encourages new faces to fill our senior-year classes—faces that have only sporadically appeared there in the past.

Traditionalists worry that the advocated multicultural education changes would weaken our national integrity, damage the world's most successful democracy, and fragment our polity into contentious forces splitting off in many different directions. Multicultural education, they believe, would destroy the unity of belief and loyalty to the nation that should be the primary teachings of the public schools. Multicultural education would allow each group of people, defined by ethnicity, to go its own way, neglecting in the process our national unity of purpose and democratic ideals.

Curiously, this message, advocated in national policies for the past dozen years, has stressed primarily the economic purposes of schooling and has only begun to mention the necessity of an educated populace to participatory democracy in reaction to perceived threats to that purpose from multicultural education. Advocates of multicultural education seem to pose such a threat when, in their most radical moments, they announce that education and the content of school curricula are fundamentally racist and must be changed completely to teach each ethnic group to take pride in its ethnicity and learn in school about its ethnic heritage at the expense of learning about a more general American culture. What has been taught in school until now, say such writers, is that white Anglo-Saxon culture is the equivalent of American culture, and they reject that as no longer acceptable for children of other ethnicities. There can be no unity of belief and loyalty in the United States, they claim, as long as the content of school remains primarily a content that leaves out and disrespects the cultures of its minorities.

The charge of racism does not sit well with education leaders of any kind in this country. Our national habit has been to think our public schools have offered the best opportunity to shape a liberal democracy in the history of the world, and hence our public schools are fundamentally the seat of liberal reform—the ills of society, its inequities, its poverty, would all disappear from the democracy if only we could find ways to educate all Americans equally.[3] An educated populace, in Thomas Jefferson's terms, would become a populace capable of carrying on the work of the democracy. An educated populace, in Lyndon Johnson's terms, would also overcome economic inequities and provide equal opportunities for economic success to all citizens. If only we could ensure that all children graduate from a good high school, our country would become a stronger democracy and an even greater economic success, for each of its citizens and for the nation as a whole.

Many multicultural-education advocates, however, believe that a stronger democracy and equal economic opportunity will never be achieved as long as school disregards alternative ways of knowing, believing, and feeling. Ways of knowing, they say, are intimately bound up in culture: how people use language, how they come to understand who they are, how they got to be that way, and how they characteristically shape their visions of the world. Those ways of knowing differ from ethnicity to ethnicity. Anglo-Saxon ways of knowing are only one set, which happen to conflict with other ways of knowing peculiar to African-Americans or Native Americans or other ethnic groups. To continue to impose Anglo-Saxon knowledge and ways of knowing on all of these Americans would be to assume that Anglo-Saxon ways are better than other ways, to disrespect other ways, and hence to be racist.

Those who oppose such ideas countercharge that to define knowledge by ethnicity is itself a racist notion, one which assumes that knowledge is inherent in race and ethnicity instead of being universally available to all. Multicultural education ignores what we all as human beings and as Americans hold in common, in favor of highlighting differences. American public schooling should have as its primary focus the teaching of what we share, not what divides us. The forging of a single nation out of the world's most diverse population must require that public schools take us as we come in all our multifariousness and make of us a single people. Certainly, we need to be sensitive to the need to include more knowledge about the histories of minorities and women than schools taught in the past, but that should not alter our fundamental purpose of teaching how eventually we all come to be Americans and to share a common democratic purpose.

Both sides of this debate have clashed over a profoundly important question having to do with who we are as Americans, what we hold in common, and the extent to which public school is the crucible in which that commonality is forged. The major differences between those who hold opposing positions in this debate arise over a question of ownership of the curriculum and therefore over the stories we choose to tell our children about America and Americans.

This debate has arisen recently because we have actually begun to realize the dream of educating all Americans. This nation has a tremendous success story to tell about education. In 1820, 70 percent of American workers were farmers or farm laborers. By 1870, 50 percent worked on farms and 10 percent held white-collar jobs, while the rest worked in factories and mines, on railroads, and in other industries. By 1960 less than 10 percent worked on farms, while 40 percent held white-collar jobs,[4] and today, less than 3 percent of Americans designate themselves farmers. In 1870, when the vast majority of America labored in factories and on farms, only a total of some 80,000 adolescents were enrolled in 500 high-school academies nationally, and most of these private schools could be found in the Northeast. In 1870, 16,000 students received diplomas—only 2 percent of the population of seventeen-year-olds. Of these, most continued on to college. High school, just 120 years ago, was not an end in itself but academic preparation for college and a professional life. Only forty years later, in 1910, 1.1 million Americans were enrolled in high schools; of these students 90 percent were in some 10,000 public high schools, all of which had come into being in that forty-year period. Some 15 percent of children aged fourteen to seventeen were enrolled, most no longer headed for college. These schools were an end in themselves, providing the foundation for children destined to go into the working world only after an extended education.

By the end of World War I, most states had enacted compulsory school attendance laws, and school enrollments vastly increased. But those laws could not indefinitely hold the children of the poor, whose work was needed in the grocery store and steam laundry as well as on the farm and in the mills to supplement the family income. The 85 percent of young Americans who did not enroll in high school in 1910 had to make their way in the economy through work, not education. That 85 percent included European immigrants of all kinds—Italians, Slavs, Jews, and Scandinavians as well as newly annexed Mexicans in the Southwest and West, Native Americans, Chinese, Japanese, and the vast majority of whites of English, Irish, and German descent as well. In 1910, although high-school populations had grown hugely compared to the previous generation, it was normal to work. It was abnormal to go to high school.

High-school attendance in this century has very much to do with the kind of work and the amount of leisure available to children. When child labor laws were enforced early in the twentieth century, it became less possible to supplement family income with their labor. High-school enrollments exploded between 1900 and the 1920s, as a result. These years also saw the beginnings of the Great Migration of blacks from the farms of the South to the industrial cities of the North. But the black population that moved north found itself trapped in cities whose manufacturing base was already faltering. Jobs for unskilled labor were declining in Chicago, Philadelphia, and Milwaukee as early as the 1920s. The Great Depression ruined marginal family farming as well as manufacturing industries in large parts of the country, sending new waves of unemployed whites as well as blacks out on the road in search of work. High-school enrollments continued to grow, ironically benefiting from the bleak work prospects of young, unskilled laborers. They stayed on in school for want of anyplace better to go.

While high-school attendance continued to grow steadily throughout the 1930s, significantly fewer than the majority earned a diploma. The great change to high school completion by the majority of teenagers occurred after World War II. Prosperity did it—a prosperity that created a booming economy, plenty of jobs, and the high wages that enabled most Americans of all races and income levels to keep their children out of the labor force until their late teens. While ideas of whom to educate had been evolving since the major growth of public schools at the turn of the century, revolutionary changes began only after World War II. Millions of G.I.'s returned from war to a country that wanted to build a strong peacetime economy but worried how to convert its immense war industry to peaceful purposes without suffering the catastrophic joblessness that had prevailed in the decade before the war. The solution was the G.I. Bill: the United States sent its young returning soldiers to college.

Until the late 1940s only a tiny minority of the nation had gone to college. The G.I. Bill taught the nation to believe in higher education for the majority. Ordinary men who would never have imagined that a college education was either possible or necessary found themselves capable of further study. The war had matured them, shown them a larger world that they would never have discovered in their home towns, and enlarged their visions of their own abilities. A nation of white men was transformed from the breadlines, soup kitchens, and despair of the 1930s to the corporate offices, confidence, and belief in progress of the expansive 1950s. The women who had riveted warships and conducted the business of the country during the war returned home, donned their aprons, and started producing the baby boom that, throughout the 1950s and 1960s, so increased the numbers of children that they threatened to burst the seams of the nation's public schools.

The industries that had vanished in the dust of the Depression and left a populace unhoused and unable to find work never reappeared. In their place came a new postwar economic expansion that could afford new jobs only for a more highly educated populace, one ready to expand America's power to world-wide cultural and economic leadership. American mass marketing, mass entertainment, communications, and advertising turned us into a consumer economy at home and an expansive economy abroad. We were ready to Americanize the world, and we went to school to prepare ourselves to do so.

Children of the 1950s and 1960s in turn grew up in households that expected from the start to send them to college. White America built and bought suburban homes, commuted to the cities to work, and enjoyed a prosperity and belief in America's greatness unprecedented in the history of the world. It all seemed normal, despite the too-recent memory of the ills of the 1930s. That had been an aberration, it seemed, in the strong America that could provide economic well-being for everyone. We were all going to enter the middle class. School meanwhile reinforced this image of the greatness of America, its political and ideological triumph, and its moral righteousness in an otherwise benighted world.

By 1957, the changes wrought by World War II and the G.I. Bill, domestic prosperity and the end of the industrial era, found 90 percent of adolescents aged fourteen to seventeen enrolled in high school. Many stayed longer because compulsory education laws in many states now kept children in school longer than in 1910. But 62 percent of those enrolled graduated. In 1940, 15 percent of the eighteen- to twenty-one-year-old population had gone to college. In 1959 that proportion doubled, largely due to the G.I. Bill; in 1960, 35.5 percent of the population eighteen to twenty-one went to college.[5] The high-school diploma had been, from 1900 to 1940, a final certification before work for almost all of the middle class. By the 1960s it was beginning to look as if even that was not enough. Most now began to assume that the majority of the population would go on, if not to college, at least to some form of postsecondary instruction in preparation for a career.

But what is true for the population at large is not true for specific minority groups. People of color did not partake fully of the prosperity that suburban white America was beginning to enjoy. We revolutionized who went to school and for how long for the white populace, but we had to go to court to do so for the black populace, not just once, but again and again in the 1950s and early 1960s, until we had learned to revolutionize our thinking about all Americans and put them all in school. In 1954, the Supreme Court dismantled separate schools for black Americans. After *Brown* v. *Board of Education,* public school meant public schools for all, white and black alike. Yet nearly forty years later, the full impact of that decision has not been realized.

While graduation rates have slowly but steadily improved for all minorities, large numbers of Hispanic, some African-American, and many Native American children have been left behind. With an overall urban school drop-out rate of one-third, as many as 45 percent of Native Americans drop out before earning the diploma. Such minority groups, moreover, dispro-portionately find themselves in classes for low achievers. One-fourth of all Native Americans and one-third of Native American boys are in special education classes. Those few Native Americans who make it to postsecondary education tend to be women in their thirties, who earn their diplomas through the General Education Development (GED) program. According to 1990 census data, however, 26 percent of all American nineteen-year-olds have not completed high school.[6] Belated attention to minority school completion rates did not occur until the 1960s. In studying differential school success for white and black populations, we learned that such success had more to do with the economic success of the population as a whole in a particular school building than with personal attributes of race or class of individual students. The 1965 Coleman report, *Equality of Educational Opportunity*, told the Congress of the United States that the nation's schools were still segregated, that they closely resembled each other in terms of how they were organized and what they taught, and that the ways in which they differed (e.g., library collections, teaching staff, spending) had little impact on differences of student performance. What made a difference for any one child was the extent to which that child attended school alongside others who were affluent. A black child—even a poor black child—in a middle-class school had a greater chance of academic success than a rich white child in a school largely filled with children of the poor.[7]

By the mid-1960s the War on Poverty was in full swing. It sought to address the economic woes of the inhabitants of cities, who were overwhelmingly poor and often black, left behind by white flight. The schools became the focus for social policies that sought to remedy the wrongs left unresolved by the courts. As a nation, we had already decided that everyone should finish high school. But not everyone conformed to the image of the white middle-class Americans for whom academic study was designed. Head Start would help prepare children suffering the deprivations—particularly the cultural deprivations—of poverty to enter school with the kind of knowledge white middle-class children got at home. Readiness for school meant knowing the names of colors and numbers before first grade and interacting with adults in ways acceptable to the norms of school. The poverty programs of the 1960s for the first time provided federal tax dollars to schools to serve the poor. The Elementary and Secondary Education Act of 1965 and its various programs provided money to states and districts based on poverty formulas that put extra resources into schools to compensate for children's deprivations. These programs defined the problem of lack of student success as lack of children's knowledge, for which school could compensate. The education revolution was in full swing; everyone would go to school, but school would not change its habits to accommodate everyone. The burden of change rested on the *children's* need to change to fit in.

Despite the War on Poverty, even despite the gains made for children in Head Start and its successes in remediating math and reading, poverty persisted and got worse. By the early 1980s the Secretary of Education, Terrell Bell, announced that ours was "a nation at risk" because our public schools had lost their capacity to produce a well-educated populace. Bell's report heralded a decade of changes. He told us that all our schools were failing, that even in white suburbia the best that could be said of schools was that they had declined from striving for excellence to being content to wallow in mediocrity. We asked too little of our students and we got what we deserved. We needed to strengthen our standards everywhere, get rid of the free-for-all education of the sixties that had produced the shopping-mall high school, and get back to basics. The states responded with a will. State legislatures launched new testing programs meant to shake up lackadaisical districts and improve their results. Getting those reading and math scores up was the new battle cry heard in state after state. Publishing all the districts' scores side by side allowed us to embarrass those districts that failed to do a good job. The districts responded in many places by throwing away electives and making sure all the teachers taught the standardized curriculum the state was going to test. "Drill the skill" was the order of the day as teachers prepared their charges for the tests.

But these national responses to the call for improving our schools continued to disregard the nature of the target population of schoolchildren. In the period 1971–80, 78.6 percent more immigrants entered the United States than had entered in the period 1950–60. From 1900 to 1980 the white population dropped from 87.7 percent to 83.1 percent of the total, while citizens of other races increased from 12.3 percent to 16.9 percent, exclusive of the 8.1 million Hispanics who were designated "white" in 1980.[8] Twice as many different nationalities resided in the United States by 1980 as had in 1920, partly as a legacy of the changes in the Immigration and Nationality Act of 1965 that equalized ceilings for countries in Europe with those of countries from other continents. Nearly three times as many immigrants entered the United States in 1980–89 as had entered in 1951–60. In the earlier period, 48 percent of the immigrants were of European extraction. In the last decade only 10 percent came from Europe, while nearly 80 percent came from Latin and Central America and Asia.[9]

This new diversity was more equally distributed across the United States than ever before.[10] Not just port cities, but the whole of the interior of the country began to see new faces in neighborhoods, at work, and in class-rooms. Just as the U.S. population became more diverse than ever before in its history, the national call for school reform resulted in curricula more restrictive than they had been in the 1960s and 1970s, demanding more testing, more standardization, more containment, and less diversity in what was taught. The diverse population did not in this case cause the restrictive school reforms, but the effect of such reforms was to fall on a more diverse population than ever before.

Despite the increase in testing and standardization, the children of the poor went on failing disproportionately, even when the state tests were so easy as to be laughable measures of knowledge. The same districts that were at the bottom in the seventies stayed at the bottom in the eighties; the chil-dren of the poor and the children of minorities kept dropping out. Research showed they started giving up in third grade, were mental dropouts by sev-enth, and left at the first legal opportunity to do so in tenth. The racial differ-entials in high-school graduation rates persisted. According to the Children's Defense Fund only 58.4 percent of black eighteen- and nineteen-year-olds and 52.4 percent of Latinos of that age have diplomas. By the ages of twenty and twenty-one the gap narrows significantly for whites (85.2 percent with diplomas) and blacks (81.5 percent) but stubbornly remains at 54.9 percent for Latinos ("An Advocate's Guide to Improving Education," September, 1990).[11]

Throughout the 1980s substantial gains were, however, made. The Scholastic Aptitude Test (SAT) scores of black children rose steadily in math and English, and their drop-out rates fell.[12] Minority college participation rates also showed major gains.[13] Improved family income, raised expecta-tions for college attendance, and possibly affirmative action seem to have increased the proportion of Americans who were ready and able to go on to higher education in the last decade.

Many teenage dropouts find an alternative way of earning the diploma later in life: in 1989, 81.1 percent of nineteen-year-olds, 86.5 percent of twenty-four-year-olds, and 86.9 percent of twenty-nine-year-olds had com-pleted high school.[14] For members of the working poor who cannot afford to stay in school until their late teens, it has been common practice to drop out before receiving a diploma and then to return to earn an equivalency diploma if and when it becomes economically important to do so.

Despite the very high number of GED equivalent diplomas earned by older adults, we prefer to educate all Americans in their teen years. Fifteen percent of our children still drop out of school.[15] Why can't they, like the rest of the population, succeed just as well in school as we and our ancestors did?

Why should there be any need for special changes in our successful formula, our tried-and-true method of Americanizing everyone?

There are two differences between this last 15 percent of schoolchildren today and the immigrants and the poor of the past. First, in the past we did not in fact ever expect the poor to finish school. We expected them to drop out, to go to work, and to succeed economically so that, perhaps, their children or grandchildren would have the leisure to afford to finish school. Immigrants were once content to postpone for a future generation what they did not expect for themselves. But now we are looking at the first generation of the poor who are expected to finish school whether or not doing so is economically viable for them. They are being asked to believe that school itself is the route to the middle class. Although this can be true, it has more often been the case that the capacity to go to school for twelve years was the *result* of having middle-class means. We now seek to educate the poor through the end of high school for the first time in our history—the first such attempt by any nation in the world.

The second difference between the poor of today and those of the past is that the poor Italians and Irish and Jews and even Scandinavians of the past were "voluntary immigrants," to use the phrase of anthropologist John Ogbu: people who chose to come to America to seek their fortunes or escape the ills of their homelands, although they might suffer both racial and other forms of discrimination when they came. Americans of African descent never chose to come here. Native Americans never chose to be Americans. Many Hispanics were incorporated into an America that annexed formerly Mexican territories.

More important to their perception of school than their involuntary origins, perhaps, is the fact that generations of these groups have earned diplomas without it making a difference to their social or economic status. Furthermore, many members of these groups perceive the educational opportunities available to them as below par in comparison to what is available to other Americans. A recent Gallup poll reported that 83 percent of American whites believe that blacks and other minorities have the same educational opportunities as whites. Only 38 percent of blacks believe these opportunities are equal.[16] Such differences in perception signify a serious rift, matched by the differentials in drop-out rates between whites and blacks, differences in achievement, and ultimately, differences in hope for the future.

If the political leaders of this country and the population as a whole genuinely want all children to graduate from high school, then we must all of us take a very careful look at what divides us racially and ethnically in our perceptions of the current state of education and in the remedies needed to achieve our goals.

At present, the division seems to run along the following lines. Those who are successful and empowered seek to reinvigorate the common core of learning that has served them well for 150 years; they believe in the American dream of individual effort and hard work paying off with academic and economic success. Those for whom such effort, work, and achievement have not resulted in economic success, even after generations have gone by, take issue with the common core of learning because they see it as one of the ways in which white America excludes them from the promise of education. They seek to bring collective pressure to bear on changing the common core of learning, believing that success will come only from group solidarity. They feel the myth of individual success will not apply to them as long as racism obliterates the unique merits in individuals by lumping them together in ethnically stigmatized groups.

In all the raging debate about the schools, we have heard much about race and ethnicity and little about class, yet class also persists in defining much of what school is about. Multicultural educators, angry with school ways, often ascribe to racism school's will to make children learn middle-class manners and morals, sit still, dutifully complete mindless tasks, follow orders, and restrict expansive habits. Such teachings originated, however, in classism. Confusions of this kind occur when, as often happens, the poor who are the targets of school reprimands happen also mainly to be black or other minorities.

This becomes an important issue to keep in mind if we remember that the purpose of the revolution in schooling is to reach the remaining one-fifth of our population, the children of the poor, and to help them find a way to stay in school until graduation. While much of the contention over how to go about doing that has to do with cultural differences deriving from ethnicity, some of the difficulties children experience in school also have to do with class issues. Our intention, as a nation, is to educate a social class that has never in history been educated before. I believe that in order to do this, assumptions about schooling and the links between education and middle-class ways need to be reexamined very carefully.

Education in the world has undergone two major changes in the past two millennia. In the first phase, literacy and numeracy were necessary for two purposes: to conduct the administration of wealth and power, and to preserve and transmit sacred texts. Educated clerks and accountants have always been needed to carry out the first purpose and priests to carry out the second. In ancient China as well as Sumeria and Mexico, writing developed and was transmitted to new generations in order to count and record food stores and other forms of excess wealth and to preserve stories about the divine origins of the kingship and the people. Not until the last few hundred years have the ranks of the literate and numerate increased significantly from a relatively small coterie.

In the Western world, the second phase of education occurred in the sixteenth century, when the Reformation and the invention of moveable type put sacred texts in the hands of massive numbers of people. Literacy and numeracy expanded well beyond the relatively few merchants and priests who had needed them until then. Protestantism brought to Christianity a will for each soul to interpret sacred texts for himself. The Renaissance also introduced to large numbers of people the possibility of reading secular texts. The middle class began to grow, partly defined by its economic place and partly by its literacy. But the texts at the center of their education continued to consist primarily of the sacred texts of the priestly class and the high-culture texts of the wealthy and powerful.

The third phase is upon us here and now in democratic America. Literacy and numeracy and the texts on which we center their acquisition should be available to all, we say. Yet the texts we use in teaching literacy and numeracy still seem to be partly descended from the priestly and royal purposes of ancient days and partly from the creations of the literate middle classes of the past few hundred years. Because of this history, the texts of school seem to concentrate on matters alien to the poor—to fail to give them voice. If we are seriously going to try to educate this last 20 percent, we need to consider how we are going to assist them in finding their voice so that they too can contribute to the dialogue through which educated people interact with each other across the ages. The revolution that wants all children to be successfully schooled suggests that the poor must enter that conversation and thereby make a new literacy and vision for us all.

In order to enter that conversation all students will need access to a powerful liberal education, but for most of this nation's history, high school curricula have not been studied by the majority of Americans. The common core that has been available to the poor as well as almost everyone else has been the elementary curriculum. As we shall see, that curriculum has never sought to develop intellectual capacities beyond minimal skills and has never contained very much of what we commonly call the Western liberal tradition.

As high schools developed at the end of the nineteenth century, a debate arose as to whether the most recent immigrants should be allowed to attend at all. The huge waves of new, diverse students threatened to overwhelm the schools. The response was a compromise: a two-track system developed in the early twentieth century that reserved the liberal arts for the elites and invented a new set of subjects called the "mechanical and manual arts" for the laboring masses. What little of history, mathematics beyond mere numeracy, science, second languages, and literature had until then existed in the common schools was removed from them, delayed until high school, and offered only in the academic track. Until World War II that content remained out of reach of 85 percent of American students. What was left in the elementary education that most Americans received bore little intellectual resemblance to what was taught in high school. That split in content between elementary and secondary curricula continues to this day. In elementary school, children read what educators and editors compose for basal reading series; they hit ninth grade and get Shakespeare for the first time. Youngsters fool around with arithmetic worksheets for eight years, reach ninth grade, and face algebra. Ninth grade is generally perceived to be a terrible year for school failure, and no wonder. Little in the first eight years of schooling prepares students for the shock of the academic high-school curriculum.

Our common school heritage, in this century as in the last, is the culture taught in the lower grades. In 1870 only 2 percent of seventeen-year-olds graduated from public and private high schools combined; 6.4 percent in 1900. Most of these were girls headed for brief teaching careers of their own. In 1898, 95 percent of all school enrollments were in elementary schools, with an average stay in school of five years. In 1920, nearly two-thirds of the relevant age group were enrolled in high schools, but only 16.8 percent graduated. Compulsory education laws by 1930 raised those figures to 73.1 percent enrolled and less than one-third graduated, and by 1940, 79.4 percent enrolled and slightly over one-half graduated. Meanwhile, for African-Americans, who embraced schooling wholeheartedly after emancipation, larger percentages (18.7 percent) attended public schools in St. Louis than whites (12.9 percent) in 1890; in 1897, 86 percent of six- to thirteen-year-old black children attended school in Philadelphia. Black literacy rose from 42.9 percent in 1890 to 90 percent in 1940, accompanied by a vastly increased high-school attendance rate.[17] By 1960, 99.5 percent of all seven- to thirteen-year-olds were enrolled in school. What they learned there, however, perpetuated the distinctions between the economic classes.

Since the early nineteenth century, highbrow subjects have been ridiculed as unsuitable for the masses, abstract studies that working people don't need.[18] Vocational education tracks satisfied the desire for a high-school education without having to offer academic subjects to the poor and people of color. Tracking into remediation and into vocational-technical programs has disproportionately kept these groups out of the academic subjects, even if they enroll in high school and even when they earn the diploma.

The question before us, therefore, is one of rethinking the curriculum for everyone—how to offer a more substantive and valuable liberal education in all the grades of school and for all the students. The task before us is the invention, for the first time, of a common core of learning that will reach all of the students and engage them all in the conversation of the educated. This is an exciting venture, and perhaps the most important revolution in the history of literacy. It goes beyond questions of economic purposes for school, even beyond national or patriotic purposes. It goes to the heart of questions having to do with civilized humanity and what it means to invite all people of all races and economic circumstances to participate in civilization.

On all sides of the contentious and acrimonious debate over multicultural education, deeply held beliefs—for some, beliefs on which successful lives have been built—are being challenged. But I hope to describe in this book a series of themes that have shaped American public schooling, creating conditions there that are intolerable for the children of the poor. Because the poor of today are disproportionately people of color, what used to be a class issue has become a race issue. Race issues surface in public schools today as never before because race issues no longer focus merely on access to the school building; they now focus on access to the school curriculum.

The themes we shall explore form a complex of ideas that shape the way we teach history, literature, and language. We shall look at the link between America's profound religiosity and its teachings about class. We will see that school has treated the poor not as individuals capable of development, but as members of groups with inherited, unalterable attributes. By embracing a religiosity that prefers the heart to the mind and feeling to thought, schools have created a curriculum designed to limit mental development. We will also examine the industrial economy that pulled the poor away from the countryside and into the cities, a schooling that sought to intervene between children and their parents, and a promise that school would provide economic salvation—a promise that has too often proven empty for children of color.

This book traces the sources of this array of themes not in the political ideology of Anglo-Saxon democracy, but in the Romantic theories of German philosophy. It shows the difficulty of creating a political definition for our nation in the face of Romantic theories of culture that carried the day and still prevail. It traces the danger that racial theories embedded in romanticism continue to inform our ideas about nationalism and to infect the school curriculum in its efforts to build nationalist fervor. Nationalism is the ultimate theme. What role has school played to create it, and how will it fare when school must include the children of the poor in its portrait of America?

The building of the nation, its public schools, and this complex of ideas about who we are collectively as Americans took place primarily in the period before 1930. The rest of this century has softened the edges and buried the themes deeply in more benign curricula than prevailed in the past. But these themes survive in too many unexamined assumptions at the heart of the curriculum. In attempting to uncover these, we will reveal the extent to which critics of our one best system of education also fall prey to the same complex of unexamined beliefs. Finally, we will sit in a borderland, where neither the civic religion school teaches nor the radical critiques of this belief system can obscure our vision, to see what possibilities for a new and different American landscape might unfold before us.

Caveats

~

Public education in the United States, particularly in districts serving the poor, has many ills we will not be able to touch on in this book. Children who come to school hungry, sick, or abused, who walk violent streets, and whose home life is in disarray suffer many social ills schools cannot and should not be expected to correct. The health, housing, employment, and crime conditions of inner-city life produce evils that cry out for attention, not just in the schools, but in other social institutions and by other social means as well. Other evils exist that this book will not address. I have visited too many high schools where a teacher never requires homework because she has only one set of books to use with four or five different classes; where teachers assign readings they don't approve of because those are the only books the school owns; where school library doors are locked or collections woefully inadequate because the school can no longer afford a professional librarian; where students have no time to take a second-language course because they have an extra requirement in remedial math; where teachers cannot take the students to museums or on field trips because there is no money for a bus; where it's impossible to teach a coherent course of study because, of the thirty students enrolled, a different fifteen turn up each day; where metal detectors are necessary at school doors because kids bring weapons; where no lunch is offered because the cafeteria too often becomes a theater for violence; where children cannot concentrate on learning because they missed breakfast, ate french fries at midnight, and were out until 2:00 A.M.; and where families move so often that children change schools six times a year and never have any teacher long enough to learn to read.

The disruptions and evils schools, especially schools serving the poor, are prey to in our times are such that it is a miracle that teachers manage to teach as well as they do. All of these and many, many more social and bureaucratic forces are at work on any given day to make teaching and learning difficult, if not impossible, for many of our children. The context for learning in our urban and many of our rural public schools is simply not civilized, yet that should not deflect us from taking a look at the content of that teaching and learning. Any reading of *Education Week,* a national journal that reviews public education for professionals, will show that most of its articles cover topics from asbestos to malfeasance of administrators to murder to budget woes—anything and everything about the politics and management of schools. All of these are important matters for concern, but what too often gets lost is the question of what and how to teach, and particularly the role of the content of school in helping or hindering children from access to learning. Remembering that social conditions and management and politics and money all have their roles to play in schooling the poor, we will nevertheless look only at the role of the curriculum in our schools.

Changing the curriculum would mean that some 2.3 million teachers, to mention only one group engaged in schooling, would need to concern themselves with the question of change as well. In my work helping teachers to identify new curricula and to try them out in classrooms, I have supported only tens of thousands to undertake a difficult, lengthy process of change. It has taken, for each teacher, a minimum of three to four years of very hard work and many thousands of dollars' worth of professional development resources to make new curricula possible. Such teachers are only beginning to demonstrate the validity of the changes they have made in the classroom. The resulting implications for the resources, time, and energy needed to make a difference for all our children are not addressed here.

Most teachers work hard to help students learn. Our nation's teachers are a dedicated, caring, hardworking lot who persist in their efforts to teach despite the vexations and interferences of crushing bureaucracies and public blame. Such work is often tedious and thankless. The teachers I have met have been, on the whole, intelligent, energetic professionals, knowledgeable in their fields, and able to face each day with a renewed commitment to taking the children one step closer to acquiring the abilities they will need for success in life. In describing the many stupidities of school in this book, I in no way wish to cast aspersions on teachers or to suggest that fault lies with them for injuring children's capacity to learn. Those injuries have mostly resulted from well-meaning but misguided policies and actions on the part of us all, from presidents to school reformers, textbook manufacturers to public legislatures. Over many years, we have built a public-school idea unrivalled in the world; we wish to make it even better, but will not be able to do so as long as poorly conceived efforts misfire in the attempt.

With these caveats in mind, let us take a look at our public schools—what they teach and how they might reconsider what they teach—to make it possible to do what has never been done before: to educate everybody, including the poor.

The Common Core
of Learning

$\smile$

To appreciate the full impact of the revolution about who should go to school and for how long, we need to remember that American public schooling has a relatively brief history. In the early years of our nation a debate about the place of education in the new democracy formed along two lines: whether the purpose of education was to preserve the fragile union by teaching a single moral vision to all, or whether education would enable the people to know enough to make their own political and moral choices.[19] By the 1830s and 1840s, privately supported schools had sprung up in towns and rural districts everywhere in the growing country, but more so in the North and West than in the South. Schools were locally devised and locally supported, principally by private subscription. In big cities, however, schools were organized by charitable groups to provide for the poor an education they could not provide for themselves.

In the decades just before the Civil War, a major movement began among reformers who wished to establish publicly supported common schools for all Americans. These so-called common schools would be regulated by the states and centrally organized; they would mix the economic classes to create democracy through rich and poor alike sharing a common school heritage. Common schools were what we now call elementary schools, and the common culture taught in them had to do with reading, writing, and arithmetic. Common schools did not generally include students of color.

The curriculum that developed in common schools was created primarily by Protestant ministers from New England and the mid-Atlantic states, where the common school movement got its start and where the printing houses existed that eventually published the textbooks for the schools. Religion thus informed much of the nineteenth-century curriculum. Pedagogy also meant a matter of repeating in school the catechistical methods of Sunday school. You learned the alphabet the way you learned the Creed, by repeating out loud a list of moral and religious precepts for each letter in the alphabet.

The Northwest Ordinance of 1787 had set the purposes of state-run schooling in the following order: "Religion, morality, and knowledge being necessary to good government and the happiness of mankind, schools and the means of education shall forever be encouraged."[20] After the Civil War, schools became less overtly religious in character, but retained fundamental assumptions of the earlier era about morality and the relation of different classes of people to morality. To be middle-class was to boast of inherited moral goodness; to be poor was to suffer inherited moral turpitude.

The poor, therefore, were considered inherently in need of school learning, whereas the middle class were considered the embodiment of what school taught. Schooling in America has a long history of promising economic and political results but delivering moral content and methods, and doing so primarily in order to change the morality of the poor to meet the requirements of employers and the government for social and political stability. Nineteenth-century schools carried out what amounted to a moral crusade against the ways of the poor; the 1960s carried out a war. According to one education historian, the curriculum consisted of a "battle between industry and idleness, cleanliness and filth, quiet obedience and unruly independence." New York City's population in 1845 was 35 percent foreign-born, but by 1855 when the common schools were in place, 50 percent were foreign-born, disproportionately poor, and crime-ridden. The schools were created explicitly to purify and cleanse the society of the filth and vice these people were believed to harbor. Taught and administered by Protestant clergy, public schools took on a missionary character designed to save the poor from their inherently evil character. By the late nineteenth century, any and all differences from the school norms of religion, of social habits, and of means were viewed as moral defects that the schools were set up to transform.[21]

At the same time schools became highly bureaucratized and standardized, offering everyone the same curriculum in organized grades and classes, using efficient methods that were not dependent on knowledgeable teachers but that did allow central supervisors and state bureaucracies to manage and control, from a distance, what went on in the schoolroom.

The content of school was seen from the start as a method of unifying disparate people with disparate beliefs and preventing mob rule. In the process, some freedom of thought and opinion was sacrificed on the alter of stability.[22] Pluralism, a problem from the start, had been explicitly rejected by school reformers from Noah Webster, who wanted to form a single national character through a unique new American language, to the present, when federal leaders and others wish to reassert the centrality of a single national heritage in school.

The tensions central to a democracy, between the need for social and political stability on the one hand and freedom of thought and action on the other, have pulled against each other in public schools from the beginning. American public schools have managed, paradoxically, to organize themselves locally but to emerge as highly conformist nationally. Without a national curriculum, we have a de facto curriculum that looks much the same in Alaska, Florida, rural Arkansas, and New York City. Some of that conformity arises because schools were founded to create it, some because textbook publishing developed a national mass market in the nineteenth century and has remained a nationwide business, and some because teaching methods developed that aimed for efficiency and control as the highest good. A quiet, orderly class with everyone doing the same task diligently became our idea of how schoolrooms should look.

Opposition to the common school movement has come throughout its history from those threatened by its conformity to a Protestant, capitalist, and English ethos—from the Irish, the Italians, even the Germans, the Chinese, the Japanese; from the workers and the independent-minded.[23] It is nothing new to find in the 1990s that both multiculturalist and fundamentalist religious groups alike consider school curricula ranged against them.

Throughout the history of public schools various ethnic and religious groups have protested against school teachings. More recently, people of color have also discovered that in order to make gains, or even to draw the attention of the otherwise indifferent white populace to their special plight, they were obliged to act collectively to protest inequities and demand reforms. Black, Hispanic, and Native American children, for example, variously experience disproportionate ills in school. Their success rates are low and drop-out rates high, and they often find themselves in low-achieving classes. Stigmatized by society and failing to find that school is as helpful in achieving the American dream for them as it has been for whites, they have formed themselves into groups, not at first of their own volition, but by the will of the white majority that so stigmatized them. By the mid-1960s the Black Power movement was asserting that a group could take on the power of the majority by aggressive rejection of everything for which the majority stood. Group activism has, since then, become a major political force in the United States not only to gain civil rights, but also social equities not attainable by law.

If school success was too slow and too discriminatory in the 1970s and 1980s, minority groups would redress those inequities by aggressive political action in local districts. Big-city systems staffed by white teachers and white administrators changed in city after city in the 1980s to black and Hispanic administrations. Aggressive campaigns to increase the ranks of minority teachers were carried out. Systems that had served mostly white populations in the 1950s were often, by the 1980s, mostly black and variously Hispanic, Chicano, or Latino depending on the terms used in various parts of the country. Asian students and other immigrants settled into districts every-where as a result of new immigration policies. Diversity became a fact of life in every state of the nation. Collective action to assert group identity took place in school-board elections, superintendents' appointments, and the extent to which community members made demands on schools to respond to the special needs of their children. Diversity, no longer a "problem" con-fined to a handful of cities, had become an issue for all Americans in schools everywhere.

Group action and group politics fix on the schools as the route to com-munity salvation. People speaking on behalf of remedies for their groups—African-Americans, Hispanics, Native Americans, and others—look to a history of success in making gains for minorities that, for the past thirty years, has depended on collective action. It's a position that says, *you* insisted in the past that we be treated like a group; now we're going to act as a group and take over. Those political leaders of our country who find group activism divisive are people in positions of great power. They have often of late included the heads of federal agencies, the governors of the states, and those academics who feel that the nation figured out how to unify itself through the schools in the period after the 1870s and should just carry on that tradition. All of these believe independent minority groups, each pulling in different directions, will fragment the society. If African-Americans take over a school district here and Native Americans there and Hispanics in a third place, and each group devises a curriculum of its own, the common cause and the common weal will disintegrate. Far better to continue to believe each of us achieves success or failure by our individual efforts, not our group affiliations, and that our schools should all teach commonly held beliefs and values. This argument on behalf of individu-alism has been offered in justification of the traditional standardized curriculum in the hope of producing a standardized populace. The contra-dictions seem to escape its advocates.

Schools were founded not to cultivate the intellectual and personal development of poor individuals, but to eliminate the collective ills of their

group—crime, vice, and immorality. Hence schooling promoted a conformity to the white, middle-class group's characteristics, so as to mend social
evils, not necessarily to cultivate individual capacities.[24] Remedies for group
ills are administered by group as well—schools have to prove they serve a
collective of the poor in order to receive federal funds to address that group's
needs. If group test scores go up, the school is deemed no longer to serve the
needy, even though individuals may still require help. It is disingenuous,
therefore, for federal officials to deplore other reform efforts expressed in
terms of group needs. Schools and government agencies have consistently
designed programs that failed to address individuals, even while claiming
that the individual was to blame if school failed to teach her.

Nineteenth-century common schools and twentieth-century school
people of all kinds also saw it as their duty to separate poor children from
the harmful effects of their families.[25] In the first half of the nineteenth century, when charity schools were just getting off the ground and existed side-
by-side with academies for which one had to pay, the major difference
between the two was that only in the charity schools was the purpose of education to intervene between the children and their parents.[26] Some teachers
and administrators of city and rural schools today continue to talk of the
harmful home environments from which the children come and their duty
as educators to intervene on behalf of the children. "They" don't speak correctly; "they" don't have a resident father; "they" this and "they" that still
characterize too many educators' descriptions of their students.

This patronizing attitude toward the lives of children has its origins in
the industrial revolution. An agricultural economy centers education and
work in the home. In an industrial society the workplace and the home split.
Parents lose their authority as educators of their young for the family farm
or store. Nineteenth-century schools intervened to educate the young in the
qualities needed by the mill and the factory. Greater literacy was required in
the industrial age; in the positive sense, schooling became necessary for
workers as well as for managers. The drive for efficient factories was paral-
leled by an increasing drive for efficient, controlled, centralized schools.
More and more family responsibilities were taken on by schools and by the
state bureaucracies that ran them, at the expense of family responsibility. To
learn meant to leave home behind.[27]

School was often designed to insure that the destinies of children would
match their origins. Individuals were perceived to be limited in their
capacity for development to the extent that they were members of groups.
Class, race, and sex could so limit development; schools were at once universal and limiting—open to all but differential in treating the poor, those of

color, and women. Schools were more free and fair here than anywhere in the history of the world, but they were not free enough.

In the twentieth century, I.Q. testing and tracking into different programs of study have given a scientific patina to the nineteenth-century belief that group membership limits individual potential. For most of our century, testing and tracking have resulted in children of the poor and minorities ending up in curricula that destine them for low-level working lives.

Much of the current dispute over the content of school curricula either takes issue with or wishes to reassert the traditional content of the Western, liberal arts education in history, literature, and language. These three areas of the curriculum, more so than mathematics, science, or any other subject, have been used over the years to construct the national identity and to assign to individuals their place in it. In order for us to understand more clearly the curriculum we have in our schools, for good or for ill, we will look at each of these subjects as they were shaped by American public schools. The history we taught in the past, the changes it underwent as public schooling came into being, and the current efforts of many to tinker with it today, will form the subject of part two. The question of how schools developed and whether they taught a canon, or limited list, of literary works, and the uses to which literature has been put in public schools will come under scrutiny in the third part. The fourth will review the troubled history of language in our public schools, from the Revolution to the present day. We will see how language learning of all kinds, including English for native speakers, English for children of immigrants, and second languages for everybody, have bumped along a rocky road for more than 200 years, reflecting changing ideas of the relationship of language to nationalism.

History, literature, and language form the core of what public schools select to teach from out of all of the humanities. The humanities usually designate all studies that deal with human, rather than natural, creations. They also define what we usually mean by *culture*—the acquired attributes of a people living in society with each other. The sciences and mathematics, physical education, and all the other subjects taught in school also make up part of the culture peculiar to school; I do not treat these, however, although they are of equal importance not only to school culture, but also to the need for curriculum reform that I hope to prove in these pages. School culture, for instance, too often praises achievement in sport above achievement in academics, feeding a society that ranks these different achievements accordingly. School culture also differentiates its expectations for achievement in math and science according to race and gender. But because most of the debate over multicultural education concentrates on the content of history, literature, and language, I leave math and science untouched in this book.

In the fifth part we will take a close look at the multicultural-education debate in America. Knowing the history of the humanities as they have been shaped by public school, we will be better able to understand where the terms and forms of this debate came from. In the final part, we will see if we can elaborate some conclusions as to how U.S. public education might develop in order to achieve its aim of reaching the entire population.

Schools have failed the poor, but in the process they have failed all of us. The minimalist common culture taught in our schools is often too poor in spirit, intellectually thin, undemanding, and plain dull to excite anyone at all about the idea of learning. Our problem is less that school teaches too much Anglo-Saxon culture than that it teaches too little of any culture.

This country has done more to educate more people of diverse backgrounds than any other at any time, but much still remains to be done to transform our schools into genuinely democratic institutions. In the final part of this book we will also look at some ways in which teachers in schools are beginning to realize that dream. Their work and the work produced by students in their classrooms fulfills the promise of our revolution by allowing the West to enter a third phase in the history of literacy. The first phase served the powerful and wealthy; the second, the middle class; this last will serve the poor. This is the revolution that says that education begins when children take something they know as a starting place from which to discover what they don't yet know. This is the revolution that begins with particulars and with the cultures of the children and follows a skein of thought until it leads to the general. This is the revolution that brings the children of the poor into the conversation of a civilization they will help us to construct.

II

HISTORY LESSON

*Our country, right or wrong! When right, to be
kept right; when wrong, to be put right!*
CARL SCHURZ

American Mythology

~~~

When we send children to school we expect that much of what they learn there will help them to understand what America is, how it got to be that way, and how we come to think of ourselves as its citizens. This instruction primarily takes place in the branch of learning schools call the "social studies." Since the 1920s, when the term first entered school curricula, it has become a catchall for a broad array of humanities and social sciences, including civics, psychology, economics, anthropology, and human relations. To most of us, however, the heart and soul of the social studies are history and geography, with the major emphasis on narratives chronicling the European encounter with the North American continent, its colonization, the establishment of an independent United States, and its subsequent history. Secondarily, our children also learn something of the history of the rest of the world. This part will focus on the way in which the narratives of U.S. and world history have been constructed in our schools, the mythology of America and Americans that these narratives seek to instill, and the vexed problems these mythologies create for a diverse society.

Every school district and every state has developed lists of things that are supposed to happen in social studies classes, and while these lists differ somewhat from place to place and grade to grade, a general pattern seems to prevail. One of the great oddities in the pattern is the repetition of American history. In fourth or fifth grade, the school year begins with stories about Columbus and his three ships and Queen Isabella's jewelry and ends somewhere around the Civil War, after which things get a bit muddled. Then in eighth grade, we do it all over again: there's the Niña, the Pinta, and the Santa Maria, and off we go, ready for Jamestown and Plymouth Rock and the Colonies and the Revolution, and so on until June. But wait—we're not done yet. Along comes eleventh grade, and we're back to Columbus again. Each offering of the course seems to be unaware of the previous offerings and unconnected with the social studies preceding and following it.

The reason for the thrice-told tale has more to do with the history of the schools than it has to do with sensible pedagogy or the subject matter of history itself.[1] Until very recently the majority of Americans dropped out before high school, so we were obliged to teach what history we expected them to learn beforehand. History was taught in fourth or fifth grade to catch most students. In an even earlier era when there were no grades in school, young people attended school as best they could; for these children, American history began and ended with the course now taught to nine- and ten-year-olds. Later, eighth-grade U.S. history was added as a school-leavers course when the grades were organized. But the high-school course was introduced anyway, possibly because neither the course in elementary school nor the one in eighth grade was very demanding.

World history doesn't usually get taught before high school at all. Either in ninth or tenth grade, most American schoolchildren encounter a social-studies course that attempts to encompass the history and cultures of the world. You may remember it—that's the course that starts with the Ice Ages in September, tells you about cave-dwelling early *Homo sapiens*, leapfrogs to the glories of ancient Egypt and the pyramids, takes a slight turn to explore the origins of democracy in fifth century B.C.E. Greece, swims through Rome (there was a Republic, then an Empire), takes a breathless jump to the later Middle Ages and northern European cathedrals and the Crusades, and then settles comfortably into the Renaissance. At this point there are often a few brief forays into China and India (Confucius, Buddha), and if there's time, we go back to pick up some bits of the Enlightenment. After that, if we're lucky, we get to World War I or June, whichever comes first, and we've learned the history of the world. I taught a college freshman who once began an essay, "In the Middle Ages during the Renaissance . . ." I suspect he was absent on a Tuesday in ninth grade and missed one of them. The real point of the gallop through world history in the tenth grade is to set the stage for the triumphal entry of American democracy in the eleventh-grade history course and to trace its lineage through selected moments of earlier peoples and places. In such a scheme, Egyptian, Greek, and Roman glories and the high points of Northern European civilization are picked out of all the possible things one could learn about Western history in order to prepare the reader for the capstone event, the United States and democracy.

The narratives of world and U.S. history taught in our high schools are meant to sketch the lineage of democracy from ancient times to the American Revolution. Ironically, the same bits and pieces of Western history made up the narrative taught in the former Soviet Union to lead to a very different climax. The Soviets also traced their lineage from Egypt to Greece to Rome and to the Middle Ages and Renaissance, but the crown of their story was the triumph of socialism, after which (until 1985 when *pérestroika* opened new historical possibilities) the heavier emphasis was on the socialist history of the people since 1917.[2] The arbitrariness of the end point of these two narratives and their highly similar plots up to the critical moment of World War I serve to point out that history as taught in schools is not inevitable or God-given. The extreme compression of world history into a single year of high school leaves the student with a vague impression that Egyptian and Athenian culture of specific periods are "ours," that the history of "our" people is triumphal, and that the lineage we share is one that defines a progress since time immemorial toward the whole purpose of civic and cultural history, which is the happy democracy in which we live.

The U.S. and world history taught in most schools constitute a series of stories that have, over time, become a part of the American myth. *Myth* in the sense in which I will use it is not the same as *fiction*. Myth is narrative we believe in as truth. In that sense, Parson Weems's old story about George Washington and the cherry tree is a myth. It was repeated in countless textbooks for well over a hundred years because of its power to unite the symbolic, virtuous Founding Father with the idea of childhood truthfulness, and thereby to unite private, individual virtue with an ideal national character and civic behavior. The story's power depends on the reader's willingness to believe it, regardless of whether it is fact or fiction. Most adults over the age of thirty today will have heard or read the story in school. Historians have discarded it from the textbooks, but it prevails as part of the American myth with which most of us grew up.

The discipline of history as practiced by historians is very different from history as national myth-building. History as a subject continuously reviews, researches, and unearths the documents and events and evidence of the past to explain anew who we are and how we got to be this way. History interprets the evidence of the past; it teaches the nature of that evidence and methods for sorting through and selecting it in order to retell an old story or fashion a new one. All history is artifice. The principles each historian uses on which to base her selections of evidence from the past will determine the kind of history she will write. The point of history is in the creation of narrative to interpret the past and explain subsequent events, but the provisional nature of history has never been adequately taught in American schools. Now when many minorities discover that the stories told in school are indeed myths that they do not happen to believe (that is, no longer myths, but fictions), they are eager to substitute "truths" of their own.

History, designed to tell us who we are and how we got to be that way, is also supposed to teach us how to become citizens of a democracy. A distinguished group of teachers and scholars called the Bradley Commission on History in the Schools believe our democratic heritage and the history of how it came into being is the equivalent of "a common religion or a common ethnicity" binding together our enormously diverse country.[3] In our democracy, there is no king to represent us, religious practice is supposed to be separate from all government-run enterprises, many different ethnicities cohabit, and many citizens are foreign-born; the only commonality holding us together as a nation is our democratic ideology, heritage, and practice. If we all learned how democracy came into being in school we would have a shared purpose, shared vision, and shared future, even though we might differ each from the other in many other ways.

The democracy that gets taught in many American schools, however, becomes a matter of "facts," and democracy's meaning often languishes in textbook-dominated classrooms. Apparently at least 60 percent of high-school class time in social studies is spent using textbooks. Covering the material—just plain getting through a long, tedious list of topics—is the major driving force for harassed social-studies teachers, especially in high schools.[4] Even though students have studied American history twice before, high school assumes that nothing much has stuck with them from previous courses.

Studies show that what teachers do in class is generally to conduct *recitation discussions,* a method most of us remember well from social studies. The way this works is for the teacher to have a particular answer in particular words in her head and for her to ask a question that she wants students to answer by supplying the words she already has in mind. As an example, one fifth-grade teacher asked his class, made up entirely of African-American children, to respond to the following: "Our nation is a nation of _____." He kept calling on child after child, running through raised hands until one of them finally gave him the magic word, *immigrants.* As one can readily see, it's not a sincere question when the questioner already knows the answer. It's not an honest discussion when students are asked not to think, but to remember what was said in class earlier or what the book said. Recitation discussion invariably ends up teaching "right" answers to questions and persuading kids that there are right, knowable answers in history.

Calling the United States a nation of immigrants is an interpretation that ill-describes many Americans, including African-Americans, who feel *immigrants* connotes only people who have chosen to move to a new place. Nevertheless, recitation-discussion methods, which dominate our classrooms, suggest that the textbooks and teachers "have the answers" and that simple, short answers can supply all the important things one needs to know about history.

Some years ago, social analyst and historian Frances Fitzgerald wrote a remarkable book called *America Revised* in which she reviewed social-studies textbooks, pointing out how dull, unreadable, and generally unhelpful they were. How many of us ever pick up a social-studies textbook to read for self-improvement? It seems strange that opaque, dense books unworthy of our adult time are required reading for children. Textbooks are written and revised by committees with an eye to the largest possible market, indeed for markets dominated by states that adopt particular books—list them as approved for all their districts. California, as the single largest state choosing books for all its districts, dominates the textbook industry. Texas, the second largest book-listing state, is nearly as influential. This means that social-studies books simultaneously have to avoid offending school boards and parents in Lubbock and in Marin County. And having been written to sell in Lubbock and Marin, they have to do for West Virginia and Detroit as well. The harried social-studies teacher either knows very little about history himself and therefore depends on the textbook, or has so much to cover that he daren't depart from the book's breathless romp through time in order to get to World War I by June. As a result, most social-studies teachers would define *curriculum* as the contents of a textbook. The picture we get of what goes on in school history today, then, is one of a textbook-dominated pedagogy that believes in right answers to historical questions despite the fact that sometimes these right answers are patently wrong.[5]

If the books are dull and sometimes wrong, what does get taught? Or better, what gets learned? All hands agree that what gets taught is less history than "civic virtue,"[6] and civic virtue may not necessarily depend on getting your facts straight. When community norms rule, historians (presumably the experts at history) are largely ignored. As Fitzgerald puts it, "texts are written backward or inside out, as it were, beginning with public demand and ending with the historian."[7]

The story told in school is a story with plot. The "nation of immigrants" myth, for example, tells a success story when you look at the rise of disenfranchised European peasants to positions of political power and wealth in this country. The story's success plot disintegrates, however, if Native Americans, African-Americans, and other Americans of color are considered to be a part of that story. Defining "us" as immigrants leaves a significant number of Americans entirely outside of the plot. It leaves every child in that fifth-grade classroom out of the triumph of the American story.

Americans of color are tired of being taught about an "us" that patently excludes them, distorts their role in America's past, or patronizes them too easily. A few Americans of color have come to loathe those success stories about the triumphs of the West and to reject such stories wholesale. The Western Civilization myth that says Egypt gave rise to Greece and Rome and ultimately to the Western, capitalist, democratic nation-state, seems to claim all these events as white triumphs. It seems to say that Africans only appear as pre-human skeletal remains in the Great Rift Valley, as victims of the Atlantic slave trade, or as problems in the contemporary Third World. Native Americans only turn up in this story as "pre-Columbians" or as generalized wigwam dwellers, and America before the European encounter is described as empty, with no permanent structures or civilizations. Native Americans are described as people of the past, as if they no longer live in our land, as if they had vanished mysteriously from the face of the earth.

Hispanic children encounter a schooling that glorifies Columbus and the Queen of Spain, but then drops the Spanish story completely, as if Spain had no further import for the North American continent. The Spaniards continue to be regarded as having lacked the farming and settling instincts of the virtuous Plymouth brethren—Spaniards, we're taught, were less interested in settlement than in bullion, hence their moral failure to strike roots in the American earth and their morally appropriate defeat during the Mexican War. A 1986 Silver Burdett elementary-school history book, for example, goes on for several pages about the conquistadors and their search for gold in the Americas. Only one line is devoted to Spanish missionaries, and there is one (negative) statement about Spanish colonists ("nearly two centuries passed before Spain made serious efforts to colonize this northern fringe of its empire"). Yet later in the text we are told that Western architecture, cowboy culture, and longhorn cattle are all the effects of Spanish colonists. In other words, the Spanish colonists themselves never appear in the book, only their remains. In all, this passage takes up five pages. The English story, however, is the real story, which comprises many subsequent chapters.[8]

Such stories are being challenged by new materials. In another elementary schoolroom in the same town where African-American children are being asked to describe themselves as immigrants, a remarkable fifth-grade teacher has provided her students with documents describing European migrants entering Native American territory. The contemporary account, from papers written by Native Americans, describes their conviction that the Europeans are coming to steal their children to eat them. The Native American parents hide their children in pits in the earth camouflaged with branches. The teacher asks the children to create a theatrical scene acting out the encounter. Two children who have both been described as lacking reading comprehension skills perform a scene in which it is clear they understand fully that both the Native American and European characters misapprehend each other. When they charge each other with inhuman atrocities, the two children act out not just the words of the text, but also the fear, ignorance, and misunderstanding buried in those words. These children have gone far beyond reading a text to believe in it. They have read critically and have provided the class with an interpretation of the text. That interpretation shows that the fear of the writer has turned the "other"—in this case, the European—into a cannibal. Fear and mistrust have taken shape as myth.

Fifth graders who can read and interpret original texts such as these have gone far beyond what most textbooks expect. While history as a discipline is a matter of learning how to construct interpretation, history as a school subject is a matter of learning how to repeat someone else's interpretation. Both students and teachers are cut out of the entire historical interpretive process. The myths in the texts, powerful and difficult to dislodge, serve their purposes so well that for most Americans they constitute foundation truths on which their beliefs about America and about themselves as Americans have been built. At key moments in this history, however, children of the poor and children of color are being asked to consent to myths they find untenable.

Native Americans for instance, are palpably here in the flesh, not just on reservations, but mingled in among the population everywhere in the country. Native Americans inhabit pueblos in the Southwest that have been continuously occupied since ancient times. They have left stone monuments, inscriptions, and artifacts as testimony to a complex and sophisticated civilization over many hundreds of years and even millennia. Hispanic peoples settled the West long before the English finally settled the East. Not just conquistadors, but missionaries, herdsmen, and farmers came to the Western Hemisphere in the sixteenth century. The first American universities were founded in Spanish, not English, America: San Marcos University was chartered in Lima in 1551 and the Royal and Pontifical University was established the same year in Mexico City. Today it is called the National Autonomous University of Mexico. Both substantially predate Harvard Yard. Such materials and others can be found only in a handful of new textbooks, such as the Globe Book Company's "Mosaic of American History" paperback series, one of which details *Hispanic America to 1776* (Englewood Cliffs, N.J.: 1993).

Alternative views of history question the inevitability of what we were taught in school, and therefore seem un-American. For the majority of Americans, including many Americans of color, alternate visions are disturbing, even wrenching. But if we are to acknowledge the real diversity of our country, our school history must change. Such change is not necessarily the precursor of the decline and fall of America, but an opportunity for renewal.

Telling Stories

⟡

Every story has a point of view, a "we" from whose perspective the tale is told. School stories have generally reserved that privilege for white Protestant Americans, but there are multiple perspectives from which to learn the stories of U.S. development. Shift the perspective over and tell the American story from the point of view of a pueblo dweller in New Mexico whose ancestors have been there from time immemorial; shift it again to tell the same story from the point of view of the African-American who dwells today on a patch of land that was once a South Carolina plantation, where his ancestors were chattel; shift it again to tell the story of the Jew whose ancestors were among the first Spaniards to arrive here because 1492 is a year of infamy, when Jews were expelled from Christian Spain and became enforced wanderers in a hostile Europe; shift it again to tell the story from the point of view of the Chinese laborer who is imported to work in Mexican California in order to establish a U.S. presence there and make it easier to wrest that land from Mexico—tell any of these stories or tell them all and America becomes a very different country from the one described in school.

In world history, many other perspectives are also possible. The Western Civilization story pays attention to the Mediterranean world in very odd ways. We're taught about Egypt, Greece, and Rome only as long as it is convenient to do so from a Northern European perspective. After the "Fall of Rome"—that is, its disintegration under pressure from the northern European barbarians—we skip in silence to the twelfth-century Renaissance, some eight hundred years later, as if nothing of consequence to the West happened in the intervening centuries. Worse, we teach "the Renaissance" as if learning were an entirely European and Christian discovery.

Another perspective could center the history of the world on the triumph of literacy, for example. The preservers of what later became high European culture throughout that lightly skipped eight hundred years were Arabs and North Africans, Islamic and Jewish, builders of a complex and sophisticated culture during a period when much of Europe contributed little to the advance of knowledge. If civilization is primarily a story not of democracy alone, but of literacy and self-determination for all, the story need not lapse in the period from the early Church Fathers to the cathedrals. In that period there is an important story to tell, albeit a Mediterranean story that is not always a Christian one.

One might teach twentieth-century U.S. history as the century of African-Americans. This is the period when African-Americans have struggled with the immensely important question of how to be Americans and how to extend the story of America to include them. It is also the story of world dominance for African-American culture. As the millennium ends, not a soul in the world lacks access to the rhythms and cadences of African-American music. Rock music was heard in Tiananmen Square. One would be hard put to find an equal to this cultural export.

Teaching history is a matter of choosing perspectives from which to tell stories. Whoever gets to choose which stories will be told in school also gets to choose the mythology of America—what it has been, what it is, and what it hopes to be. In the beginnings of our Republic when the common-school movement was gathering strength, several ideas about school coincided to create the kind of history teaching we still, to a remarkable extent, see in classrooms at the end of the twentieth century. Up until the 1830s and 1840s the major divisive forces in the new country had to do with regional differences: of economic interests among the North, the South and the West; of class between property owners and labor; of outlook between agrarian and commercial interests. The common school, which in its original conception really meant what we now call elementary school, was designed to unify the country and overcome these regional and class differences. Racial differences were not at that time seen as amenable to such a process; common schools on the whole were not available to people of color, whether enslaved or free.

The new Republic, in trying to define itself, did so largely at first by trying to prove how different it intended to be from the European models that preceded it. Europe was always at war; the new American federation would, in contrast, stand peacefully united and God-directed. By the end of the nineteenth century, school taught that to be an American one had to reject Old World customs and habits, including the ethnic and national animosities of the Old World that immigrants had brought with them. It was to be a country united by common faith in an American creed.

The common-school movement consciously structured the unity of the country around a myth of common origin (the English settlement of this country from East to West[9]); a common, generalized Protestantism (viewed then as nonsectarian because it overcame differences among Protestant sects); and a conservative ideology that protected property, enhanced industrial development, and reduced the threat of labor unrest and radical change. These themes were developed consistently and in tandem through the content of school, the methods of school, the structures of school, and school laws and edicts at state and local levels. Schools were created to teach a coherent way of being and a single identity for Americans regardless of class or regional differences (in the early nineteenth century) and despite ethnic differences (in the early twentieth). The late twentieth century, however, can no longer reconcile this singular identity in the face of ethnic and racial dissent.

The Model American
Takes Shape

~~~~~~~

*When I mention religion I mean the Christian religion; and
not only the Christian religion, but the Protestant religion;
and not only the Protestant religion, but the Church of
England.*

MR. THWACKUM, THE DIVINE; *TOM JONES*

Beyond the skills of reading, writing, and calculating, U.S. schools have
never offered academic subjects like history as discrete, sequential courses of
study throughout the grades. In this, American schools differ markedly from
European schools, where subjects hold their own from the earliest years
through the end of secondary education. Part of the reason for this quite
large difference has to do with the populist purposes of American common
schools. In eighteenth-century Europe as well as America, young children
were tutored at home if they were wealthy, the youngest of all in "dame
schools" run by local women who earned their pin money by teaching toddlers their letters. Very few children could afford to attend any kind of
school beyond this. European school institutions were universally designed
to prepare boys to enter universities, and universities saw their task as
preparing upper-class young men either for the ministry or for a gentlemanly, leisured life. Since advanced schooling and the universities were primarily geared to the needs of the church, school learning was designed to
prepare one to read the sacred texts and theological commentaries of the
church. European schools taught classical grammar (Latin and Greek) from
the earliest years, mathematics, ancient history, geography, and "natural philosophy," or what we would call science. These subjects were offered every
year to all attending boys. Schooling leading to universities in Europe was

above all an invitation into a common set of references revolving around Greek and Latin classical texts. You were a gentleman partly by birth and partly by virtue of your familiarity with a shared set of readings and the culture you shared with other gentlemen. Except for the clergy, therefore, a liberal education was never meant to be practical preparation for a career.

Until the late nineteenth century, *history* meant either sacred history or classical history. Modern history (since the Fall of Rome) only gradually became a university subject. The first professorship of modern history was established at Cambridge University in 1724; the first general history professorship (ancient and modern) was not established in the United States until Harvard did so in 1839.[10] Modern national histories only began to appear after European nations began to define themselves as modern nation-states, an idea that began to be forged in Britain in the early eighteenth century and in Germany in the later part of that century. The British created their idea of nationhood out of three key Protestant texts: Foxe's *Book of Martyrs,* Bunyan's *Pilgrim's Progress,* and the Protestant Bible. These three shaped a narrative of the British as a Chosen People in a Chosen Land whose greatest duty to God and country was to defend the world against tyranny and Popery.[11] This image was passed along wholesale to American schools through the influence of transplanted Puritan teachings and texts. As the United States began to organize its idea of itself as a young nation and its idea of how to forge an American identity for its citizens, a second influence came—from German philosophy. Georg Wilhelm Friedrich Hegel (1770– 1831) and other German thinkers in the late eighteenth and early nineteenth centuries identified a nation's people with a glorious past and a common great destiny for the future. Such ideas strongly influenced the New England transcendentalists and the founders of the first U.S. public schools. Modern history became a major vehicle through which schools could transmit concepts of national origin and destiny. The young United States took its model for self-definition as a nation from these two sources, the British God-given mandate and the new German Romantic ideas of nationalism. The schools would make the nation.

The Republic's past was brief, of course, at the time of the formation of common schools. Colonial and early U.S. schools continued the British habit of teaching classical and sacred histories as part and parcel of a story that saw British Protestantism as its culmination. For lack of a U.S. history, the new Republic's schools explicitly taught British history. In the first decades of the nation, moreover, few schoolbooks had been published in the United States besides the most basic ABCs and Noah Webster's "Blue-backed Spellers." From the early nineteenth century through the 1840s, the history textbooks used in America were by and large reprints of British publications picked up there by American clergymen.

The writers of the textbooks most often appropriated for early American school use were most frequently Scottish Presbyterian ministers, whose ethos derived from a Protestant dissent, not unlike Puritan dissent, from the Anglican orthodoxies of England.[12] When these Scottish textbooks arrived on our shores, usually carried here by dissenting American ministers, they were often reprinted with the American ministers' names on the title pages.[13] The clergy were usually the most educated residents of rural and small-town America and the most likely to be called on to run schools.

Dissenting Protestants—Puritans and Presbyterians alike—revered education and viewed Scripture as a direct source of truth and knowledge as a form of piety. Education was the business of the ministry, and their job was indoctrination. There was no room in such a view of education for further dissent, or for diversity, which would threaten the special covenantal relationship between the people and their God.[14] The common-school movement began in New England and was most heavily influenced in the East and West by the traditions of education that derived from dissenting Protestant thought.

The strong Presbyterian influence on American textbooks continued to dominate the teaching of history for almost a century thereafter; William Holmes McGuffey (1800–1873), the great originator of homegrown American textbooks, was also a Presbyterian minister. McGuffey's textbooks dominated the school market for seventy-five years and strongly influenced textbook content well into our own times. Dissenting church doctrine dominated our nineteenth-century curricula. While the Protestant Bible and *Pilgrim's Progress* were staples of early U.S. education, the content of American history as taught in schools throughout the nineteenth century was also largely to be found in the school readers. *Readers* were anthologies of poetry, political speeches, parts of plays, and bits and pieces of philosophy, history, and all manner of subjects. Then, as now, very few works of any length appeared in them whole. Schools used only a handful of textbooks of any kind in that period, usually amounting to no more than a speller, a reader, and sometimes a geography. The readers, therefore, virtually constituted the school curriculum. The readers devoted half of their space to war and one-fifth to government and politics.[15] They also taught about America's heroes by means of moral tales invented for the purpose, and included many songs, hymns, and prayers.

The readers offer an ideological portrait of America that carries on the British Protestant cause against the Spanish and Popery, even though American history books began the story of this country as if it had no European context. As a result, Americans never learned much about the struggle between England and Spain for domination of the Atlantic or about the religious context in which that imperial and commercial rivalry was set. For Renaissance England, it was the Queen as Defender of the Faith—the Protestant faith of the Church of England—who sent Sir Walter Raleigh on his travels; for Counter-Reformation Spain, it was Philip II and Catholicism that aimed at ruling the Atlantic waves. Carrying on that European rivalry, American schools took on the British cause along with the British textbooks. The Spanish were portrayed as cruel and bloodthirsty, the English as peaceable settlers and farmers; the Spanish were evil Catholics, the English the divinely guided forebears of Americans. The earliest textbooks did at first admit that the Spaniards founded colleges in the Western Hemisphere; these books were quite expansive in their treatment of French explorers and detailed the broad variety of Native American peoples, governments, and customs.[16] Generosity toward American civilizations other than the English, however, disappeared later in the nineteenth century. Yet even in the earliest books, the two oldest settlements in U.S. territory, St. Augustine and Santa Fe, were not mentioned. The Spanish and French were described as adventurers, and only the English as establishers of homes.[17]

In reality, by the time the English began to settle in North America, Spain had colonies as far north as Chesapeake Bay. The English knew full well when they arrived that they were pirates in Spanish territory.[18] The mythology of British destiny ignored the immense building program of the Spanish Americas, which by the 1620s included some seventy thousand churches.[19] No American textbook made any distinction between the rapacity of the conquistadors and the efforts of missionaries to settle and establish Spanish civilization in the Americas.

The building of cities, churches, and civilizations in the Western Hemisphere by the Spanish has been consistently ignored in favor of the story of the 1607 Jamestown settlement and the 1620 Massachusetts settlement. Earlier Spanish and French settlements are described as having been done in by vice, laziness, famine, and disease. Although early U.S. textbooks admitted that some Puritans were intolerant and practiced witchcraft, by 1925 the Puritans were being described as benevolent founders.[20] Portraits of the English that still bore the marks of Revolutionary animosity were transformed in the late nineteenth century into admiration—which prevails even now.

One wonders if some of the anti-Hispanic feeling in this country today may derive from this school "creation myth," which divinely sanctioned the English Protestant settlements and vilified the evil Spanish Catholics. That evil was to be eradicated by the Mexican War and subsequent annexations of Mexican land in the treaty of Guadalupe Hidalgo in 1848. We taught that this country was settled from East to West by the English and their descendants, a teaching that disregards the civilization that Spain brought to the South, Southwest, and West. Imagine a history of the United States that started with the settlement at St. Augustine and proceeded to talk about the fifty-five years of Spanish interaction with the Western Hemisphere before the Puritans made it to Plymouth Rock. Imagine a history written by a Spanish missionary working with Central and Southwest Native Americans instead of by a Presbyterian minister adapting British books for use in American schools merely by changing the author's name on the title page. Imagine a U.S. history that starts ten thousand years ago, before the Europeans learned to sail out of sight of the shore, and dwells at length on the first settlers in the hemisphere and their civilizations. Such histories are now just beginning to be called for in our schools, most notably in the recent California state requirements for social studies, and to be produced by a handful of publishers.

Honorary Englishmen

~~~

World history has an equally peculiar history in the schools, but in order to understand how it is that Greeks and Romans have come to be considered honorary Englishmen, we have to remember how Greeks and Romans entered modern European schooling in the first place. The Church held the monopoly on schools throughout most of the history of the West from early medieval times. If you were literate at all, you were probably a priest or a monk; the books you read were books about religion written or copied by other priests and monks. The language in which you were literate was Latin (and, sometimes, ancient Greek), because of the linguistic heritage of the Roman Empire and the languages of the basic Christian documents: the New Testament, the Church Fathers, the Mass, and the discourse of the Church in all its theology, forms, rituals, and administration.

The great change that began to secularize schooling in the West came with the Renaissance rediscovery of secular Latin texts and Latin versions of Greek texts, long preserved in the non-Christian Mediterranean, but "lost" to the less civilized North. Humanist scholars of the Renaissance, preeminently the great Dutch scholar Desiderius Erasmus (1469–1536), offered a vision of a different kind of education, which had reference to the secular world as well as the religious and explored linguistic, political, literary, natural, psychological, and philosophical realms in addition to the world of faith. Latin and Greek texts in these fields, long considered merely pagan, became the central texts of a universe of learning that opened up a new kind of education for the first time in a thousand years in northern and western Europe. Erasmus returned in 1516, for the first time since St. Jerome, to the Greek sources of the New Testament and edited a new version of the sacred text. Being literate in Renaissance Christian Europe still meant being literate in Latin, however, and continued to do so well into the nineteenth century.

Between the fifteenth-century explosion of classical secular learning and the early eighteenth century, European schools focused almost entirely on biblical and classical history, literature, and languages. Caesar and Herodotus defined history for the younger readers, Livy and Thucydides for the middle years, Tacitus for the more advanced.

It was not until the late seventeenth and early eighteenth centuries that some Europeans began thinking they might want to augment their study of the ancients with some consideration of the postclassical, modern world. The debate over the relative merits of ancients and moderns raged in Britain for many years and in some sense continues on into our own day with reference to literature; the debate has hardly begun to take shape with reference to history.

The founding of this nation took place in a time when the history of the Jews as received into the Christian Testaments was of equal importance with the classics to British compilers of world history textbooks. At the end of the eighteenth century, explorers and the first archeologists were just beginning to search out ancient sites and monuments in the Near East, identifying and collecting evidence of ancient civilizations. This research focused on the dual origins of European culture: the Graeco-Roman and Judeo-Christian remains. Archaeology, like school history, dwelt on these two ancient civilizations to the exclusion of all else in the search for the European creation story. At the heart of the Judeo-Christian universe are the biblical documents as transmitted by Christendom; at the heart of the Graeco-Roman universe are the humanistic texts so explosively rediscovered in the Renaissance. Both the biblical and classical foundations of Western civilization place the book at the center of culture. Writing and commenting on written discourse are what scholars and theologians *do;* they form the center of study whether one is destined for a life in the monastery or on the battlefield, the bourse, or the home farm.

The double axis of Western thought entails two central debates: the debate between received biblical truth and the pagan, secular truths of the Graeco-Roman world, and the debate between the ancients collectively, both Christian and secular, and the moderns—between the foundation texts (the "canon") and the pressure to extend canonic status to events in the modern world. Most of this debate comes down to our own day as a largely literary fight. But in teaching history, the debate was early resolved by virtue of the fact that for many European nations, legitimacy of political power depended to a great extent on the transmission of religious legitimacy. European states justified themselves on the basis of their historic links to a sacred foundation. French history as taught in schools, for example, begins with the pope's crowning of Charlemagne in 800 C.E. World history as taught in the classroom has to do with the Christian world, which takes its political, economic, and social coherence from those moments of Christian triumph that simultaneously celebrate national triumphs. Up until very recently, the justification for a world history that moved from biblical history to Graeco-Roman, to the Middle Ages, to the Renaissance, to the Reformation, was a story with a plot describing the triumph of nations in determining their individual religious, and hence political, destinies. It is a story that leads up to the triumph of the Protestant empire in the American hemisphere, and the Protestant, democratic apotheosis of the modern world. In nineteenth-century American schools, the primary purposes given by the authors of world histories for the study of the subject were the inculcation of religious belief and patriotism.[21]

The people who created the common schools for all Americans worried about maintaining stability, taming any would-be tendencies to radicalism that might change the political framework of the country and its growing organization of wealth and power. Fashions in history—for instance, the late eighteenth-century fascination with the newly accessible, exotic Far East— meant that earlier in the nineteenth century, world history books included material on the Far East. Later in the century, however, the Far East gave way to material on feudalism and the medieval European period,[22] just as fashion among the artists, writers, and philologists who led nineteenth-century Romanticism took up medieval themes in painting, poetry, architecture, and language history. Neo-Gothic architecture spread across the American landscape, darkening churches and college halls; Poe raved about darkness; and dictionary makers searched out medieval root words in the Teutonic proto-European languages. As this focus on the medieval European past intensified, nationalism and the rise of nationalism became the dominant theme and indeed the purpose of history as taught in school.[23] Later nineteenth-century books on world and U.S. history and geography sought to connect legitimacy of the political order—i.e., the nation-state—with transmission of religious legitimacy and racial coherence. If the English were the best, it was because they carried the torch of the highest form of Christianity and were racially superior to all other peoples. The schoolbooks justified their national fervor on the basis of both religion and race.

But these ideas about race were invented neither by the English nor by the Enlightenment, although many justifiably angry people of color in the United States today blame both. Racial arguments for nationalism largely came from German Romantic idealism. "Germany" in the eighteenth century consisted of a collection of dozens of principalities and states with no larger, coherent political shape except the acknowledged fiction that they were what remained of the "Holy Roman Empire." From the time of Frederick the Great of Prussia (1712–1786), German-speaking intellectuals and political leaders agonized over the lack of national unity among the scattered states, urging the people to struggle to put together a powerful, pan-German nation.

German Romantic thought of this period had an immensely powerful influence on American philosophy and American schools.[24] They don't teach you about German influences in America any more; they stopped in about 1918. But German Romantic philosophy, German university research, and Prussian school methods for teaching the masses were among the strongest influences on American thought and educational institutions in the nineteenth century. If you wanted an advanced degree you went to Germany to get one, and hundreds of America's professors did so. If you wanted to be modern and scientific, you learned how from the German thinkers. If you wanted to organize efficient classrooms for large numbers of charity children, you adopted Prussian methods of education. If you wanted to know how to create a nation out of a regionally divided, fractious bunch of states and a unified populace most of which consisted of laboring poor from diverse religious and ethnic backgrounds, you turned to German thinking on how to define a nation through its state schools.[25] The idea of a nation depended on tracing the origins of the populace to a glorious past, bound by shared race, religion, and language.[26]

Among the American enthusiasts for German philosophy were the "St. Louis Hegelians," a group of Western thinkers who adopted not only a passion for the German greats from Goethe to Schiller to the Schlegels, Fichte, Schleiermacher, and Hegel, but also adopted Germany's adoration of the Greek ideal of Plato, Aristotle, and the historians and playwrights of ancient Athens. For a nation to form, it needed an Homeric bard, or prophetic poet, to tell its history, create its language, and express its greatness. Homer did it for Greece, Goethe for Germany. Shakespeare was England's bard, who turns up as a *Romantic* poet after the Schlegels had finished with him—a poet of the people, a poet of passion, a poet through whose transforming vernacular language a people came into being. The St. Louis Hegelians were so taken with this idea they even read their Shakespeare in Schlegel's German translation. One of their number, William Torry Harris, became U.S. Commissioner for Education, bringing his Hegelian ideas with him into office.

German Romantic ideas pushed American thought toward the necessity of forming a national identity through a search for the ideal. Fichte's *Addresses to the German Nation* (1809) and Hegel's *Phenomenology of Spirit* (1807) were interpreted by the St. Louis Hegelians as an agenda for "forging a genuine national personality out of political and cultural fragments, a national identity that would assume a role in world history." While such a search had grown up in American thinking long before this, the new

Romantic ideals set in motion teachings that had an ultimately insidious effect on American beliefs about race and class. Germany and the United States shared a need to forge nationhood in the nineteenth century; each saw itself as potentially shaping a new world order for the future through that national destiny. The St. Louis philosophers and educators found Hegelian ideas suitable for supporting a philosophy of nationalism that presupposed a racial and class-biased theory. White supremacy and Protestant religious supremacy suited this agenda.[27] Neither Germany nor the United States had geographic boundaries to define them (as England did), or historic domains of a single, unifying monarchy (as France did). Nationhood for Germany would depend on shared race and language. In the United States, Noah Webster's case for a new American language to define an American character strongly influenced the schools. Jean Hector St. John de Crèvecouer, an eighteenth-century immigrant farmer, puzzled over the American problem of race at length, concluding that the new race was to be made up of the mixing of peoples whose common heritage was to be ideological, not cultural.

That ideology, however, did not take center stage in American schoolrooms. What was offered instead was a religious and moral education that emphasized ideals, holding up examples of meritorious behavior that schoolchildren were taught to emulate. You would become an American to the extent to which you resembled the ideal. Into schoolbooks then crept, by the 1830s and 1840s, a history and geography strongly influenced by German Romantic racial theories. All races on earth, so the teaching went, could be ranked in hierarchies, with the English and German races on top and the African at the bottom, with everyone else arranged according to their resemblance or lack thereof to the ideal. History allied English and German racial superiority to a superiority of language, religion, and behavior.

Defining the American nation soon also came to mean defining its territory. The United States rightfully, so we began to believe, included the lands that eventually stretched from coast to coast and from a truncated Mexico in the south to the 49th parallel in the north. This territorial definition of America was taught in school as the religious destiny of a people under God's leadership.

While race theory developed in the early Romantic era, it only became crucial to the formation of nation-states after the 1860s. If we look at both Europe and the United States, we can begin to see why. We all learn in school that emancipation occurred during the Civil War. What we don't learn is that serfdom was abolished in Russia in the 1860s and that certain administrative restrictions on former serfs in the Holy Roman Empire remained in effect until 1871; in the Hapsburg Empire, Jews first achieved full civil rights in the 1860s. Central and Eastern Europe, like the United States, discovered themselves as modern nations partly by virtue of granting these freedoms. But in all of these nations white Christians found themselves unwilling to acknowledge the other—whether Americans of color or Austrians who were not Christians—as full equals. The laws of the 1860s allowed former serfs and slaves to mingle freely with the rest of the populace, so social strictures took the place of legal ones to preserve distinctions of place. Race theory blossomed just as civil status was granted to all.

After the Civil War had tested American unity and identity to the utmost, an even stronger urge toward national unification via the school curriculum took hold. The second half of the nineteenth century was a time of enormous population growth, of westward expansion, of industrial development, of massive immigration, and growth of cities. With all this came a change in the citizenry, no longer primarily or purely landowning, agrarian, or of northern European extraction. The new populace seemed a threat to the old established interests.

Racial theory helped define the German nation that emerged out of the Holy Roman Empire in 1871; racial theory helped justify European imperialism around the world in 1870–1914; racial theory helped to forge American nationalism just as emancipation and new immigration patterns threatened to overwhelm the old American identity. In the period 1870–1914 in the United States and in the imperial nations of Europe alike, official national traditions were invented. The Daughters of the American Revolution was founded in 1890. This is the period when flag rituals, national anthems, and patriotic holidays came into being, cultivated as unifying elements whereby the masses of the new electorate—sometimes Catholic, sometimes African-American, sometimes laborers from new places of origin—would bind themselves to the idea of the nation.

Psychology and anthropology alike were announcing that the human animal, far from being primarily rational, as the Enlightenment had believed, was primarily irrational, as Freud and the folklorists were proving through their researches into the darkness of the soul and the prehistoric past. The masses of new voters were believed to represent these unruly, irrational characteristics. In the United States, where no official state religion was permitted, a new civic religion was born to keep them obedient; fealty to flag and national hymn and country replaced fealty to lord and priest and parish. In the words of one analyst, "the educational system was transformed into a machine for political socialization by such devices as worship of the American flag, which, as a daily ritual in the country's schools, spread from the 1880s onwards."[28] The flag became paired with the Lord's Prayer. Public rituals became the rule by which to judge Americanness. The use of the English language was also important. For British subjects, right of birth determines Britishness plain and simple; such is not so clearly the case in an America where, in the period in question, you were as likely to be foreign- as native-born. The new rituals helped provide the solution.

U.S. education toward the end of the nineteenth century became the vehicle for an intense nationalism when Catholics and Jews and Slavs in the East and Chinese in the West entered the country in large numbers, and when massed labor was imported to our cities, mines, and mills. Having just established common schools for all Americans, America now conceived of the idea of public high schools and proceeded to build them on a massive scale.

Even though the new high schools were not designed as prep schools for college, they had nowhere to turn to invent a curriculum except the college preparatory models of existing academies. Certain subjects were appropriated by the new high schools and disappeared as a result from the lower schools. One of these was world history, another foreign languages. American history as a one-year course of study was added. The high-school curricula that emerged were not well integrated with those of the common schools, even though high schools became the next step after common school for an ever-increasing proportion of our population.

In the 1890s and the first decade of the twentieth century, university-based historians gathered repeatedly to define a history curriculum for the schools that would be research-based, go beyond mere memorization, and empower America's newly enfranchised citizenry. The recommendations of these committees noted the oddity of the school curriculum then prevailing, which saw the world from the point of view of northern and western Europe when city schools were filling up with children of southern- and eastern-European extraction,[29] who found themselves in high school as a result of the new child labor laws—laws meant as much to keep adult wages high as to take better care of children. The professors recommended a solid history curriculum that would make more sense to the children being taught; but their ideas were swept away by the time we entered World War I. By 1916 the "progressive" education movement was in full swing. "Social studies," albeit a history-centered social studies, took over, and "history" as the principal way of organizing knowledge of human communities gave way. By the 1920s, America had decided that high school should recognize that most Americans were not interested in intellectual pursuits—or not suited for them. Individual social adjustment and conformity to an idea of American social behavior, rather than the study of history for its own sake, became the major purpose of the new social-studies curriculum and of school in general.

In 1918 an entirely new and entirely American way of thinking about school appeared. The *Cardinal Principles of Secondary Education,* published by the U.S. Department of the Interior's Bureau of Education, pronounced the purposes of schooling to be health, command of fundamental processes (such as reading, writing, and calculating), worthy home membership, vocation, citizenship, worthy use of leisure, and ethical character. Of all of these, citizenship was probably considered the most important. Nowhere in this list is the student perceived as having to *know* anything whatsoever.[30] Being a good American, therefore, meant being comfortable with the status quo—adjusted, contented, and minimally educated in the three Rs, but not necessarily knowledgeable. Although history continued as the backbone of the social studies, it played a much smaller part in the overall purposes of school than in the 1890–1920 period; in a sense, history as a school subject of some rigor had existed in American schools for a period of less than thirty years.

The social adjustment purposes of public schools in the 1920s were bolstered by the massive adoption of I.Q. testing, first used on a large scale to test army recruits in World War I. America went "science" crazy in this era—another legacy of German cultural influence—and I.Q. testing became a national craze for determining which children were to get the academic preparation for college and which were to get the new vocational preparation that had been added to the high schools to prepare children for a life of labor. Stephen Jay Gould's *The Mismeasure of Man* brilliantly describes the way I.Q. tests enabled America to find a "scientific" justification for its prevailing racism and classism. The tests then and for much of the rest of our own century have served to confirm the social purposes of school; to justify the educational separation of laborers, who need not know anything, from leaders, for whom knowledge was reserved. High schools now provided two or more "tracks," or curricula, for students—one for those headed to college, one for those headed for a life of labor, and increasingly, a third, "general" education track for those headed for white-collar jobs. The National Center for Research in Vocational Education published a report in 1992 that shows U.S. schools still persist in believing that students have innate abilities or lack thereof, that those abilities are based on students' social backgrounds, and that social background should determine access to academic subjects in school. This demonstrates an institutional race theory that seems to inform most decisions about the amount and quality of academic learning available to the poor and minorities right up to the present moment.[31]

The social studies movement of the 1920s to the 1950s stressed school subjects designed to pacify dissent, although Frances Fitzgerald did find that earlier in this period individual historians had managed to write books that differed in ideology one from another.[32] But dissenting views disappeared entirely with the advent of the Cold War, when history in the schools became a tool of U.S. foreign policy. The 1950s saw history books obsessed with U.S. power, with the flag and other patriotic symbols, and with "our" rightness as divinely ordained.[33] Fighting the Cold War meant telling schoolchildren about the rightness of our system and the evils of all others—especially, of course, totalitarian socialism. The 1960s challenged that self-satisfied picture by pointing out that the implied "we" of the textbooks described a non-Hispanic, white, male, middle class that left out the majority of Americans, if by majority we include women as well as people of color. When we lost our faith in America's divine purposes on Vietnam's battlefields and could no longer see this country as the savior of a benighted world, the triumphal image the 1950s texts had tried to convey began to retreat.

Mid-nineteenth-century writers had spoken of conflicts in the American West between the indigenous people and the eastern migrants; later writers described the East-to-West migration as if it took place in an unpeopled landscape. And we have already seen that the French and Spanish were first vilified and later eliminated from the western and southwestern lands by the textbooks.[34] A vast publishing industry depends today, however, on offending as few Americans as possible, resulting in textbook writing so bland that virtually no information is conveyed. Mass marketing of textbooks has homogenized our history, stilled the individual voices of historians and historical figures alike, and banished thought, excitement, and conflict from a subject that above all others surely ought to consist of all of these.

As historian and textbook writer William E. Dodd once noted, "If the history of the United States were written exactly as it happened the author would probably be landed in jail."[35] Historians' goals have repeatedly been thwarted by public opinion—opinion based on feelings and wishes rather than on historical objectivity. But historians themselves have changed their dominant theories about how to write history since the profession first organized itself in the 1870s.[36] History as a discipline has had a vexed relationship to nationalism and the construction of the nation. U.S. schools have not, on the whole, taught history in order to cultivate thinkers, doers, dissenters, or makers of democracy. Rather, they have assumed the United States to be a fine place to live as long as everyone agrees to be content with the status quo, salute the flag, and thereby become an American.

At the heart of this picture of the United States and its place in the world lies a profound, abiding, and consistent distrust of the American people. This distrust virtually says that we do not believe we can be a single people unless we all subscribe to a singular way of life, that the majority of the people should conform to an image of America that has never been true for all of the people, and that the majority should learn no more in school than what will content them to conduct their lives of labor without complaint.

In the last few years, however, voices have been raised to reconsider the place and nature of history in our schools. New York State and California, the largest and most diverse of our states, both revised their social studies curricula in the late 1980s. The Organization of American Historians, the American Historical Association, and several other groups that brought scholars and teachers to work together have recently engaged in a flurry of activity to reinstate a rigorous history in the schools. The textbook industry, responding to the California demand for a history that will treat of minorities, of the Native American and Hispanic past, of the European encounter, and of the minority contributions to our history, have at last begun to give us textbooks more worthy of our children's attention. Many of these new efforts to revise the history taught in our schools try to respond to minority demands for inclusion, balancing these with a central teaching of the democratic ideology and heritage. Many of their recommendations and curricula remain subject to intense debate among historians, educators, politicians, and the public. The debate centers on the mythologies to be taught.

The Pastoral Ideal

God the first garden made,
And the first city Cain.

ABRAHAM COWLEY

One of the persistent themes in America's mythology is that the ideal America can be found in its landscape. "America the Beautiful" is a paean to the landscape; George Washington is revered for being the landed, farming-patriot-turned-general—the ideal American;[37] our dream of American life is of a home moated by grass and stuffed with the furnishings of country living. When we think of "the poor" and of "minorities," we do not think of either as inhabitants of that pure countryside, despite the fact that most of America's poor are indeed rural inhabitants and most are white, according to 1990 census data. Yet, "the poor" and "minorities" have come to be associated with each other and with cities—and cities are associated with evil.

In biblical terms, the farmers and herders were the good guys (Abraham and his family) and the denizens of the cities of the plain were the bad guys. The first murderer became a city dweller. Biblical and classical images of countryside purity and associations with an unspoiled, prelapsarian Eden figured largely in the early English settlers' notions of the American continent. Although America was proud of her cities in their early development (Boston and Philadelphia were often called the New Athens—the seats of learning and publishing, as well as the birthplace of the new democracy and its burgeoning commerce), such images soon faded as large numbers of non-English, non-Protestant immigrants and free blacks began to fill up their streets.

Schools did much to foster the image of goodness prevailing in the American landscape and evil overrunning the American city. The pastoral ideal leaves the poor stranded. They're the ones who came too late to grab the land. But when they must live in cities in order to work, the poor come in touch with the intellectual elite, and it is always elites who romanticize rural ethnics as having a special holiness.[38] Rural landowners are understandably suspicious of cities, where the powerful intellectual and labor coalition is formed.

Anti-urbanism is close to, if not the same as, anti-intellectualism. Whereas great cities and the root word of *civilization* have meant the same thing in the past—where seats of government, commerce, culture, and intellectual progress have associated together—America has in many of its institutions divorced these elements from each other. The capital of the country was eventually placed not in a thriving metropolitan center but in a swamp, where its federal government functions are divorced from the actual living city, which is now almost entirely black and Hispanic. The first federal attempt to provide for education created the land-grant universities, whose purposes were to promote agrarian learning in locations set deliberately far from cities.

If you persist, as American textbooks have, in telling the history of America as a history of settlers and farmers and landowners, you tell a story about the English and sometimes about Germans, Norwegians, and Swedes. You tell an anti-Spanish story too, because it was the Spanish habit to express its New World civilization in towns and through church architecture more often than in the countryside and farming.[39] If you told the story of America as a story of its civilization—its cities—you would be telling the story of Catholics and Jews, Hispanics and Irish, and a story about African-Americans. This is also a story about how labor left the land and subsistence farming to seek work in the cities.[40] For Chinese as well as African-Americans, the landscape never was an agrarian ideal; it was abandoned in sorrow for the possibility of work in the urban centers. Asians were singled out by laws in the West that prevented them from owning land. These stories certainly get told in our textbooks and classrooms, but they're told as if they were subordinate to the true, real story of the ideal land that frames the larger picture. For America's minorities, the agrarian ideal never was a possibility, for the land had all been taken by the time they got a chance to look around them; for Native Americans, the land that they had freely inhabited became a landscape drowned in tears.

In the nineteenth century the U.S. population was indeed almost entirely rural, but in the twentieth century it is not. Just as immigration and migration were beginning to turn the tide between majority rural and majority urban, the sons and daughters of the Revolution took fright and organized themselves into patriotic and exclusive clubs to glorify the colonial, agrarian, racially pure past.

The colonial past entered our schools as a deliberately created mythology beginning at the end of the nineteenth century.[41] The colonial revival was largely created by hereditary organizations that set out to distinguish their position in the class structure in the face of overwhelming new immigration patterns of the period after 1890 and the migrations of African-Americans out of the South. Wealthy industrialists caught fire from this idea to conjoin their own new wealth with the pure colonial past by creating monuments to the Eden myth of early, pastoral America. John D. Rockefeller's pet project was the creation of "Colonial" Williamsburg; Henry Ford's was Greenfield Village. Both, built in the 1920s, were designed to homogenize the diversity of the colonial past, and were in reality fictions rather than restorations. Both suggest a racially pure colonial heritage.

Perhaps the supreme moment of late-nineteenth-century colonial invention is the "Liberty Bell," originally cast to commemorate the fiftieth anniversary of William Penn's 1701 grant of a Charter of Privileges to Pennsylvanians. Dragged out of its obscure resting place to decorate a re-creation of the Revolution, dusted off and enshrined, the bell has become the supreme icon of the American creation story, mythologized as a Revolutionary icon by the colonial revival of the late nineteenth century.[42]

Along with the invention of a pure colonial past elevating British origins, we were taught in school to revere the American landscape as a mark of the divine presence.[43] This was not a landscape as it came wild from the hand of nature, but a cultivated landscape, where the farmer carried out God's will. Such themes took their origins from the Puritans' sense of divine purpose in cultivating American soil, but they were transmuted in the nineteenth century by Romantic ideas of nature as the visible manifestation of the invisible and divine.

These images of a pastoral America continued to inform the stories told to children even as America industrialized. Throughout the nineteenth century and well into the twentieth, schoolbooks held up the pastoral ideal and vilified the city. The independent farmer not only was supposed to be the typical American—and he was, until late in the century—but such an enormous amount of children's reading was associated with rural themes that childhood itself became associated with the out-of-doors,[44] and this at a time when schools were being organized in the cities for the express purpose of getting city children off the streets, out of sight, and inside. It must have been an odd experience in the 1850s to be the child of factory workers—oneself, often, at least a part-time factory worker—and to have held up for one's admiration children who spent their time with chickens and ducks, ponds and sleigh rides.

A landowning, farming ideal is a conservative ideal. Once the Revolution was accomplished, freedom was to be seen as established for all time by 1783, never thereafter to need further attention.[45] We were all to settle down and become Americans, which meant conservators of property. The "all" of "us" were those who either were white propertied Protestants or could be persuaded by school to behave as if we were.[46]

The conservative story of America taught in school respected property and the leadership of the many by the few. Progress was a *national,* not an individual promise. The morality preached by the textbooks repeatedly told of thrift and industry as among the highest moral characters the laborer could acquire, a thrift and industry that promised a lifetime of labor rather than a goal of riches, the acceptance of such a life as good, and a willingness to yield leadership to those with more property and, almost by definition, more virtue. In the enormously popular McGuffey readers, the lessons taught were those of a morality of property.[47]

In the higher readers, those for the fifteen percent of students destined to attend high school in the nineteenth century, Hamiltonian political philosophy prevails and the Jeffersonian past is played down. The principles of property are married in the McGuffey readers to principles of unity, preservation of the Union at all costs, and to the religious purposes of the country. God is invoked not only as the preserver of the Union, but also as the maker and preserver of distinctions between rich and poor. The McGuffey readers aligned the judiciary, the clergy, property, status, Whighery, and conservatism in a powerful alliance defining America. This alliance was created single-handedly by McGuffey's powerfully influential textbook series. It put God and property on the side of the very idea of America. This set of textbooks was successfully marketed throughout the country to the majority of our schools partly because they clearly corresponded to the desires of the majority to legitimize an industrializing society.

McGuffey's readers urged the social virtues of obedience, temperance, modesty, brotherhood, kindness, and veracity in lesson after lesson, and sold forty million copies of these lessons from 1850 to 1870, sixty million more from 1870 to 1890, and even fifteen million from 1890 to 1920.[48] After McGuffey's influence tailed off, the *Cardinal Principles,* or domestic virtues of the social adjustment curriculum, took over. The common culture sold in school created an image of an American content with his lot in life and with the manners and behavior to prove it. This culture was so firmly established by the end of World War I that it prevailed until the foreign and domestic policies of the Vietnam era finally called the question in a way that could not again simply be ignored.

A recent review of textbook practices suggests that these books continue to define curriculum and constitute very big business based on large adoptions by the twenty-two states that choose books for all their schools (the other half leave adoptions of books to their districts).[49] The commercial publishers define now, as they did in McGuffey's heyday, a virtual national curriculum not subject to a democratic process but to the marketplace. The national pastoral ideal has proven very difficult to realign, but it must change if we are going to imagine ourselves all as Americans—city dwellers and laborers, the rural poor as well as the landowners.

And Forgive Us
Our Trespasses

❧

When the common schools were formed the only models available on which to shape them were religious schools. Many of the forms and rituals for instilling patriotism and national identity were drawn from the religious instruction that had shaped education throughout its history. The flag ritual as an opener to the school day came late in the nineteenth century, but children prayed in school from the earliest colonial times until the 1960s. Although we no longer overtly teach a generalized Protestantism, its particular religious purposes structured early schools and American myth-making in schools to an enormous extent.

Voltaire and Tom Paine, for example, were pointedly left out of our stories about the making of the new Republic. Despite their influence on the Revolution, their radicalism and deism were unacceptable to the ministers who wrote textbooks and taught school. When Paine and Voltaire were mentioned at all by the early writers of schoolbooks, it was only in order to argue strongly against them. Heroes were described so as to link the American story closely to a religious cause. Washington, for instance, was portrayed in ways that connected our political history with Revelation.[50] Instead of teaching the history of the Revolution as a result of Enlightenment secular ideas, we taught ourselves a Revolution that derived from religious righteousness.

Protestant Christianity, and more particularly, dissenting Puritan and Presbyterian Protestantism, is described in nineteenth-century textbooks as truth, necessary for virtue and the basis of civic progress. Histories and geographies alike repeatedly contrasted the virtues of dissenting Protestants and the religious toleration and freedom they brought to this country with the evils of European and especially Catholic states. The textbooks ignored Puritan intolerance.

To quote Ruth Miller Elson, the doyenne of schoolbook historians, the schools taught us to believe that we were "the chosen people of God." Washington was portrayed as a latter-day Moses leading us to a promised land, the Constitution his stone tablets, transmitted to an elect people with divine blessing. "Thus the United States is a Protestant nation with a divinely appointed mission" and "American nationalism and religion are thoroughly interwoven."[51] In the words of William Holmes McGuffey's *Second Eclectic Reader,* published in mid-century, our founding "fathers passed through a great many trials . . . the Lord blessed their labors and smiled on them."[52]

The early Presbyterian domination of the schoolbooks, including the Reverend McGuffey, inculcated a Calvinist doctrine of innate damnation for the majority. Most children, and especially poor children, were assumed to be inherently bad. The purpose of school was to convince them they had no hopes of salvation. After the 1850s, McGuffey's books were re-edited by Methodists whose milder attitudes toward children changed the attitude of school teachings to strengthen the innate virtues of children. Such strengthened virtue depended on persuading them that their parents' customs were evil. Methodism, the frontier doctrine, took over when western publishers—particularly the Cincinnati publishers of the McGuffey readers of the 1870s and after—took over leadership of the textbook industry from the earlier eastern monopoly.[53] If the attitude toward children softened with Methodism, it still plainly told children of the poor they were fundamentally flawed because of their poverty. By 1890, the McGuffey readers and the American Book Company, their publisher, controlled 75 to 80 percent of the American schoolbook market. By the time the trust busters broke apart this monopoly in 1910, the push to Americanize and homogenize the enormous new influx of immigrants from southern and eastern Europe was in full swing. Although McGuffey no longer monopolized the schools, all textbook writers were responding to the schools' wishes to transform their motley populations into "Americans" along non-Hispanic, white, middle-class lines. McGuffey's original myths, legends, and heroes were eventually replaced by mild-mannered, middle-class stories,[54] but the religious instruction of all Americans, although less overt than in earlier days, was nonetheless firmly in place. The model American was a Protestant, and the task set for the schools was to help all children fashion themselves in this image.

McGuffey, who created the American identity very nearly single-handedly, still evokes nostalgia in many a citizen today. His books, re-edited several times in the second half of the nineteenth century, consisted of a primer and six "eclectic" readers. Since mid-nineteenth-century schoolrooms were ungraded, students proceeded from the easiest—the *First,* largely written by McGuffey himself—as far as they could go before leaving school.

Current-day nostalgia for McGuffey—and beyond McGuffey, for a "common core of learning" that many a traditionalist wishes would return to our schools—remembers a time when nearly every American schoolchild got his Patrick Henry straight from the reprint in the McGuffey reader. Parson Weems's tale turned up here. So did the Lord's Prayer. So did Blackstone and other conservative interpreters of our early Republic.[55]

Alas, the majority of students in U.S. schools before 1900 never got past the *Second Eclectic Reader,* or at most, partway into the *Third* before leaving school permanently to enter the workforce.[56] The legends, heroes, and extracts from Scott, Mark Antony's speech, Longfellow, and Whittier didn't turn up in the early readers at all. Those books were almost entirely made up of prayers, hymns, moral tales, and saccharine sentiments urging virtue and restraint, written expressly by McGuffey himself and his later editors. No great literature or history was to be found in the books the majority of Americans read in school. Through the *Third Eclectic Reader,* a seemingly inordinate amount of space is devoted not just to stories about beavers building industriously or rich children paternalistically lending a hand to the virtuous poor, but also to the dangers of drink. It seems odd now to see an ABC book give so much space to temperance and stories of the just deserts accorded to drunken young men, but these early readers were being read by twelve- and fourteen- and sixteen-year-olds in many a school where the pressures of farm and factory work meant spotty attendance and correspondingly slow progress in the readers. The common core of learning never prevailed for the majority of schoolchildren beyond the simple moral pieties of the lowest of the readers.

As long as most American schoolchildren were descendants of northern and western Europeans and were therefore both Protestant and white, the forging of an American identity had to do with overcoming relatively fine distinctions among nationalities and Protestantisms. But by the end of the nineteenth century much sharper differences had to be overcome if the model American identity was to prevail. By then, nationality and religion were both believed to be genetic traits.[57] Descriptions of these characteristics were primarily taught in the geography books, but they spilled over into the histories and readers as a set of assumptions, prejudices, and stereotypes. The geographies stressed "cultural" geography, teaching the habits of people in various countries. Italians, for instance, were happy-go-lucky, lazy, prone to vice, and Catholic; the Swiss were industrious; the Africans the lowest of the low; the Jews untrustworthy; and so on.

Given this picture, it was clear that American schools did not expect descendants of Africans, Jews, Italians, and so on ever to become truly American. They couldn't really aspire to the ideal; they just didn't have it in them biologically. Nonetheless, they were all taught by school to behave *as if* they were Americans. Our national virtue depended on our capacity to reject ourselves, to obscure our ethnic and racial affiliations under a mask of national identity. This was perhaps the most outrageous of all the fictions taught in school, since it gained strength in the curriculum just as children of diverse races, religions, and customs began to make their presence felt in the public schools.

Such race theories began to take hold after the Civil War, when the need to bind up the fractured nation was at its height. The ideas came from German race theories invented to assist that nation in forming a unified state through a unified definition of its people. Aryanism and the search for an Ur-civilization to predate all European civilization is the child of Romanticism, not of the Enlightenment, which cared little for race as an argument. Only after 1870 did the general meaning of the word *race* come to be a subset of the human species based on physical characteristics. Before then, the word generally meant simply progeny, such as the entire human race, or the race of the Marlboroughs (the family's offspring), or (metaphorically) the race of sports enthusiasts, and so on.[58] It meant, in effect, breed, without any pejorative connotations. But nationalism, a word also postdating 1870,[59] imperialism, colonialism, and slavery needed a racial theory that would explain why everyone was "equal" but not everyone would participate equally in the attributes of the new nation's character. Daughters and Sons of the Revolution defined the limits of full participation. The geography books hastened to explain how it worked.

In our own times ideas about innate superiority have been expressed in two ways: in the belief in the superiority of America to all other countries and systems; and in the idea of fixed, innate I.Q. and "aptitude." Curricula devised to match children's differing abilities, disabilities, and disadvantages maintained those disadvantages from one generation to the next. For the poor, history curricula taught you to believe in the white, Protestant, male-dominated political structure. History was not, by definition, something you or your ancestors participated in. Nineteenth-century books were full of absolutes and certainties about the relationship between love of God, love of country, individual virtue and "the perfection of the United States."[60] The *rightness* of the United States and all its actions continues to inform twentieth-century schoolbooks without having to be stated quite so often.

Heroes and a cult of heroes and legends became the major vehicles for inculcating U.S. history for the majority of schoolchildren. Heroes as representatives of political states have always helped to define those states, and through poetry have always helped to bind the allegiance of the people. In America, textbook editors rejected Walt Whitman's epic offerings, choosing instead to anthologize his patriotic Lincoln elegy, "O Captain, My Captain." I was amused to see that Diane Ravitch's recently published *The American Reader* reprints it along with Whitman's "I Hear America Singing," a sentimental paean to happy folk at work.[61] The poet's more radical celebrations of the diversity of America, never found acceptable for schoolchildren, remain generally neglected.

Heroism was also a central necessity of Romanticism, and particularly of the Romanticism that justified imperialism in Europe and America in the later nineteenth century. The movement to unify Germany entailed the creation of epic Wagnerian heroes; the establishment of a United States as an idea in the absence of any length of history entailed a substitution of heroes for history. The Founding Fathers, the legends about Washington, the canonization of Franklin and, later, Lincoln—the very naming of high schools the length and breadth of the land (it's a poor community indeed that lacks a Washington or Lincoln High School)—were the content of history education. Today many a traditionalist continues to urge that heroes and legends should return to our schools in force, especially for our elementary-school children, again as a substitute for history.[62]

Un-Americans

The English, the English, the English are best,
I wouldn't give tuppence for all of the rest.

MICHAEL FLANDERS AND DONALD SWANN
"A SONG OF PATRIOTIC PREJUDICE"

The image of America inculcated by the old legends and by the entire mythology of history in school leaves out the majority of Americans. The origins of the anti-Catholicism of American schools in the religious warfare of Reformation Europe have been mentioned. Anti-Catholicism played itself out in the schools in negative portrayals of Catholics, Catholicism, and nationalities associated with Catholicism, from the Spanish to Latin and Central Americans to Hispanics in North America, the French, Irish, Italians, and so on. It also resulted in mayhem and bloodshed in big cities over school curricula and in a continuing uncomfortable relationship between public and parochial schools to this day.

Nineteenth-century schoolbooks taught that Catholicism was subversive, and in fact, un-American.[63] After 1870, such teachings calmed down, for by then Catholics had started their own schools in the big cities and post–Civil War sectarian controversies generally receded as issues of race and nationality gained urgency. Anti-Catholicism left an enduring legacy, however, in the absence from our schoolbooks of attention to the real achievements of Catholicism and Catholics and in the presence of a success story that is essentially the story of the Protestant apotheosis in the New World. In Catholic schools, moreover, children were told that Jesus gave sanction to American patriotism.[64]

Also left out of the ideal America were those peoples considered to be of inferior race. One of the definitions of progress for America came to be the extermination or subjugation of such races. Ruth Elson notes that Native

Americans simply vanished from the schoolbooks, but not until they had first been transformed into "savages." Early in the nineteenth century descriptions of the many different Native American societies abounded in the histories and geographies, but they later faded away. As Native Americans were portrayed as obstacles standing in the way of progress, so their disappearance was first divinely sanctioned in the schoolbooks and then exterminated from the memory of school.[65]

The Jews began the nineteenth century as a religious group and ended it as a race.[66] This confusion of nature and nurture, a convenience of certain aspects of Romantic racial theory, has been turning up frequently in current-day discussions of schooling by and for minorities. By ascribing religion to inheritance, racial theorists of the last century could justify as divinely sanctioned both the privilege of the Protestant majority and the powerlessness of others.

Before the Civil War, the "Negro" was simply the most "degraded" of peoples. After emancipation, innate inferiority continued to be assumed and was indeed bolstered by some interpretations of Darwin. It is fascinating to note how often Darwin was (and for some still is) perceived as blasphemous except in those cases where his work could be twisted to provide "scientific" support for racism. Having emancipated the slaves, the schoolbooks ceased to mention the subsequent fates of blacks.[67] Until the 1960s, textbooks often left the entire history of African-Americans out of the story of our country's history.[68]

The 1870s brought a xenophobia that grew to its apogee in the 1920s and reappeared again in the 1950s, making it clear that only one type of American was truly a patriot and that conformity to that model was essentially a matter of inheritance. The period 1870–1914 saw the beginnings of global mass migrations on an unprecedented scale, particularly in the United States where Europe's huddled masses yearned to live and where African-Americans were beginning to participate in the American polity. In the face of such social upheavals, those with precarious holds on a little bit of the good life may have turned reactionary to preserve what they had. Xenophobia was the result, and xenophobia was taught in school.

History became fixed in place. The Constitution became a reverenced, if little discussed, symbol. Liberty and freedom were preached in school at the same time as they were clearly limited in reality to those who were capable of its fullest inheritance. The message in the schoolbooks was that "only eternal vigilance against unidentified enemies will preserve freedom."[69] America became a bark of freedom in hostile seas, needing to keep a stern lookout both for enemies from without and the even more insidious enemies within.

It is worth dwelling on the 1870 to 1914 period because in that time the United States consolidated its territory, its nationhood, its idea of nationalism, and its public schools. There were protests from historians that American supernationalism would cut us off from the rest of the intellectual world, but they went largely unheeded.[70] The history of the schools since then is a series of variations on a theme. Many writers have tried to suggest that the teaching of history got its death blow in the 1920s and thereafter, when "social studies" reduced the subject to mere socialization for motley Americans. Little history, however, and much national myth has *always* been the staple of U.S. education, *for the poor and laboring classes,* including all people of color. They stopped going to school just when history began to be taught in earnest, in high school.

In high school, moreover, the history taught has tended more and more to elevate English origins and to imagine the democratic idea as an English inheritance from the Greeks. The English "love of liberty" was taught in the nineteenth century as a *racial* characteristic. But British history prior to the end of the nineteenth century rarely mentioned Magna Carta. By the height of our American love affair with our British ancestry in the 1890s, British history was being searched diligently for evidence of democracy.[71] Magna Carta emerged, was reified, and stands today as an icon to be carted around the country as H. Ross Perot, the Texas billionaire, did for the celebrations of the 200th anniversary of the Constitution.

The second group to be raised up by late nineteenth-century historiography, and nearly to the same heights as the British, were the Germans, described by American histories and geographies as industrious, honest, thrifty, inventive like us, and praiseworthy above all for their philosophy and learning. Equally admired was German glorification of war and of military heroes.[72] For that matter, the schoolbooks' only French hero was Napoleon, for similar reasons. This admiration for German militarism, the elevation of the heroic father figure who was fierce and victorious in battle, and the racial basis for such admiration that equated individual heroism with the racial character of his nation, are part and parcel of Romanticism, which transformed the story of America.

Coloring Within the Lines

Question: What do you think of Western Civilization?
Gandhi: I think it would be a very good idea.

Until the 1970s Africans, Asians, Native Americans, and Hispanics in the New World had very nearly vanished from U.S. history textbooks,[73] and at the same time the poor and the laboring classes of all colors and nationalities became invisible as well. Under serious and unrelenting pressure from vocal minorities, textbook companies have made changes in their practices of inclusion and states and school districts have woken up to a need to change the stories told about American and world history. The seventies saw the ethnic-heritage movement take fire, fueled in part by the immensely popular television version of Alex Haley's *Roots*. Ethnicity became a fad for everyone, as we happily got back in touch with customs and traditions that our parents and grandparents had as happily shed on first becoming Americans. The seventies and early eighties also saw the rise of fundamentalist movements everywhere in the world as people reacted to the homogenization of modern American culture, which they saw as a threat to ancient beliefs, ways of being, and identities. To reject American culture—the culture of mass marketing, democracy, and emancipation of women—was to reject both modernism and the secularism that modernism entails. In the United States, that rejection came from the so-called moral majority, which reacted against the removal of prayer from public schools, fled the newly integrated schools of the South, and set up Christian schools where prayer, creationism, and other fundamentalist beliefs could be restored to the curriculum.[74] Ironically, in the 1980s multiculturalism often repeated this pattern, setting up a similar desire to escape the threat of being swamped by a generalized American culture by putting traditional cultures of the various ethnic groups in its place. Afrocentrists, for example, and the moral majority alike reject the secular, rationalist education that leads to modernism and with it an undifferentiated, mass American culture.

By the mid-1970s, many voices began to call for multicultural education in the schools, to broaden the history of our country to include the accomplishments of people other than its military and political heroes. New forms of history being explored in universities were turning up information about people of all kinds whose individual voices had hitherto been less available to us than those of published white males. Social history, local history, domestic anthropology, women's history, and Chicano and African-American interdisciplinary studies, to name a few, flowered in the 1970s and 1980s. We learned far more than we had ever known before about ordinary people, how they lived, and how their work, their migrations, the products of their hands, their wishes and their beliefs, made up an exciting, new, and richly patterned texture for history to study. Such history was less about heroes or nationalism than it was about groups and developments that cut across national borders or focused on different horizons. This new history has only just begun to affect school teaching; in general our schoolteachers went to college before it came to fruition in the academy. The new history does, however, feature prominently among historians who began to work with teachers in the 1980s to reconfigure the social studies.

In the early 1970s conservative textbook companies introduced changes cautiously. Careful of their profits, they just colored in a few faces in the illustrations, but even these were at first sold only regionally in the more progressive sections of the country. Textbooks then began to include heroic African-Americans and others, including women, at various points in the history they told. New York and California, our two most populous and diverse states, are also two of the states that regulate schools most strongly from central offices. They have recently undergone a difficult process of revising the teaching of history in a much more thoroughgoing way than has ever been attempted before. Both states have commissioned scholars, teachers, and community representatives to reconsider history with a view to including all of America's peoples while keeping an eye on careful historical scholarship and balance.

The backbone of history as conceived by public schools to date has been the idea that individual virtue represents national virtue. The individual connects to the state via the Protestant idea of an elect people, each one of whom participates in the body of the elect through his individual conscience and resemblance to the ideal. The very source of minority discontent with American schools, however, comes from *group* power and group identity, which dissents both from the national ideal and from nations built of individual successes. The California *History–Social Science Framework* and the New York State *Curriculum of Inclusion* both attempt to meet the obvious need to revise our ideas about who is an American and how America got to be this way, by casting much wider nets than our public schools have done in the past. But both of these state reforms have caused serious dissatisfactions among minorities convinced that the curricula remain basically ethnocentric—that is, primarily a tale told from a European-American perspective. Traditionalists also worry that the new curricula are divisive when they debunk old myths without sufficiently replacing them with a new civic religion in which the entire country could happily believe.

The new California *History–Social Science Framework,* first issued in 1987, restores history to the heart of social studies education. It asks that history be "a story well told," avoid surface skimming in favor of in-depth study of a smaller list of topics than has heretofore been the case, hopes for multicultural perspectives rather than white ethnocentricity, wishes to teach "ethical understanding and civic virtue," highlights our democratic values, studies the Constitution and Bill of Rights, and includes the history of religion.[75] The new curriculum has been acclaimed by many of our country's foremost historians and educators as the best available model to date for a strong, sensible, and useful social studies.

The new framework begins California history with the story of California's indigenous people rather than with European settlers from the East, and it puts the whole of U.S. history in the context of world history instead of artificially removing it. In addition, the world history to be offered traces the histories of African and Asian civilizations as well as those of Europe.

Such major shifts in perspective ought, one would think, to appeal to minorities in this country whose stories had heretofore been slighted. But when California's Department of Education began conducting hearings on textbooks to support this curriculum in 1990, not only minorities but also traditionalists found much with which to quarrel. The Houghton Mifflin social-studies textbook series matched California's radical shift of perspective by portraying Native Americans, Africans, and Spaniards as early inhabitants of Florida; not until the fifth chapter does the book get around to Columbus. Despite this major change in the American creation story, many minorities attending the hearings on textbook adoption for the new curriculum claimed that the new books were still racist. The story being told, they felt, was basically one that tells of the triumph of Western ideas. They even claimed that to describe Native American migrations from Asia to the American continents is racist. They wanted history to be told from the perspective of the group being described, and for each group's version of history, whether Hispanic or Native American or African-American, to be given equal credence by school. A *single* narrative or story, as called for by the California *Framework*, would by definition, therefore, be racist. More moderate critics of the framework and its accompanying texts came from minorities who believe that only good things should be told about each minority group. Such a position substitutes for history, in one commentator's words, a "plea . . . for the public equivalent of love."[76]

A traditionalist historian, Arthur Schlesinger, Jr., asserts, however, that U.S. history is essentially a continuation of European history and to deny this is to falsify history. Schlesinger is quite contemptuous of "the fallacy of 'the superior virtue of the oppressed.' " He goes on to argue for a teaching of the history of democracy as a "creed" and talks about "belief in one's own culture." Without this, he sees the old melting-pot metaphor yielding "to the Tower of Babel."[77] Schlesinger's preferred metaphors make it clear that he considers the multicultural challenge to traditional history a challenge to the old faith.

Minority groups opposed the new textbooks for their failure to make myth out of minority ways of life, and Schlesinger opposed minority dissent by insisting on belief in a shared culture and creed. These two views form the crux of the current debate about U.S. history. The Houghton Mifflin series took a centrist position, endorsing neither creeds nor mythologies while attempting to refocus the center of discussion on the many peoples who interacted in U.S. and world history. These textbooks were adopted for use in the Los Angeles Unified School District in spring, 1991, despite all the furor.

In New York, the State Commissioner for Education had to convene two committees to evaluate its new "curriculum of inclusion" for social studies, in 1989 and again in 1990. The first group issued a report containing strong charges that the schools taught Eurocentric racism. When a new committee was convened, it issued a report on the history curriculum from which two members, notable historians Kenneth Jackson and Arthur Schlesinger, Jr., publicly demurred. The first report wanted to teach Iroquois origins of American democracy; the second points out that some U.S. minorities are in fact world majorities. Jackson, Schlesinger, and Mario Cuomo, the governor of New York, all worry that the new multicultural history advocated by the commission could Balkanize our country.

We are obviously in a state of some turmoil about our teaching of history. Much of the trouble, it seems to me, comes from Romantic ideas on both sides. Schlesinger and others are right to accuse radical minority groups of wanting to romanticize "the people," a German Romantic *Volk* that never existed but was idealized as the embodiment of racial virtue. Minorities are right, however, to charge that given our rapidly changing demographics, the Eurocentric story line still continues to ring false as the only possible story that could be told about America.

Part of the trouble comes from the definition of history as story. A history whose purpose is the justification of the triumphant nation requires a plot that turns out well for us, the good guys. Unfortunately, the evidence on which history is based has no plot.[78] It is, in some ways, "one damn thing after another." Historians impose plot on evidence in order to interpret causality—to make sense of the disparate evidence of the past and to work backward from a known conclusion to its probable causes.[79] What has happened in academic history is that the old, big syntheses of history of the 1950s that told a story of American triumph can no longer be written. Those plots have been called into serious question. No new syntheses of history have yet fully been produced to replace them. This leaves schools in a quandary. Multiculturalists keep asking for multiple histories, each told from a different perspective because no single new story that combines all the different possible stories has yet been imagined. One historian, Thomas Bender, believes it is indeed possible to write a new, unified history that will tell a single American story. He suggests, intriguingly, that it is possible to take all the social, local, feminist, Chicano, African-American, and other such histories and fashion from them a single narrative that describes the ways all social groups interacted politically in our history. Such a synthesis would show how political history is a product of social interactions. Bender would call such a synthesis neither social history nor political history, but a history of "political culture," connecting the private world of the social group with the public world of power and showing how all Americans partake fully in the history of the nation.[80] Until such a new synthesis is written, however, we find ourselves mired in a struggle between those who defend the syntheses of the past and those who so far have seen no alternative but to call for multiple, disconnected histories of individual social groups. If Bender's idea for a new kind of narrative history that will weave these disparate stories together is feasible, then we must call for academic historians to work on this as their highest professional priority.

Many historians have been working closely with teachers over the past decade to reconsider what the social studies should teach in school. The National Commission on Social Studies in the Schools (NCSS) asked historian David Jenness to conduct a dispassionate inquiry into the history of the social studies as background for the work of the NCSS Task Force on Curriculum. Jenness reminds us in his book, *Making Sense of Social Studies*

(1990), that historians like to claim that history sets us free, but the way it has been taught in school, history has been used to bind us.[81] Arthur Schlesinger, Jr., for instance, suggests that teaching a democratic creed will bind us together as a nation much in the way that the earlier nation-building myths of school were meant to mold a unified people.[82] This tension between the freedom of democracy and the need for bonding in a nation has been a problem with history teaching in schools from the start. I would suggest, however, that there is only a problem as long as we fail to believe in the students' capacity for judgment. It's the old eighteenth-century argument all over again: how do you make a republic out of a motley assortment of people? Do you educate just a few of them as leaders and the rest as followers, or do you educate all of them for democracy, trusting all to have, as a result of education, the capacity to act responsibly? Those who insist on a return to legends, heroes, and a belief in America as a special, exceptional, and morally right nation and the past as a fixed, finished, *true* story are taking a position that brooks little argument, dissent, or even discussion of the past. Such a position implies a lack of trust that the students will behave like good Americans unless they are wholehearted parties to this set of beliefs about America. It distrusts students to look at the evidence, draw their own conclusions, and still behave like good Americans. It distrusts their intellects and, ultimately and ironically, their individuality.

The National Commission on Social Studies in the Schools' report of 1989 brought together professors and teachers from all over the country to imagine an ideal social studies curriculum for all Americans. The Task Force on Curriculum called for a coherent course of study from kindergarten to twelfth grade, with the core of it as history and geography, but not neglecting civics, government, and other related topics. The task force also made a strong argument for the full integration of American history into world history.[83]

Another group, the Bradley Commission on History in the Schools, again composed of scholars and teachers, produced a report in 1988 that firmly called for more history in the social studies and more school time for history. They advocated, like all reformers of history teaching from the days of the 1890s reform committee to the present, less emphasis on facts alone and more on understanding.[84] This was a call also for a broader, more inclusive history, but one that places the story of Western Civilization at the heart of world history. Their Western Civilization repeats the story of progress from Greece to Rome, the Middle Ages, the Renaissance, the Reformation, and the English Revolution, a story with which we are familiar. The Bradley group also calls for greater attention to Asia, Africa, and the indigenous Americas.

Individual historians writing for the Bradley Commission commented on the report's call for more history, representing a variety of ideas about what kind of history should be added to our school curricula. Gary Nash wanted to replace the Great Man theory that believes political leaders are the principal makers of history with a democratic history that looks at the collective, group histories of farmers, laborers, women, and so on. In the same book Charlotte Crabtree, who currently directs the federally funded National Center for History in the Schools at UCLA (in which Professor Nash holds the principal academic leadership) wanted elementary schools to return to the myths, legends, and heroes of yore. And Ross Dunn wanted broad global themes to become the organizing principles for teaching history.[85]

The Bradley Commission seems to accommodate a variety of positions on what we mean by history, yet their overall recommendations are for a retelling of the triumphal story of the West and a return to heroic tales for the youngest students. David Jenness, in contrast, believes that narrative history is the most complex history of all, requiring highly sophisticated critical abilities to discern it as history rather than accede to it as a matter of faith. Such stories, he feels, are best left to the oldest, most sophisticated students, not the youngest or most naive.[86]

Tom Holt writing for the College Board in 1990 suggests a history that invites students into the act of interpretation and story telling—one that teaches students by including their active participation in history. Holt's idea is to emphasize the art of interpretation of evidence and the construction of narrative argument to invite students into the act of constructing history. His approach would enable students to understand history from the inside out. What yet remains to be addressed in such an approach is the question of the larger narrative that structures the students' work. Someone ultimately must decide which documents should be studied and what shape the course of study will take. We are always thrown back on the need for some kind of narrative framework within which teachers and students can proceed.

Beginning in 1990, the federal government sponsored the "America 2000" goals for education in the new millennium. The states' fifty governors worked with the president to highlight history and geography as two of the five "core subjects" of national curriculum improvement. The "America 2000" plan said nothing about changing the history content of school; it sought instead to establish national tests that would enable us to measure our progress toward improvement. Yet debate rages among politicians and educators over what kind of tests to use. In the absence of a viable new way of teaching and testing history or of anything like consensus on what constitutes American history, federal agencies, leaders, and advisors may prevail with their preferred versions, which say that the American heritage of democracy should form the centerpiece of history teaching.[87]

All the calls for experimentation and reform reflect the complexity and difficulty of the issues to be resolved in teaching history in our diverse society. The terms in which the debate has been set seem to suggest that we must choose between a history that praises individual freedom along with the democratic ideology or one that is subject to many differing group perspectives contending for mastery. Amy Gutmann, a philosopher writing on democratic education, suggests that rather than having to choose one or the other view, we need to realize that democracy functions best through their constant interplay. Other writers call for an education of enculturation that teaches both the value system of the majority and a hearty skepticism about it. Yet other writers point out that as long as the structure of school is itself authoritarian, democracy can never truly be taught there.[88] To fail to believe and act on the belief that all students are capable of learning is to fail to teach democracy.

Teachers themselves are highly sensitive to community norms and carefully structure what they teach to comply with these norms and expectations. The populace generally does believe the stories they were taught in school. Teachers are overwhelmed with prepared materials: heavy textbooks, ancillary teaching tools, and district guides. They're required to "cover" so much that the inevitable result is superficial, factual recall for short-order tests. Despite their best efforts, many social studies teachers generally feel their courses are inadequate to the serious study of history and geography, which they would like to teach through major interdisciplinary themes and ideas. The pressure to cover too much results in a minimum actually being taught.[89] New demands for alternative perspectives or for meeting multiple sets of standards (or both), are seen by social studies teachers as merely add-ons to an already overstuffed curriculum. Contending with the demands of community groups, state regulations, district requirements, new standards, and old textbooks, teachers are left to fend for themselves to make sense out of all this for their students.

In the process, what suffers most is the democracy everyone seems out to save. American students generally have a poor understanding of democratic processes, including democratic dissent. Indeed, we seem to be teaching our children that real participatory democracy is at odds with national allegiance. Studies show that, for African-Americans, civics courses in school tend to increase loyalty and conformity rather than active, participatory democracy.[90]

Finding a way for all Americans to participate in the democracy rather than merely to treat it unthinkingly as a creed would be the centerpiece of a truly multicultural education. Amy Gutmann's *Democratic Education* urges that the aim of our public schools should be to prepare the populace for each citizen's equal opportunity to exert the rights and responsibilities of citizenship, rather than the lesser task of preparing students for equal opportunity for economic success. Current federal arguments for public education, however, consistently stress economic betterment for the individual and economic competitive advantage for the nation as the twin goals of school. Capitalism, or the "free market economic system," is constantly urged on schools as the corrective to our national economic woes. Unfortunately, like the democratic heritage, teaching in these fields has come in the form of prescription and consent rather than through analysis. If we fail to teach a democratic process, we fail to teach the capacity to think and to judge in any subject, and our nation of diverse people will lack those critical capacities when most they and we need them. An education that took democratic ideals seriously in the methods and content of history instruction would by definition become a curriculum of inclusion for all.

Formulating a new, inclusive approach to history might involve a more coherent placement of U.S. history in the context of world history. World history continues today generally to be taught as if *we* were the single goal toward which all before us were striving.[91] Current events, global education, and "world cultures" programs in schools, on the other hand, tend to be ahistorical as they focus on issues in the news and cross-cultural comparisons. Such studies gained some popularity in the 1970s and 1980s in states and districts seeking to teach about global patterns and global communities in an increasingly closely knit world economy and environment. Such approaches may have their merits, but they generally avoid serious attention to the historical causes of contemporary issues, and they also tend to reveal our old biases.[92] At their worst, global courses just try to teach kids to like everybody.[93]

Since history teaches us to define ourselves and our place in the world, history has become the weathervane of our popular beliefs, turned this way and that by contending theories of education, contending beliefs about what constitutes our common culture, and contending desires for power among racial, ethnic, and class groups. In the face of mounting demands for very different images of America, teachers in practice most often stick to the textbook in hand, rarely straying from its platitudes and avoiding topics, like religion, sex, and money, that might cause controversy. The old textbooks tried to avoid assigning blame; the new ones try to make everyone feel good about themselves. Throughout, the poor are perceived as suffering from a causeless affliction that needs to be cured.[94] Real ideas and the texts in which they were explored by writers and thinkers over the centuries are largely absent from the schoolroom. Modern teachers are so anxious to attract a flicker of student interest, they too often substitute video and fiction for the study of historical texts themselves. For all the veneration of the greats of history, few of their writings find their way into the classroom where students could read them and judge for themselves. Elementary social-studies classrooms teach young children to believe eternal verities; then high school teachers find it next to impossible to get the students engaged in debate about the tough and interesting questions that history raises.

The Riddle of History
in a Democracy

School districts, especially urban ones sympathetic to the need to address the ethnic makeup of at least their own student bodies, hasten to fiddle with the social studies curriculum to appease community wishes. In one big-city system, such haste recently resulted in a slapped-together teacher's guide to Puerto Rican culture, written apparently with little scholarly or community consultation. Among other howlers, the published guide claimed piñatas appear as traditional Christmas fare in Puerto Rico. Outrage from the Puerto Rican community revealed the school district's mistake. Another urban district is in the process of creating a multicultural curriculum by "infusing" perspectives and beliefs of Africans, Asians, Native Americans, Hispanics, and Pacific Islanders into the existing Eurocentric curriculum in all subject areas. Besides a monumental confusion of race with culture, this curriculum seems to be yet another over-hasty compilation of beliefs with little attention to historical scholarship. Indeed, historical scholarship is perceived by the compilers as just another Western notion, of no more value to schoolchildren than any other belief system.

In their haste, school districts respond to new minority demands in their communities by replacing the old racist myths of the nineteenth century with new myths of "the superior moral qualities of minorities," as if all whites were uniformly oppressors and all the oppressed were uniformly in close touch with natural inherent virtue.[95] This extension of Romantic idealism and the racist theories it gave rise to repeats a Manichaean view that sees either all good or all evil in the protagonists of history rather than deal with the muddles and confusions and difficulties of real life.

What, then, should we do with history in the schools? I suspect we need to find some way of teaching the practice of history using the materials of the past from the United States and around the world. The practice of history differs considerably from the transmission of myth. It consists of the capacity of students to interpret the past, thereby making themselves a part of the narratives they create. Students will still need guidance as to which documents to read in order to fashion their interpretations, and the documents chosen should be drawn from the source texts of political and social history. They might include professional historians' interpretations of the past. But the students' job will be to interpret the texts of historians as well as other sources of evidence. The fifth graders who acted out their interpretation of a Native American description of the European encounter were doing just this. So was a class of urban high-school students I observed recently who read letters and proclamations relating to an incident in British Indian history and who watched brief passages of a film on Gandhi's Great Salt March. The teacher then asked them to write—in full sentences—their interpretation of what they had seen and read. Writing enabled the students to form a clear argument concerning the evidence with which they had been presented. Only then did the teacher open up the classroom to general discussion. The students were highly articulate, having had a chance to interpret texts and formulate understandings for themselves. They asked good questions—of the teacher, of each other, and of the texts. Those questions resulted in a tentative thesis, formulated by the class as a whole, concerning British uses of power in India. Every student in the room was actively engaged in the construction of historical interpretation.

The teacher chose the texts to present to her class, as well as a method of teaching that placed her students in the role of active historians. The teacher's choices of texts were based on decisions made by a group of teachers who wanted to investigate questions of political power in a course on modern history. The decision to use an example from India was based on a state mandate for all students to learn about India at a particular time in the tenth grade. The state provided a framework, or general outline, of the material to be taught, but the teachers in that particular school devised a course of study that would allow students direct access to the raw materials of history and opportunities to interpret it.

By picking and choosing our history to suit our nation-building needs, we constructed myths that are no longer tenable. The current controversy over history in the schools will not be resolved if some of us doggedly stick to beliefs unacceptable to other groups, while others insist, like many a Third World, postcolonial nation, on rewriting history to suit one or another subgroup.[96] I can imagine, however, a history without textbooks and without unacceptable ideas of nationalism, yet with a capacity to form the citizenry of a democracy. I trust in our democracy, in the capacity of our children's minds, and in their ability to become committed citizens not because they've been taught a civic religion but because they've read the texts, considered the evidence of the past, argued, experienced, and thought it through, developed the critical capacities to make responsible judgments for themselves, and arrived at interpretations of history that depend on a commitment to the processes of democracy. Western Europe itself, in this era of confederation, is moving away from the ultranationalisms that have caused worldwide grief in our century. The Council of Europe's education newsletter announced in 1990 that "History should no longer be presented mainly from a national point of view."[97] That's an astounding recommendation, but one that holds the clue to our future as well.

Nations are imagined communities, fabulations based entirely on shared beliefs.[98] Minority discontent with school is very much a discontent with the historic association between race theory and nationalism. The discontent of the poor and the workers is equally a discontent with a schooling that has preached democracy and practiced paternalism. If the children of the poor and the workers demonstrate their distaste for such stories by showing their backs to school, we should not be either surprised or discouraged. We should instead sit down with them to craft—for the first time—a history that makes sense for building not just a nation, but a democracy.

III

FIRING THE CANON

A Bible for every family, a school for every district,
and a pastor for every thousand souls.
Rev. Lyman Beecher

I did my B.A. in Ethnic Studies in the early sixties;
only they didn't call it that back then.
They called it "English."
Tony Cade Bambara

The Machine
in the Classroom

Six times in the last year, during visits to elementary and secondary class-rooms, I have witnessed the "simile and metaphor lesson." This is the vocab-ulary lesson in which students are taught to distinguish between similes (comparisons of unlike objects using *like* or *as*) and metaphors (compar-isons of unlike objects without a comparative). In all six cases, the teachers I watched neglected to tell the students that these comparisons are of *un*like, concrete objects; that they are only two forms of figurative language out of many that could be taught; or that to teach such vocabulary at all constitutes the final contemporary remnant of classical rhetoric left from a nineteenth-century curriculum almost entirely based on formal rhetoric.

One teacher, described by colleagues as the "best language skills teacher in the school," handed students on the left side of the room a series of large cards on each of which the first half of a phrase was written. Similar cards, each bearing the second half of the phrase, were handed to students on the right side. The class was a "Chapter I" remedial reading class for eighth graders, some of whom were obviously sixteen and eighteen years old and who had been in such classrooms repeatedly for years without managing to learn to read well. A student on the left would be asked to read from her card. She would happily read, "Pretty as a _____." Then the student on the right who had the "correct" fill-in for the first student's blank was supposed to raise his hand.

One very tall, mustachioed eighth-grader had the word *ox* on his card, and he wanted desperately to be "right," so he raised his hand and read it off. That wasn't the answer to "Pretty as a _____." The teacher called on one student after another on the right side of the room; finally one who wasn't in the mood for raising his hand that day was found to be hoarding the word *picture*. And so it went. The left side of the room had cliché after cliché on their cards; my friend with *ox* kept trying to offer the all he had, but was continually "wrong." He'd been dealt a bad hand. "Strong as an _____" never came up before the bell rang.

Chapter I of the reauthorized bill of the Elementary and Secondary Education Act of 1965 is the nation's largest program for remediating children of the poor. Schools must prove children in their care are poor in order to qualify for the money, which is often spent on specialist reading teachers who pull students from regular classrooms for extra reading or "language skills" instruction. Chapter I funding is also closely linked to standardized tests required by federal administration of the program, so the instruction in the classroom is virtually all geared to coaching for the tests. I have seen high-school Chapter I classes where a five-page version of Melville's *Moby-Dick* was the text. Students were then expected to go to math classes where they were given math textbooks that I find unreadably dense and English classes where, when the unvarnished Shakespeare turns up, students' eyes glaze over.

Such conceptions of language and reading contaminate the curriculum for all. Students who are deemed not to read well based on standardized test results and grades—and who qualify as poor in the eyes of the federal government—end up in Chapter I reading programs that take language apart into tiny pieces. The idea seems to be that students should proceed from small fragments of language to larger units later on. Such approaches to reading remediation have infected all but honors English in most American schools.

Students are confronted with such instruction in English classes daily and throughout their schooling. They are presented with grammar workbooks, "basal" readers, and basal worksheets in first grade, to discover that most of English consists of vocabulary, connect-the-word lessons, and reading for the purpose of answering questions at the end of the chapter. According to one researcher, no more than 3 percent of student work in high school involves writing a paragraph or more. A 1990 survey shows that seniors in high school are required to read no more than ten pages a day for all their school subjects.[1] These disassembled forms of language and literature are often the exclusive form of instruction offered to the children of the poor. Children who use rich figurative language in their homes and on the street, who engage happily in word play, who love stories and poetry in their natural settings, are turned into dolts in classrooms where English and reading are transformed from subjects of wonder into punishments for the uninitiated.

A major new movement in language and literature, particularly at the elementary level, but also appearing sporadically in secondary schools, has begun to take hold in many classrooms around the country. In this "whole language" movement, teachers have begun to approach reading and writing "holistically," meaning they promote extended reading for pleasure and enlightenment and frequent writing for fluency. Such teachers fill their schoolrooms with trade books rather than textbooks. They read to children and encourage children to select their own reading, urging students to record personal reactions to their reading and other experiences in daily journals and discussing their reading and writing in small groups. Such teachers refrain from correcting mechanical errors on the first draft of student writing, preferring to encourage students to shape their ideas in larger ways before worrying over details. Whole-language teachers try to develop students' personal needs to read and write rather than impose artificial exercises on them from on high.

Students like the one who could not figure out how to get his ox to fit into a pretty picture fare very well in whole-language classrooms. One such student, who had gotten to ninth grade with little experience of reading or writing, found herself in a literature class where the teacher orchestrated multiple opportunities for students to read a diverse array of African-American, British, and world literature and where the teacher insisted on extensive student writing every day. Writing in her journal one day, the student told of plans to go to college and promised she would never forget the teacher who, in ninth grade, finally taught her how to read.

We repeatedly wring our hands over the tragedy of children reaching ninth grade—or even twelfth—without having learned to read. The peculiar nature of English language and literature instruction that still dominates in most classrooms and the history of why these subjects are structured to disassemble language rather than to create it will be taken up in this part.

In the beginning of the nineteenth century, American schoolbooks on rhetoric analyzed the beauties of the great writers of the past. Homer, Virgil, Milton, and even Voltaire got a hearing in books originally written for university audiences in Scotland and England. Up to forty-two different figures of speech were identified and memorized by high-school students in the period.[2] By the late nineteenth century these writers had disappeared from the rhetoric classes, now called "composition," and access to style came only from lists of definitions of rhetorical terms.[3] Composition had split off from reading. The final remnant of this rhetorical approach to writing can be seen when a puzzled teenager is asked to understand a figure of speech divorced from its context, isolated from any writing purpose, and cut into two pieces of paper, half of which is left in someone else's hands. Meaning could hardly be more thoroughly banished from such a classroom if one had deliberately set out to remove it.

Literacy as an act of personal salvation for all of the people became a possibility when Martin Luther put a vernacular Bible and its interpretation directly into Protestant hands. The United States came into being partially as a result of widespread literacy and the capacity to make individual decisions based on the reading of complex texts. But the subsequent history of schooling in America has, for a variety of reasons, retreated significantly from such a generous attitude toward the people and their intellectual development. Romantic nationalism, the professionalization of English studies, racism, and scientific determination have over the intervening years conspired to detach most Americans from interpretive reading of texts.

From the Renaissance to the twentieth century, if you were the son of a gentleman and destined to rule, "grammar" school meant Latin and Greek grammar. You spent most of your school hours turning classical writing—history, literature, essays, poetry—into grammar exercises, parsing sentences to show you could name the parts of speech and memorizing long passages to show you "knew" them. Much of American education in the past and still today equates "knowing" with knowing "by heart." We still search literature for the answers to questions—answers that can be memorized, selected from a list of four possible choices on a machine-scorable test, marked on a grid with a number two pencil: answers that are "right."

Except for the prose in basal readers, no literature was ever written for such purposes. Like the other arts, literature has only been allowed a place in school learning if its purposes can be described in the interests of national culture and moral development. While many writers have, throughout history, explicitly written in order to glorify their nations and national heroes or to establish the history of the people and their divine origins, such purposes have become dominant for literature in school. Closely linked with national purposes for studying literature are moral purposes, and in the case of American public schools that has meant the religious purposes closely allied with our nineteenth-century nation building.

English departments in both universities and high schools trace the American tradition of literature—the canon—from the masterworks of Europe to the Puritan writers of the seventeenth century, through the twentieth century in a line that admires highly wrought language and formal structure. This American literary tradition is primarily a white and male tradition. A very different lineage, however, that comes from American writers of color and women, has begun to be explored; it includes many works that draw on different language traditions and forms, including oral literature, and a focus on subject matter that often differs from that in the canon.[4] I hope to show, however, that *canon* as applied to the literature taught in public schools has a literal meaning. Throughout our history, the Protestant Bible and Protestant prayer have constituted our basic school texts and have subsequently shaped English studies as a whole.

When in 1963 the Supreme Court removed Bible reading and prayer from public school, we realized a loss of common culture, a common set of literary allusions, and the common core of learning of school. "English-Language Arts" as most schools call "English studies" thereby lost their anchor. The debate about the secular literary canon rises at a time when we encounter students who no longer share a memory of having recited the Lord's Prayer in unison every morning and no longer receive a regular dose of Bible reading in school. Indeed, since the New English Bible has replaced the King James version in Sunday school and church, new generations of schoolchildren are unable to spot Biblical references in the English and American Puritan tradition. So even as a literary text, the language of King James' biblical translators has largely been lost. We need to reconsider seriously what place literature should take in our schools in the absence of a religious purpose, even though serious change may not come for a long time. This part will, further, consider the ways in which literature was removed from elementary schools and reserved for the high school, thereby effectively barring access to complex language and alternative visions for the laboring poor. This isolation from literature still prevails in the huge differences between elementary and high-school curricula and between the literary offerings to be found in academic and vocational tracks.

The Canon

❦

Opposing views of the canon and its appropriateness in school teachings have a long history. *Canon* originally referred to the biblical texts chosen by the Church Fathers as Holy Writ, to be included in what Christians call the Bible ("apocryphal" texts, such as the Gospels of Thomas and Peter or the Book of Tobit, were left out). When applied to secular literature, the *canon* refers to received writings bearing the approval of the educated elite of the Western world.

Two sets of texts and their accretions of commentary stand at the foundation of Western Civilization: the Judeo-Christian historical and religious foundation texts and the priestly commentaries that have accumulated around them over two-and-a-half millennia, and the secular (pagan) texts of the ancient Graeco-Roman worlds and the commentaries that have been devised for them over a similar period of time. Written texts, whether sacred or secular—their authenticity, their meaning, and their transmission from one generation to the next—have until very recently been acknowledged by scholars, educators, parents and legislators alike, as what we mean by *education.*

Current patterns of American schooling have a deep history in the very origins of mass literacy in Western Europe. In the early sixteenth century, Martin Luther advocated overcoming the separation of the people from direct contact with their God by giving them direct access to the Bible in the vernacular. Up until his day, only the priests and monks and a tiny proportion of the Christian upper class and Christian, Islamic, and Jewish merchant class were literate at all. For Christians, moreover, literacy meant Latin, and sometimes Greek and Hebrew. Most people learned from hearsay, whether through sermons in the church or public pronouncements in the village square. Luther, who saw the priests and monks as unnecessary mediators between the people and their God, developed his ideas at the very moment when the technology of the printing press had only just been put together. Perhaps the first true publicist of the modern world, Luther was able to bring out a Bible in German and thereby let loose a revolution in literacy that ultimately proved unstoppable. When William Tyndale produced the first English translation of Scripture in 1535, he was burnt at the stake and his book was destroyed in its Continental warehouse. Foxe's *Book of Protestant Martyrs* quotes Tyndale, whose language we still read in the Revised Authorized Version: "If God spare my life, ere many years I will cause a boy that driveth the plough shall know more of the Scripture than thou dost." Erasmus similarly had visions that the ordinary farmer or weaver would "sing parts of [the gospels] at his work" (preface to 1516 New Testament).

Popular literacy and the existence of a Bible in one's own vernacular language were connected closely from the start. The Protestant Reformation produced Bibles in every modern European language and many minor dialects by 1570. The Counter-Reformation's missionaries reacted by traveling to America, Asia, and Africa to create alphabets for languages they found there and to learn the writing systems of the Chinese so as to produce Bibles in all of those languages. Religious tracts for the poor were pioneered in England in the 1620s, just when some Puritans were getting ready to cut off King Charles I's head. The Age of Discovery, of European expansion, of the printing press, the Bible, and the Reformation are all the same age. Literacy was offered to the world's population within a few generations. The fervor with which missionaries introduced biblical literacy wherever ships sailed was partly a measure of the newly discovered power of religious literacy and partly the result of fierce international economic competition among Reformation and Counter-Reformation groups alike. Along with the relatively cheap availability of printed books, the Reformation brought at the same time battles for national independence from the Vatican. England emerged from the sixteenth century with a Protestant head of state and hence national Protestantism. The Vatican fought back with a zealous territorial expansion to convert heathens everywhere to loyalty to Rome.

When U.S. history skips lightly over the history of the Reformation and its close associations with mass literacy, Protestantism, and nationalism, it leaves unstated the single most powerful influence on the formation of the modern world and of American education. Literacy, in sixteenth-century Europe and in twentieth-century America alike, holds a basic Protestant tenet: the ability to read the Bible. It remains even today the primary reason adult illiterates give when asked why they turn to literacy programs for help. Puritan education and the pre-Revolutionary textbooks consisted almost entirely of overtly religious teachings. Despite the gradual secularization of U.S. schools over the years, current lessons about literature still bear the traces of their Calvinist and Methodist origins. The Bible remained until thirty years ago the central literary text of school.

Just when the earliest colonial schools were being organized, a European debate arose as to the place of the classical, secular texts in school. In the eighteenth century, writers and thinkers of all kinds engaged in what Jonathan Swift called the "Battle of the Books." The "Ancients" had come to be venerated as the source of all learning, while the "Moderns" had not as yet gained a firm position in universities or in schools. School learning meant Homer and Virgil and Livy and Tacitus and Euclid, to the exclusion of Shakespeare and Milton and Pope and modern historians and scientists and mathematicians. Early eighteenth-century poets looked over their shoulders at the monumental achievements of the ancients and the Renaissance and, seeking popular sales, translated the classical Greek and Latin into English and other modern European languages for the first time. They were motivated to reach wide new audiences unschooled in the classical tongues and to appropriate the classics into English cultural nationalism. The move to the modern vernacular—Dryden's Virgil, Pope's Homer—reflected a new literacy that began to take hold in post-Reformation Europe. A populace that had learned to read by reading the Bible in the vernacular now demanded secular reading matter in the vernacular.

Alexander Pope was one of the first writers to make a living selling his translations to the newly literate public; most poets of earlier generations had depended entirely on noble patronage. Shakespeare, of course, had made a very good living putting on plays for a largely illiterate, general audience. But printed poetry and then prose fiction in English is the story of a growing eighteenth-century middle class and its appetite for modern, secular writing.

The argument over the ancients and the moderns was transported to the newly established American republic after the Revolution. Benjamin Franklin was one major advocate for a modern education in English in what we would now call high schools. Instead of students spending years studying classical languages, Franklin's plan would have emphasized translations and practical studies of all kinds to prepare young people for a life of commerce or industry. His proposals for a model school, however, were soon overruled by the trustees of the academy he helped found.[5] While a modern, English curriculum was offered, a second track in classics was added because many parents still believed a classical education was synonymous with advanced education, and because the universities both here and abroad stipulated a classical background as an entrance requirement.

Meanwhile, the argument between ancients and moderns was taking on a new shape in the later eighteenth century in Europe, where German philosophers, poets, and literary critics were inventing Romanticism. There Goethe, Schiller, and the Schlegel brothers were puzzling over the question of whether it was possible to have a great poetry without a great nation, or a great nation without a great poetry. Their model was England, where they saw Shakespeare taking his place beside Homer and Virgil; yet Shakespeare was not a writer of the court, nor a writer of the nobility, nor an epic poet celebrating a single national hero. He was a man of the people, whose vernacular plays were designed as popular entertainment for all ranks. Shakespeare was adopted by German thinkers as the preeminent and first Romantic writer, one whose work represented, knit up, and expressed the nation of England and its general populace, not just its upper ranks. August Wilhelm Schlegel, the elder of the two brothers (who between them gave lectures on and translated many ancient and modern texts, including the *Bhagavad-Gita* and the works of Calderon), translated Shakespeare into German.[6] This translation and the Schlegels' lectures on Shakespeare created a Shakespeare worship in Germany that outdid the already great admiration for his work that had continued in Britain ever since his lifetime. Shakespeare became the great Romantic figure so desired by German nationalists, who in Goethe soon discovered a similar, founding poet for the German nation.

Romantic education, which is education for nationalistic purposes, was also used in the nineteenth century to make ever finer distinctions between classes of people. Educated people shared allusions from literature in their social discourse not available to those lacking such an education. The common culture so lamented by traditionalists was never a democratic culture. Democracy of knowledge meant the shared beliefs taught in elementary, "common" schools, not the culture common to the tiny percentage that continued its education in the academies.

A new nation needed a literature that was nation-defining and a schooling that inculcated common beliefs in the young. In early U.S. charity schools, the forebears of urban public schools, the formation of the American republic was seen to depend on a literacy to be achieved through Bible reading in English, and correct spelling and pronunciation. School children would spend most of their school time memorizing and declaiming carefully selected texts. The nation-defining literature primarily came from patriotic speeches, but the overwhelming majority of reading material came from Protestant prayers, hymns, and biblical texts. In a sense, the biblical material became the national literature of America, following the strong Puritan tradition of defining the nation as a special redemptive inheritance from God. This was the new American canon in English. For most of our nation's history, schoolchildren had "copy" books, not notebooks; copying—good, clear handwriting—was deemed the goal of English studies. Getting by heart the speeches and essays of patriots and the poetry of sentiment, and declaiming these in a standardized American English, were the purposes of the texts used in school. Morality based on biblical texts built good character and citizenship. Charity-school leaders did not expect the children of the poor to become themselves makers of poetry or leaders of the country.

If the basic reading texts in U.S. schools were biblical, the model for fiction in school was the moral tale or lesson deriving from the kinds of tales told in Sunday school. In 1816 the American Bible Society was founded for the express purpose of placing a Protestant Bible in every schoolroom in the United States, a campaign that continued successfully throughout the nineteenth century. Between 1780 and 1800, charitable societies had been founded to create "Sunday schools," originally not schools carrying out the work of churches, but schools run by secular groups that often met in church halls, to provide general education for working children on the Sabbath.[7] The purpose of these schools was as much to keep poor children off the streets on their one day off from work as to provide them with literacy via a healthy dose of Bible reading. These Sunday schools were later extended for week-long attendance. Major school systems in some Eastern cities, such as Philadelphia, got their start in the Sunday schools.

The mixture of Bible reading and moral lessons for the poor came from the philanthropists' view of poverty as a moral defect. Failure to act middle class was considered an inherited characteristic that could best be corrected if the children were separated as much as possible from the vicious influence of their parents. The heavy moral tone of Sunday-school stories was designed to help such children mend their evil ways.

Sunday-school literature became a staple of schooling. One learned the ABCs through a literature expressly written for the poor, in which the point of the story was always to teach "the moral of the tale," written out at the end. The American Sunday School Union established children's libraries and strongly influenced "the character and tone of all children's books."[8] Since the Middle Ages most people have learned their Bible stories in fragmentary "lessons" appropriate to feast days. These lessons, linked as they are to a commemorative calendar, do not follow the narrative sequence of the Bible. Similarly, the weekly Bible lesson or verse used as the text for the sermon appears isolated from its narrative context. Sunday-school aesthetics has a long tradition of offering the people isolated fragments of texts and providing interpretations of these as the basis of moral instruction.

Common Purpose

Some were English,
plain and simply English,
and among them
they set out
with tooth and knife,
with venerable quotes,
they set out . . .
to take my poor poetry
from the simple folk
who loved it.

PABLO NERUDA

The oldest textbook in the English New World was the famous *New England Primer*, first printed in the late 1680s, which taught the alphabet as if it were a catechism:

> *A* In Adam's Fall
>   We Sinned all.
> *B* Heaven to Find,
>   The Bible mind.
> *C* Christ Crucify'd,
>   For Sinners dy'd.

And so it goes through the alphabet. The rest of the *Primer* consists of "Bible facts, Bible verses, prayers, the Creed and, in later editions, 'Mr. Cotton's Catechism.'"[9] The lives of Protestant martyrs were also features of the *Primer*. The first state to outlaw various sectarian Protestant teachings in public schools was New Jersey, which did not do so until 1844.[10] The year 1844 also saw thirteen people murdered on Philadelphia's streets in what came to be known as "the Bible Riots." By that date, Philadelphia's diverse population included a growing number of Irish Catholics whose bishops could not accept the teaching of the Protestant Bible and creed in school. Their request for separate classrooms where the Catholic Bible might be alternatively read by Catholic children led to days of rioting, the torching of a church, and death. In the aftermath the Archdiocese of Philadelphia began to set up its alternative schools, which today serve nearly half of the city's school-aged children.

Literacy in the early United States may have been largely restricted to biblical literacy, but it was hugely successful. For the northern colonies, nearly all of the white male population was literate before the Revolution, whereas only half of the males in England and France were to achieve literacy half a century later.[11] The Revolution in America was in fact sustained by radical pamphleteering and newsprint, and might not have prevailed without the avid readership that literacy created. Precisely this triumph of radicalism through literacy in the white male populace prompted fear among our country's leaders immediately after the establishment of the new republic. Schools were quickly organized along conservative lines to consolidate a sense of national unity and to stabilize the young nation's integrity.

Schooling also consolidated along the lines of moral education directed at the poor from on high, a tendency one can find in state-regulated schooling in most countries. Such moral education is designed to encourage a willing, obedient work force and to avoid the dissatisfactions that might come from too much education.

Many Americans preferred the idea of leaving the laboring masses of people in ignorance, whereas school reformers advocated education as a vaccination against threatened unrest in the new society. Early America saw a major debate between those who feared education as the precursor to further radicalism and the common-school advocates. Common-school advocates established tax-supported public schools by promising a populace that would be loyal, patriotic, and models of unambitious good conduct. But as late as 1830 the *Philadelphia National Gazette* still ran editorials advocating that laborers and women had best remain uneducated.[12] The slave-holders of the South, of course, also advocated no education for African-Americans, rightly fearing the power that literacy entails. And modern-day book censors continue to argue that a little learning is a dangerous thing. In the 1991–92 school year, book censorship—primarily motivated by religious objections to content—reached a ten-year high. Literary classics as well as contemporary writings suffered at the censors' hands.[13]

The public schools were created despite strong arguments against education, not to enlighten or empower labor, minorities, or women, but to control their behavior. Rote learning, discipline, religion, morals, thrift, industry, promptness, cleanliness, acceptance of one's lot in life—imparting these values became the primary functions of school in the period before the Civil War.

In Britain, private schools for laboring children created a literate working class in the first half of the nineteenth century, which in turn fueled a movement for autodidacts and a healthy appetite among workers for adult education societies. When the state took over the schooling of the laborers in the second half of the nineteenth century, however, it taught their children that they didn't even know how to speak their own native language. State schooling alienated the workers' children from education and resulted in a twentieth-century British population with an immense split between the culture of the middle class and that of the poor—the "Two Nations" of Disraeli's phrase. While less overt in the United States, stamping out the speech habits and behavior of the poor has always been the business of school. And the poor increasingly came to mean immigrants, so that stamping out speech habits meant stamping out the culture of origin in order to make them "Americans." In urban and rural schools today one hears the poor disparaged for chaotic family life and impoverished or disadvantaged language.

The poor have always been a problem for schools and have always been blamed for failing to be middle class instantly upon entry to the school building. The speech and behavior of poor children have always been different from those who have had the leisure and opportunity to develop these through extended formal study. School teachings about language have defined disruptions between children and parents, school and home, high culture and popular culture. They have also defined and institutionalized a cultural rift between the social classes in the name of creating a common culture. Such a common culture approached the education of the poor with the goal of preventing them from behaving in ways different from the middle class. It viewed the poor as a problem to be solved by preaching and catechism, not by broad reading, reflection, or analysis.

The Development
of School English

~~~~~~~

By the late nineteenth century most high schools and academies in the United States offered two tracks: a classical program emphasizing Latin, Greek, and mathematics, following a pattern to be found in similar schools in Europe; and an English program covering a broad array of modern subjects, including modern languages and bookkeeping.[14] Neither track built on years of preparatory study. Then as now, the early years of school attended to little more than what we currently call "basics," the reading, writing, and arithmetic that saw its highest goal as the reading of newspapers and the capacity to do simple computations.

In 1894 a committee of university presidents strongly recommended that secondary school take up the study of modern (postclassical) literature.[15] At that time, the very idea that literature could be a subject of study was a novelty. In the period 1905–20 the idea of the tax-supported high school emerged as vastly increased numbers of students appeared prepared to attend. A battle for the high schools ensued, resulting in a compromise that rearranged the two tracks of study. The academic subjects that fulfilled college entrance requirements were reserved for the few.[16] Those not destined for higher education were allowed to remain enrolled, but placed in a different course of study; as a result, some of the mathematics and the foreign languages that had been taught in the common schools were removed, to become the exclusive domain of the college-bound in the high school. Access to serious study of the liberal arts therefore began to be restricted for the general populace able to attend high school just as they were beginning to be able to afford to let their children benefit from an extended education.[17]

There was some confusion at the turn of the century as to what English as a subject might become. Harvard's entrance examinations consisted of essays to be written on a published list that, in 1885, included *Macbeth, The*

Merchant of Venice, the first two books of *Paradise Lost*, an essay by Emerson, George Eliot's *Silas Marner*, and Dickens's *A Tale of Two Cities*. Submission, sentiment, dissenting Protestant thought, as expressed by these writers, made a canon of value for our new nation: Harvard's examination books became the high-school literature curriculum.

Silas Marner presents a wonderful metaphor for the evangelical purposes of schooling in America. A perennial feature of high-school reading lists until the 1960s, the novel is atypical of George Eliot's work. It is a simply organized moral allegory quite different from the complex and massively intellectual explorations of social, moral, and philosophical issues to be found in her other novels. *Silas Marner* tells the story of a weaver who rejects his Puritanical faith after being badly cheated by a man he had considered his closest friend. He moves from the dark industrial city to a quiet village, a place that seems to represent all the virtues of an older, preindustrial rural England. There, after first becoming a miser who lives only for his work, Silas finds consolation and redemption through the love of an orphaned child.

Silas Marner's story portrays a theme central to the educational goals of American schools. The superiority of the heart to the head and the superiority of feeling to thought set the true course on the road to salvation. Published in 1861, it almost immediately found its way into schoolrooms, where it sat comfortably alongside the moral allegories of Hawthorne and McGuffey. The poor weaver's quiet acceptance of life's vicissitudes is rewarded with the most precious gift of all, the love and devotion of the child. The wisdom of simple folk gained through feeling rather than theology becomes the true guide to a life well lived.

Everything the schools could possibly want in a novel was to be found in *Silas Marner:* submission to labor, the rewards of keeping to your station in life, the advantages of not thinking or knowing too much or looking into things too critically, the salvation of work, the superiority of country to town and of mild Methodism to the older, more severe forms of dissent. For a hundred years Americans were offered this novel, not because it was a curiosity by a major writer, not because it would sharpen students' minds, not for its place in literary history, but because its moral message suited the Sunday-school aesthetic of public education for the working classes. Of all the books on Harvard's list, *Silas Marner* alone showed a major drop in frequency on high-school reading lists from the early 1960s, when it was ranked third, to the late 1980s, when only fifteen percent of schools in one study continued to teach it. This was also the only top ten selection in the high schools between 1907 and the 1980s written by a woman.[18]

Hawthorne's shorter moral allegories found their way into McGuffey for much the same reasons that *Silas Marner* was taught; *The Scarlet Letter*, another staple of English classes, depicted an America that had happily softened its Christianity since Puritan times. Dickens appeared in school to reinforce ideas of the heart's wisdom. These workhorses of the English curriculum turned school ideas of literature and reading into an extension of moral character formation, carefully selected from among all the possible stories and poems one could have chosen for any other purposes. Pope's *Essay on Man*, asserting the need to accept the rightness of the world order, was taught—not his satires, which lashed out at the vice and folly of society. Children were taught in the nineteenth century to look for the moral; now they are taught to look for the theme. It's the same approach, as if literature were a practical guide to forming the reader's character. Poor Americans whose primary or only acquaintance with literature came in school might be excused for thinking it hardly worth the effort. Although the causes of illiteracy are far more complex than just a question of the uses to which it has been put in school, some attention to those uses must be given if we are ever to convince students of the value of the enterprise of extended attention to the complexities of thought and language that literature demands.

In 1926 the College Board first introduced the Scholastic Aptitude Test (SAT), which began to take an increasingly important role in college admissions.[19] The SAT, it is vital to note, is not a test of specific knowledge, such as whether one is familiar with *Macbeth* or *Silas Marner*. It is designed to test general aptitude for study by looking at a student's facility with mathematics and language. One needn't read any particular set of books before taking the test; the SAT stresses vocabulary and grammar to a great extent in its verbal section. This major change in college entrance testing matched closely the 1920s move to an education for the majority that had less to do with the subjects of history and literature and more to do with social adjustment. Although *Silas Marner* and *Macbeth* continued to function as staples of high school study, their original purpose was vitiated by the new kind of test.

In the school debate over the literary canon, the most important recent research seeks to be reassuring to traditionalists by reporting that major English and American literature selections taught in school have changed little from the beginning of the century until the present.[20] The study of book-length literature taught in U.S. high schools recently prepared by Arthur Applebee seems to suggest that high-school students are reading today what they read in the past. The study mentions in passing that not all students read very many book-length works of literature; these are generally withheld from "lower track" students. Indeed, lower track students get to read fewer classics and more contemporary literature than the college-bound. By studying only book-length works, however, Applebee misses most of the reading that's assigned in schools from the anthologies—the shorter pieces. The study forgets that most English teachers are stuck with anthologies for decades at a time as the only available literature; the anthologies dictate the curriculum. Applebee does provide an enormously diverse list of titles each taught by fewer than five percent of the teachers, which suggests that when teachers can select one book or two outside of the anthology, they range very widely indeed among Western classics and contemporary selections, U.S. and world writers, men, women, and people of color.

Is there a received canon of reading? If so, who gets access to it? These are vexed questions. One researcher studying the same data as Applebee comes to the opposite conclusion, claiming there is no identifiable canon.[21] All of this research assumes that teachers get to choose what they teach—and they do not. None mentions the real heart and soul of canonical school literature—the Bible and pious literature closely related to the Puritan tradition. The problem of the canon and the dissatisfaction felt by the disenfranchised in school is not a matter of this or that particular writer or particular book. It's a dissatisfaction in general with English studies as encompassing an exclusive tradition that leaves out many Americans. The school canon assumes for all Americans a comfort level with a generalized Protestant, middle-class, white, New England, and British identity. Most important of all, however, is that even this tradition has been too often withheld from the poor, who have only been offered the workbooks and the scraps and leavings of a coherent study of language and literature.

To the extent that high-school academic tracks have been defined by college entrance requirements, the high-school canon in the academic preparation courses has a close dependency on subjects as they have been defined by college departments. Increasingly sophisticated departments of Black Studies, Puerto Rican Studies, and Women's Studies have, since the late 1960s, opened up whole new territories of literature in America that were until recently terra incognita. Leading the call for loosening the grip of canonical English studies on the curriculum, such research has become strident in its denunciation of Western hegemony. Part of this movement includes an assertion of equal status for hitherto neglected writers of color, women, and other "alternative" voices, also asserting the legitimacy of media other than the printed text. Women's Studies has searched out a rich history of diaries, letters, and other documents never published in the lifetimes of their writers. Analysts of African-American and other cultures have been developing ideas about aesthetics that depend less on printed text than on oral culture, ritual, dance, and music. They tell us that the canon has elevated a Western print culture that is peculiarly a white male phenomenon, while ignoring the visions of those who never made it into print or whose work cannot be reduced to print. To study the poetry of the published few, they assert, is to ignore the creative genius of the unpublished many.

Such an attack on the text-centered Western world seems like a deathblow to the Judeo-Christian, Graeco-Roman core around which Western schools and universities were founded. University-level English studies, however, have been with us for a very short time—only a hundred years in the eight-hundred-year history of Western universities. In that century English studies have suffered a troubled and internally conflicted history. Gerald Graff, a historian of the profession, reminds us that English and then American literature had to fight their way into the university. Such studies were originally justified as creators of national identity, but from the start the English department was always divided over whether its purpose was primarily the scientific study of the history of language or a gentlemanly discussion of the pleasures of literature. In his major book on the subject, Graff discusses at length the question of whether there ever was a canon that the profession as a whole actually professed.[22]

Once again, German ideas of how to build a nation are fundamental to understanding how literature is taught. In the early nineteenth century, there was no university study of English language or modern literature. At that time, a handful of professors held chairs in Rhetoric, the most notable of whom was Hugh Blair, a Scots minister at the University of Edinburgh. His influence on American schooling was profound, for he treated literature "as an extension of public forms of speech and argument."[23] Blair's *Lectures on Rhetoric and Belles Lettres* (1783) range broadly among classical and modern writers, providing illustrations of rhetorical strategy and treating both political and historical documents and fictive works as equally illustrative of his arguments. Blair's selections, and indeed his own writing, came to form the basis for many advanced American school readers, so that it became the habit of American schools to teach selections in anthologies rather than whole works. The method of study in American schools and universities alike in the nineteenth century consisted of memorization and declamation of Blair's selections.

The rhetorics of other Scottish and English writers adapted early in the nineteenth century for American school use established the anthology of highlights of literature as the basic tool for high-school reading instruction, but later American adaptations of these books tended to use them for memorization and elocutionary purposes alone. "Writing" in English, which meant copying for the younger children, later grew to an inordinate emphasis on penmanship, which still seems to dominate instruction in many elementary schools. High schools focused on style when they did take a look at real literature, and particularly on figurative language. The confused and fragmented uses to which literature was put, even for the academic elite, are today reflected in the often incoherent English courses of our contemporary schools.[24]

As we have seen, school literature teaching was never very closely connected with aesthetics, the enjoyment of complex language, the creation of worlds made of words, or the imaginative exploration of what it is to be human. Schools were founded in a spirit of evangelism and helped to institutionalize the evangelical movement of the early nineteenth century.[25] It should be no surprise that devotional literature continues to dominate popular taste.

Yet the adult American public in its vast energy flocked to the lyceums for intellectual development and created the world's most massive hunger for newspapers.[26] Some of the earliest nineteenth-century school readers for advanced students, adapting British books, provided a broad range of translated selections from Cicero, Livy, and Molière, and extracts from Shakespeare, Sheridan, and Sterne. Such selections declined as the nineteenth century wore on. Early readers for beginners focused on moral lessons, fables, and fairy tales. But perhaps surprising to us today is the nature and extent of the German literature included in advanced readers. Goethe, Schiller, Herder, Kant, the Grimm brothers, and Fichte were heavily anthologized. Goethe's *Egmont* and *Faust* were the most popular, but also offered were Schiller's *Die Jung Frau von Orleans* and *Wilhelm Tell*, Lessing's *Minna von Barnhelm*, and Heine's *Das Buch der Lieder*.[27]

Direct contact with major international literature became severely curtailed as the common schools developed and the native publishing industry geared up to serve it. The schools became bureaucratized from the 1830s on, and major writers were replaced by "moral and religious essays and pieces on . . . death, disease, scenic wonders, patriotism, and heroism." In 1852 the first compulsory school attendance law was passed in Massachusetts.[28] By then public schools were an American institution, and school reading was a mechanism for improving the poor. Although such improvement may have been well-meaning, if patronizing, school reading had ceased to offer opportunities for intellectual development.

As the nineteenth century wore on, the eclectic anthologies used in high schools included fewer and fewer broadly European, Near Eastern, and Asian ancients and moderns, and focused more exclusively on modern English and

American writers. The selections narrowed to increasingly conservative views. Some of the anthologies reduced the space allotted to selections of writing in favor of literary history and biography, so that histories of English and American literatures began to appear containing few literary samples, or none at all.[29] After 1920, when teachers rather than professors started to compile literary histories exclusively for school use, literary selections increased again,[30] but this was also the time when professors and schoolteachers began to part professional ways. Many professors retreated to the universities to study writers who were not immediately accessible to unsophisticated readers and to ignore writers who were.[31] Many teachers succumbed to the newly evolving scientific theories and approaches to reading.

As McGuffey waned, Dick and Jane waxed. Reading series had become big business by the time the McGuffey publishing trust was broken in the early years of the twentieth century. Scott, Foresman & Company first published the Dick and Jane series in the 1930s and dominated the market through the 1950s. The major innovation of this series was vocabulary and syntax control,[32] eliminating from early reading all the big, juicy, interesting words and structures, and reducing narrative to a monotone that no child would ever dream of reading for fun.

Those of us who did manage to grow up loving to read did so because wordplay was part of the point of reading, enjoying Peter Rabbit's "soporific lettuces" and the Kipling camel with his "great big lolliping humph." Dick and Jane purged children's first shot at reading of "difficulty," and later "readability formulas" made such purges sound scientific. The twentieth-century love affair with science and scientific-looking methods completed the work of separating children from language as it is used by powerful writers. In school one is taught that reading is a dull chore involving dull language and dull stories whose point is to answer the questions at the end. At least McGuffey tried to sweeten his moral pills by engaging children's interest in his stories. Few would remember Dick and Jane and their successors in the basal reading series with a pleasurable glow.

The factory model of school perceived reading as analogous to the assembly line. Reading could be dismembered into component parts and then reassembled piece by piece—syllables, simple words, complex words— and writing could be broken into lines and loops before whole letters; all of this could be taught in a graded system through which children moved as if on a conveyer belt. If at the same time one attacked children's own speech habits vigorously and taught them to reject their native usage of language, then all would be well. The only ones who escape this kind of "reading" are those for whom school reading is not the only literature available, who acquire a richer and fuller appreciation of it on their own or in their families or through other institutions such as the church.

The factory model, scientific readability formulas, and moral didacticism have neglected our children's mental development, but American public schools were founded more for political, social, and economic purposes than intellectual ones.[33] All of this sat well with a democracy that associated authority with the rejected Old World intellectualism.[34]

One irony of today's dissatisfaction with school is that, while critics are angry because school teaches a canon of Western Civilization, such a canon has never been successfully offered to the majority. And, as long as 15 percent drop out (the vast majority poor), and many more are disaffected, we are faced with a Western canon signally unavailable to the population protesting it.

The Longing for Heroism

Traditionalist laments for the loss of heroes and legends from our curriculum reveal a nostalgia for a time when certainties prevailed. Today's schoolbooks often avoid individual responsibility and action. The social adjustment movement in schools that began in the 1920s results today in schoolbooks that elevate peer-group, collective decision making and consensus over individual acts of charity, heroism, or daring as the movers of plot.[35] Traditionalists like Professor Allan Bloom want to return to the myths that bind us. He laments the passing of McGuffey and the Bible as foundation texts, the loss of heroes, the loss of morality and the nobility that heroes defended.[36]

Bloom is right to note that heroism presupposes a vision of a world in which an individual can represent the national polity and, through his actions, express the national will and national belief. But the literature of our culture has offered a much more complex and interesting heroism. American writers have time and again qualified the hero's capacity to enter into the American landscape without the guidance of men of color. Natty Bumppo in Cooper's *Leatherstocking* needed the guidance of Chingachgook, Ishmael and Ahab needed Queequeg, and Huckleberry Finn needed Jim. Heroism in these books is a complex matter of discovering America and its meaning through mutual, interracial dependency. Huck's escape from "civilization" and Jim's escape from slavery necessitate learning about freedom from each other. Huck and Jim are ordinary people who rise to heroism through the trials they undergo and through an understanding of how they are linked, white and black, to each other and thereby to the river and the landscape. The joke played on McGuffey and on other school literature, of course, is that Twain's twinned heroes are a bad boy and a runaway slave. In the end, it is the slave who teaches Huck a finer virtue and heroism than he can ever learn from "civilization."

The textbook heroes were never like this. McGuffey's heroes stood for unalloyed virtue, not complex interdependency. Some minority writers and critics of education, however, still wish for a heroism that imitates that of the old school books, but one which would substitute or add people of color and women to the old list of dead white male heroes. Harriet Tubman, whose staunch heroism freed hundreds of slaves single-handedly, would become a counterpoint to Daniel Boone, and Frederick Douglass would assume the mystique of a Founding Father. But American literary heroes, white or black, tend to be less awesome and capable than Harriet Tubman. The heroism of the grand gesture does not sit comfortably in a liberal democracy, seeming to hark back instead to more authoritarian societies. Captain Ahab's outsized heroism is tragic; Ishmael's survival depends on learning from Queequeg how to stay out of its way.

Larger-than-life heroes, moreover, perpetuate the romantic nationalistic purposes of school insofar as they define an ideal American whose individual action builds the nation. As Whitman discovered in *Leaves of Grass*, a named individual would constitute an anti-democratic hero, since a democratic nation subsumes the individual to its larger purposes. Whitman celebrates the "magnificent masses," and he sees the country's immensely variegated landscapes and peoples as the inspiration for a new kind of democratic poetry. It is by taking in all that is American, good and bad, black and white, male and female, country and city, that he is able to begin to comprehend the nation. That plenitude defines heroism in the very diversity of this country. Similarly, Melville's idea of the epic novel as an encyclopedia suggests that plenitude, again including a tragic vision of America, helps us to understand ourselves. Such writers dare not shirk any part of us.

Neither Whitman's *Leaves of Grass* nor Melville's *Moby-Dick* nor Twain's *Huckleberry Finn* are what traditionalists have in mind when they call for a return to heroes and legends for elementary-school children. They want instead the heroes of the school legends, from the pens of the Presbyterian and Methodist ministers who compiled elementary-school books. Real writers have much subtler and ultimately more rewarding moral purposes. If we are to have their literature in school, or any literature that takes children's intellectual growth seriously, we will have to introduce it for the first time.

The Western Civilization so earnestly defended by Bloom and the traditionalists who dominated federal education agencies in the 1980s has simply never been taught to the children of the poor. The Western Civilization being attacked by professors of African-American, Chicano, and feminist studies as the productions of racist, sexist, classist, dead white men, has never been taught to the children of the poor. We can neither condemn it for having warped their souls nor return to it to find the ties that will rebind us as a nation, because the children of the poor neither suffered from it nor gloried in it. They had no access to it in school.

I suggested in the first part that there have been two phases of literacy in the world since the Sumerians first cut reeds to make impressions in clay tablets some four thousand years ago. The first phase of literacy is the one that uses writing in the service of the rich and powerful and for purposes of worship, which are often closely related. For most of the history of the world, literacy has been confined to a small coterie of people in the direct service of monarchs and gods. The oldest poetry in every civilization celebrates heroes of the state (Gilgamesh, Aeneas) and heroes of religion (Rama); often the hero of the state is introduced as having divine origin. Such literacy is "high" culture, since it originates from and serves royal and priestly classes.

In the second phase of literacy, the capacity to read and write dramatically broadens to include a much larger part of the populace. When the Reformation, moveable type, cheap paper, translations of sacred texts into modern languages, and the introduction of secular writing of all kinds all appeared within a generation, a literate middle class was born. When that middle class came to write literature for itself, it created a new genre, the novel, to replace the epic, and a new kind of heroism, the heroism of daily life.

Perhaps a third phase of literacy is now possible. If we manage to bring the poor into the realm of readers and writers in democratic America, it is just possible they will discover themselves as a third audience for literacy. Perhaps film-making and popular culture in other media herald a new kind of art form that doesn't depend on literacy. But a completely literate America, an America of writers and readers—not just people with bare capacities to fill in job applications for work punching illustrated buttons on cash registers—could rise up to create a new literary form. And with it, I would expect to see a new kind of literary hero, neither the heroes of ancient epic poetry nor the heroines of middle-class novels, but something quite new and accessible to the new population of readers and writers we hope to produce.

Seeing into Things

Wouldn't a parson be almost too high-learnt to bring up a lad to be a man o'business? My notion o'the parsons was as they'd got a sort of learning as lay mostly out o'sight. And that isn't what I want for Tom. I want him to know figures, and write like print, and see into things quick, and know what folks mean, and how to wrap things up in words that aren't actionable.

THE MILL ON THE FLOSS

Americans have generally wished for the kind of practical education for their children that Mr. Tulliver seeks for his son in George Eliot's *The Mill on the Floss*. But they have had to settle for a high school education that's "out o'sight," mysterious, after an elementary schooling that was inadequate to the practical necessities of seeing "into things quick." For unschooled working parents who, like Mr. Tulliver, have ambitions for their children to enter the white-collar world, an education that would make their children flexible, clever, and worldly-wise, in command of language and capable of acting in the world of affairs, has remained an American dream unfulfilled. Elementary schooling has too often failed to teach the working classes the capacity to understand and manipulate language, preferring to concentrate merely on writing "like print." Powerful critical capacities take years of wide reading and analysis and extensive participation in language creation as well.

Literature in schools has been used to help bind a diverse society by selections chosen to override the divisiveness of industrial capitalism, immigration, labor agitation, urbanization, and class conflict.[37] Such a binding up has fettered our children's and our society's capacity to cope with the complex realities of life in a postindustrial age. The factory model for education never did make much sense, even in an age when most children were destined for a life in the factory. In an age when numbers of factory jobs, farm jobs, and mill jobs have been shrinking for decades, there is no longer even an economic excuse for a schooling designed to keep working people so fettered.

The model that we have lived with for 150 years of public schooling has suggested a series of dualisms, as if capitalist production were opposed to leisure, evil cities opposed to rural idylls, facts opposed to values, research opposed to teaching, and thought opposed to feeling.[38] We end up putting the humanities—literature, history, philosophy, and so on—in a category that's beyond the reach of the urban child destined for a world of work: an idea that first turned up in Aristotle's *Politics,* which claims that the humanities rightly belong to the purely leisured elite. Democratic America initially carried out that idea by keeping the real literature and learning in the academic tracks of high school where most working children can't reach it. If literature evokes yawns of boredom from students, it's perhaps because school has taught them that being an American means above all finding practical uses, including moral uses, for everything, including literature. Now we have a situation in which traditionalists lament that literature is no longer being used to teach values and reformers argue that traditional literature should be junked for having taught nothing but jingoism and narrow ethnocentrism.[39]

Such contentions reveal confusion about what literature is. Literature has an independent habit of often failing to serve ideologies while exploring new realms of being previously unimagined. It is precisely literature's tendency to break the bounds that makes it empowering and fearsome at the same time.

Literary analyst Irving Howe has pointed out that the multicultural attack on the so-called hegemony of the West is carried out in the very terms of Western thought and tradition.[40] This argument states that we don't read Western writers—or any writers—to "endorse our current . . . pieties. . . . We read them to experience otherness." The study of literature is "not a stuffy obeisance before dead texts . . . but rather a critical engagement with living texts."[41]

This view points up very clearly the failures of school, where stuffy obeisance has been the rule rather than the exception. New pieties are being offered up in place of the old ones by the new left and the old pieties are being dredged up for reinstatement by the new right. The multicultural movement has done a great service to school literature by pointing out that the old verities that shaped its canon are not inevitable and that school reading has served to alienate rather than engage all sorts of children. If we need to temper such criticism, it will not be useful to do so by pretending to an open-mindedness that schools never practiced.

Schools continue to be quite timid about whom they will admit through their portals. While Lorraine Hansberry and Richard Wright are among the fifty writers most frequently assigned in grades seven through twelve, "in schools with a fifty percent or higher minority enrollment, they rank only fourteenth and seventeenth." At the same time, Wright's *Black Boy* is one of three books most often banned by public schools.[42] Prior to 1975, literature by black writers turned up in schools only to illustrate sociology or history. Since then such writers have begun to appear in school in terms of their literary artistry.[43] Yet most teachers trained to the old school canon are unable to identify writers of merit outside of its limits and await the research being done in universities and by textbook anthologists to expand the lists of poets, novelists, and dramatists available for school reading.

Henry Louis Gates, Jr., a leading professor of literature, has been creating a new anthology of African-American writing. He points out that anthologies create canons and courses of study alike. Gates draws on alternative literary forms, traditions, themes, and linguistic structures for the anthology, which asserts the rightful place of African-Americans in literary America.[44] The work of anthologizing and hence canonizing the African-American tradition is desperately needed, and many publishers are beginning to provide Native American, Chicano, and other traditions—each in its separate book. What is worrisome about this approach, however, is the possibility it opens up for us to choose to ignore one or another of these traditions. It allows us to perceive such traditions, which we have not so far done, but it also allows us to see each as a singularity.

One teacher writing for a national education journal has described her approach to selecting literature for her students. She lets them do the choosing. "I've never met a required-book list I liked," she declares. Her successful students are those who, with her guidance, learn to make their own choices, to value book ownership, and above all to prize the ownership of book knowledge. When her students could choose for themselves, they wasted none of their choices. They learned to develop criteria, the most important of which was captured in a comment one student made to another in dismissing a book: " 'You'd only want to read that one once.' "[45]

School districts, however, still generally retain the authority to choose books for children. Those that serve chiefly minority populations are seeking out new books that mirror these cultures. A new regionalism is thus beginning to take hold, different from the regionalism schools sought to overcome in the 1850s, when they created a national, Protestant culture. The new regionalism seeks to resuscitate or create a cultural past as well as introduce a culture of the present for the racial group predominant in that region. The new regionalism is based on strong Romantic ideas about the virtue inherent in folkways and customs and the moral worth to be gained by identifying the individual with his culture of origin.

Traditionalists fear that such a move would destroy the common culture of the country. Multiculturalists argue back both that identity with the subnational group is essential to human development and must precede national identity, and also that such racially identified culture is available to all Americans, not just those of any one specified ethnic group. Multicultural reformers claim they want to create a new coherence out of differences, insisting that much of what was taught as universals in the past is accidental to only one culture, that of successful non-Hispanic whites.

Often multicultural education's embrace of new media, including non-literary arts, film, video, and literary forms such as diaries and letters, not only deals body blows to the text-centered Western perspective, it presupposes a cultural validity and separateness drawn on racial lines that may not in fact exist. Most such critiques claim a superiority of the irrational over logic and the "heart" of folk culture over the "head" of European culture. Extreme statements suggest that Europeans had no contact with their souls, unlike other peoples.

Other multiculturalists, particularly Central American and Caribbean writers, far from searching for racial purities, recognize the essentially mestizo character of their culture and glory in it. Rather than separate out what is Native American from what is Hispanic and what is African, such writers suggest we look at a literature that defines itself by its unique mixture, as if there were salvation in the creole who bears within him the cultures of three continents and peoples.[46] Yet even such writers are reminded that one of these cultures, the Spanish, was itself a product of a mestizo inheritance from Arabs, Jews, North Africans, and indigenous peoples, and that the Arabs in turn had been transmitters of East Indian, Islamic, and Greek culture to the Iberian peninsula and hence to Europe in the ninth through twelfth centuries.[47] One could presumably keep probing further and further back to demonstrate that there is no particular virtue in ancestry or culture per se; ultimately we are all inheritors of many cultures.

Mestizo thinking is an interesting broadening of our ideas about what is culture and what is not, but it continues the myth of the superiority of culture by virtue of racial origin, raising up for admiration cultures peripheral to Europe and seeing this as a progressive idea. Alas, it too is a nineteenth-century myth of the folk, searching in the past for a glorious ancestry. It may even be a secular version of the old hunt for divine origins. This is a very human form of behavior, but one which regrettably perpetuates a Romantic theory of racial superiority.

Every writer struggles to find new ways of seeing in terms of traditional forms and subjects. Understanding how writers extend traditions depends on the capacity to trace their sources. But that would suggest that schoolchildren spend their time worrying over literary histories in school, and it is not clear that literary histories of African-American, Hispanic, Native American, Asian, or other traditions should take the place of what is now taught in school. Indeed, since literary history of European literatures or even American and British literature has never been well taught in school, alternative traditions could certainly constitute a major innovation. But is that the kind of thing we particularly want schoolchildren to be able to do with literature?

In mourning the demise of the McGuffey readers, the historian Henry Steele Commager lamented that our nation has suffered the loss of "a common body of allusions" and "a common experience and a common possession."[48] That loss, however, was not sustained by the working classes. Their loss was the loss of the Protestant Bible and a handful of prayers and hymns that ceased to inform school reading in the 1960s about the same time that churches variously abandoned Latin and the Authorized Version. Restoring a common culture seems to be the despairing wish of many a reformer, either by shoring up the canon of the West, extending it to include literatures that have until recently been ignored, or by offering half a dozen separate literary canons in its place. What few seem to imagine, however, is a coherent vision for the place of literature and English studies in our schools.

Unless we learn to trust the children to seek out meaning and to shape it anew for themselves, we will continue to create English curricula that imitate the Sunday school pedagogies of the past. Children who manage to love reading seem to have developed their love despite, not because of, school. They read widely in fiction, non-fiction, comic books, and the miscellaneous materials that come into their hands. They read real books, not those whose purpose is to answer end-of-unit questions. What school can do to help all the children gain the most powerful tools of reading and writing is to take a hard look at the children who love reading and figure out how they came by it. We need to find the literature and the motivations to read that literature that will inspire children's active explorations on their own.

I once visited a middle school whole-language classroom in which the teacher was preparing her students for six weeks of intensive poetry writing. She wanted them to begin to collect a portfolio of all the work that would go into making poetry—the jottings, writings, revisions, and commentary that each student would engage in; records of the group work and commentary they would exchange; journal entries on their individual reading; published poetry; and each other's creations. A major publisher had supplied this teacher with a lavishly packaged, step-by-step, glossy, four-color kit for teaching a portfolio lesson. The teacher handed out the kits to her class and then showed them what to do. They were to open the plastic covering on the kit, remove the contents, throw everything away, and retain the folder alone. This project in poetry was to begin with empty folders. Within six weeks, the students would have full ones, made up of their own learning in the course of writing, rewriting, reading, and thinking about poetry. To be able to do this, a teacher must have knowledge, courage, and confidence, in herself, but primarily in her students. This kind of classroom will not make money for textbook publishers. It might, however, make a literature for the children.

IV

WORDS FAIL US

Introduction

❦

Most kindergarten and many first grade classrooms in our country are furnished and decorated to resemble playrooms or living rooms, with plenty of easy chairs and couches, play kitchens, circular tables with small chairs, rugs dotted around a cheerful space, and colorful decorations hanging from clotheslines and plastered on every available wall. Denim-clad teachers sit cross-legged on rugs with groups of children hovering around for shared story times or coloring at tables or building dens out of big blocks or mixing sticky messes in bowls.

Perhaps because I had visited so many such joyful rooms over the years, the combined kindergarten–first grade class in one medium-sized Midwestern city depressed me. There, a few work tables floated despondently in a sea of brown carpeting, but the message sent by the whole room was that neatness and orderliness were the goals of school. Printed posters tacked in a tidy row ten feet above the floor enjoined cleanliness, quiet, hygiene, and spelling correctness in stern sentences, giving warning from on high to the twenty tots below that virtue belonged to the grammatical. None of the children's own work was visible anywhere.

The children themselves were variously Southeast Asian, South Asian, Hispanic, African-American and Anglo-American (or in this part of the country, German- and Norwegian-American). They were, like most children I've visited in schools, neatly dressed, well-behaved, and interested in everything that might happen around them. But the grammar exercises frowned down on them from above, while the children, preliterate and unconscious of the injunctions on the posters, were shepherded from one worksheet task to the next by their rather gloomy teacher.

Twice a week this classroom gets a visit from a poet in residence. When she enters the room she brings with her a liveliness and fresh air that immediately transform the atmosphere. The children are invited to cluster around the poet as she prepares them to make a poem together. She asks them what they'd like to write about. Someone suggests a poem about a snake. They all happily agree that a snake poem would be a fine idea. They set to work. What can they tell the poet about their knowledge of snakes? The children apparently know about snakes being long and slithery, and that some have rattles. The poet writes down as many snaky attributes as the children can produce. Then she asks for language that sounds like a snake and feels like a snake. Then she asks for language that tells what a snake does. She reviews all the language the children have given her and asks them to connect up the sensual information with their ideas about the doings of snakes. By this time the poet has covered two long pieces of paper with the children's language, and quite a few circles and arrows, drawn to show how the snake's attributes connect. Many of the words and phrases are long and complex. Some are in languages other than English. The poet points out that the children have discovered that long words and a long poem make sense when one is making a poem about a long snake. The children and the poet troop off to the computer lab, where they will enter their collective ideas so that each child can proceed to refine individual notions of the shape of the poem.

The gloomy classroom full of strictures about correctness and the lively classroom full of emergent poets define two opposing attitudes toward the children of the poor and their language competence. The first says that children must set aside what they know and how they use language to fulfill language tasks that exist nowhere in the world but in such classrooms. The second says that children already know a lot about both language and the world it can describe; it encourages using language to construct new visions and meanings. The first seeks to constrain language by grammatical minutiae. The second seeks to constrain language in poetic forms constructed by the children themselves. The first disassociates children from language and meaning. The second invites children to connect themselves through language to the outer world.

Nowhere is the chasm between school and home more clear than in the ways in which language, that supreme delineator between human beings and the rest of the animal world, is used to distance children from their own cultural contexts as well as from the ways language is used in the world. Especially with reference to poor children, educators too often can be heard to say that "*they* don't have any language when *they* come here." A principal of a school in a large eastern city once proudly showed me around his first- and second-grade classrooms, where teachers were using puppets and felt storyboards to teach six- and seven-year-olds the words for colors and numbers. The principal called a child out to the front of one room to ask him his name. The child knew his first, but not his last, name. This was offered as proof of the language impoverishment rampant in this very poor neighborhood, where the six hundred enrolled children also boasted some sixty different ethnicities.

What that school failed to investigate was what the children *did* know. The child without a last name might very well know the first names of a broad range of adults in his life and even their last names as well; he might know his mother's last name and the names of various of his siblings' fathers, but be puzzled as to which of these might appropriately be added to his own first name. The question might easily not have arisen prior to his entering school. That does not mean he lacks language, nor does his inability to name colors correctly mean he is verbally impoverished.

As early as 1972, linguist William Labov published a landmark study of inner-city black English, in which he demonstrated that contrary to popular beliefs, poor black urban children participate in a richly verbal culture. "They have the same basic vocabulary, possess the same capacity for conceptual learning, and use the same logic as anyone else who learns to speak and understand English." Success in use of highly competitive street language, however, was never an indicator of success in school. Labov went on to question whether the language taught in school prepared young people to be as effective "narrators, reasoners and debaters" as working-class speakers were in their own element.[1]

In a study of black and white pre-school language use in the Piedmont, anthropologist Shirley Brice Heath studied working-class "ways with words" in her book of the same name. She discovered that language patterns in these poor communities differed radically from each other, and that neither poor whites nor poor blacks prepared their children for language uses beyond the minimal expectations of elementary school.[2] The whites more successfully matched the kind of language expectations of the early grades than the blacks, while black children were well prepared for language usages in the community that ran afoul of school norms. Heath's study showed that the cultural contexts determining language use and meaning in such communities are simply different from the cultural contexts of language use in school. For example, the black adults never asked their children questions to which the adults already knew the answers, whereas the poor white parents began such questioning practices with their infants and toddlers. The children of the former arrive at school with no experience in dealing with this kind of questioning. The white children arrive at school prepped to know the "right" answers—answers which the teacher already has in her head.[3] The white children are encouraged as preschoolers to tell sequential, true "stories" about events that have happened to them; the black children learn at home to use metaphor, to elaborate fictional stories and to use language for negotiating power. School generally frowns on the black children's stories, calling them not "fictions" but "lies," and wishing they were less elaborate, more sequential, more consistent. Ultimately, however, the language usages of the poor whites who desire to fulfill foreknown tasks and provide foreknown answers to questions are useless when it comes to complex learning or understanding of issues where there are no right answers and where a tolerance for ambiguity is essential.

For many American children, both those whose mother tongue is English and those who encounter English for the first time in school, classroom attitudes to language use and teaching amount to a direct confrontation with everything children already know about how language works. These attitudes and practices also often fly in the face of our current understanding of how children learn their own mother tongues, how language is used both in general and in particular contexts, and how one would therefore want to teach children the complex of subjects revolving around oral and written language.

A facility with language—the ability to speak and read and write well—has always been recognized as a key to both self-determination for the individual and power and status in the community. It would therefore seem reasonable to believe that a democracy, above all other forms of government, should take a keen interest in promoting language facility among all its citizens. Yet, as we have seen, much of American education for its workers and the poor has been designed to contain their unrest rather than to empower them. Language teaching in English for those whose native tongue is nonstandard has emphasized the prescriptive—"correcting" children's "mistakes." Language teaching for those unfamiliar with English has emphasized the abandonment of children's mother tongues. Language teaching to instill a second language for enrichment has been so incompetent, half-hearted, and ill-managed that few Americans gain any useful second language capacity in school. Language teaching results not in a broadening of children's minds and capacities but a narrowing of them, a reduction of scope that ultimately incapacitates a nation not only to speak, but also to think. We seem to believe as a nation that language should be plain and practical, that anything beyond this is a useless frill or a snobbish affectation. Instead of breeding up a democracy where everyone is a monarch of language, we've reduced our people to barely functioning minimalists. We have done so out of fear.

"To Guard the Avenues
of Their Languages"

Along with the idea that a nation needs a vernacular poet, German Romantic theory also suggested that a nation needs a people bound by similar language, culture, and folkways. The romanticizing of folk culture and the search for singular folk roots in language and custom proceeded apace. Napoleon's sweep across the aging Holy Roman Empire had left in its wake the flotsam and jetsam of disunited German principalities and states. In reaction, honor demanded unification. But how to effect this in a nation that never was?

What we fail to learn sufficiently in our schools is that *no* European nation in the eighteenth century had a single language or single ethnicity within its borders. Royal academies had been established in the seventeenth century to purify national languages and set language standards in pronunciation, spelling, and punctuation. Printing centers had, since the Reformation, used the dialects of the cities where they were located as the basis for vernacular spelling and the standards of usage. While all languages change constantly, print has a tendency to slow down the rate of that change. Throughout the Renaissance, European culture was primarily an oral culture. The Renaissance brought an explosion of language experimentation, but the growing literacy and importance of print in the seventeenth and eighteenth centuries began to slow down this development. On the Continent, the royal academies began the task of regulating the purity of a particular dialect and imposing this on printed matter and in administrative usage. If you wanted a royal patent for your invention or had to appear in court or wanted to print a book, you soon had to do so in a standardized French or Spanish. England alone gloried in its mongrel linguistic inheritance, boasting of a language that gained flexibility and enriched vocabulary from its multiple Germanic, Latin, Norman, and Celtic roots and its capacity to invent new words as needed. England did, however, confine printing to companies with royal permits, most of which were in London and hence printed texts in the London dialect. Print and power, literacy and the language of power, developed hand in hand.

By the end of the eighteenth century the idea of literacy in a standard, national dialect, viewed as a necessity for national consolidation, had taken firm hold throughout Europe. In America, Noah Webster took up this call in his dictionary and the "Blue-backed Speller." Webster crusaded for a distinctive American language that would cast off British English, as the country had British rule. Webster's new American language would also regularize regional dialects and spelling to match the new standard pronunciation.

Purity of language, whether Noah Webster's version or that of his contemporaries in Germany, became a central tenet of nationalism later in the nineteenth century. The idea of a nation, so the theory goes, depends on a people unified by ancient custom, language, and ethnicity. Later in the nineteenth century, this Romantic idea gave rise to an accompanying belief that national purity also depended on purity of race.

Nations in the making like to determine language policy early on. It may seem obvious to suggest that Frenchmen are people who speak French, yet in the seventeenth century this was far from the case. Neither France, nor England, nor any country in the world has ever boasted a single, universal language at the time it first perceived itself as a nation. Ideas of nationhood early became associated, however, with the need to establish a language of government, status, and power, which can then be taught in state schools whose purpose is to build the nation. The Académie Française was created in 1635 to regulate the French language by choosing one of its many dialects as the standard, reforming spelling and pronunciation, producing prescriptive rules and dictionaries, and insisting that Frenchness depended on the speaker's degree of conformity to those rules. In Samuel Johnson's famous criticism (Preface to the *Dictionary*, 1755), "Academies have been instituted, to guard the avenues of their languages, to retain fugitives, and repulse intruders; but their vigilance and activity have hitherto been vain; sounds are too volatile and subtle for legal restraints; to enchain syllables, and to lash the wind, are equally the undertakings of pride."

Johnson recognized that language in action disregarded national boundaries. Actual usage rather than imposed rules—a true democracy of the intellect—determines the history of language. Yet despite Johnson's early understanding that language is constantly changing and evolving, Noah Webster, the first American dictionary maker and would-be radical language reformer, believed like Cardinal Richelieu a century and a half earlier, that a national language could be mandated. In his eagerness to distinguish the *American* language from British English, Webster campaigned for spelling and pronunciation reforms that would override regional differences, unifying the new nation. Despite the two million copies of Webster's *The American Spelling Book* sold between 1790 and 1804, his campaign to mandate language usage ultimately failed. A few minor spellings, such as the change from the British *theatre* to the American *theater*,[4] are its only legacy. Ironically, Webster wanted his own New England dialect to form the standard for all of America; he taught children, for example, to pronounce *deaf* as *deef*.[5] Such pronunciations did not always take. His dictionary, first published in 1828, similarly sought to dictate pronunciation, spelling, and usage. It has remained the foundation for all subsequent American dictionaries. Webster, believing that America had a chance to become a perfect nation and people, aimed to reform the corrupt British language. Perfection would be hastened by the isolation of this continent from any further influences of the overthrown Old World and by strict attention to language "correctness."[6]

Johnson's successors in England meanwhile proceeded to make dictionaries illustrative of how actual writers, whom they quoted, used the language, and how successive users have changed the meanings and usage of words over time. *The Oxford English Dictionary* records the history of how writers have used words; Webster records his own ideas of correctness. Webster's enormous influence on American ideas of language has resulted in an antidemocratic idea of language that is much closer to the centrally controlled, high-status, top-down authoritarianism of the Académie Française of the seventeenth century than to the laissez-faire descriptive purposes of the modern British tradition.

Webster's authoritarian attitude to language enormously influenced U.S. education at a time when the new republic's leaders not only had a powerful command of English but also ranged easily among several other modern languages. If one needed to exercise diplomacy with the French or learn about new German inventions, one picked up the language as required.[7] Such cosmopolitanism was regarded—even in America—as a matter of course. Today we rarely bother to inquire if our secretary of state speaks the language of the people with whom he negotiates, yet Benjamin Franklin taught himself French well enough to negotiate and triumph among native speakers of that language of diplomacy. At the same time, however, Franklin was an advocate of practical education in English and suspicious of the use of German in Pennsylvania, which he saw as threatening to swamp English in his state, particularly since he viewed Pennsylvania's German immigrants as "generally the most stupid of their own nation."[8]

Language acquisition has always been associated with questions of status. The closer one's language usage to that of the seat of power, the higher one's status. High-status language is usually also associated with writing, and high status can be conferred on a people through their sacred texts. As one writer has put it, language figures in "the holy trinity" of nationalism, defined by a "holy people, holy land, holy language" that comes down to us from ideas of nationalism in the Bible. European language theorists of the late eighteenth century saw language as the key to the history of a people and therefore were keen to search out its roots as a clue to the prehistoric origins of the folk. The philosopher Johann Gottfried Herder (1744–1803) defined language as the collective achievement and soul of the people. This idea served to inspire the German unification movement.[9] Curiously, Herder wanted to discover and preserve the folk origins of the German people and to purify the language at the same time. Archaeological research and notions of language purity sit ill with each other, since language has a propensity for messy borrowings and extraneous usages. Webster picked up this national language idea, but also wished to teach the American people to purify their usage.

In early America, such ideas quickly caught on as the key to American-ization of the fragmented new states and regions: the new language would unify the new nation. Webster's theory suggested that correct grammar, virtue, and patriotism defined each other.[10] The perceived need to homogenize disparate Americans and to unify language use across regions for nationalizing purposes was seen as a major purpose of school from the start.[11] Benjamin Rush used the image of "melting" Americans "into one mass" as early as the late eighteenth century. He unfortunately also used the image of converting "men into republican machines . . . [to serve] the great engine of state."[12] In their haste to subdue radical passions and get down to the business of nationhood, our founding fathers were anxious to eliminate difference by melting it down or stamping it out. In school language teaching, that purpose has stayed with us ever since.

When English language studies were first introduced to universities in the later nineteenth century, they pursued Romantic nationalism by investigating the linguistic roots of the people. Anglo-Saxon therefore became the foundation course for the scientific study of English.[13] For ordinary people not in universities, folklore, legends, and folk song constituted the emotional and psychological living memory of the folk, according to Herder's ideas.[14] Fichte had gone in search of peasants whose language was "unspoiled" by cosmopolitan interactions, and which he elevated as the "purest" version of the language. Such ideas about the purity of the folk remain with us today, particularly among advocates of minority languages and literatures who insist that there is a peculiar virtue adhering to the historical languages of their cultural groups. German Romantic theory sanctified the study of early versions of English in America as a research subject.

Benjamin Lee Whorf (1897–1941) spent a lifetime studying Native American languages, resulting in his thesis that thought and perception are shaped by the language in which they are framed. Whorf's theories propose that scientists, for instance, trapped in the patterns of thinking defined by Western languages, are unable to perceive the natural world from more than one perspective because their thought and perception is monolingual. Whorf draws on Herder's thinking to suggest that only through multilingual, multicognitive perceptions can one arrive at broader perspectives. The sanctification of people and their perceptions can, however, work on behalf of cultural nationalists of different kinds. Emphasis on the history of folk English is now being picked up by advocates of Chicano or African-American or Native American languages and literatures as a model for elevating the distinctive aesthetics and traditions of each.

Meanwhile the schools hark back to the earlier tradition of legislating language as a means of unifying the nation, rejecting "foreign" influences and differences from the standard as corrupt.[15] Such language reformers not only want everyone to speak a standard form of English, they recognize that high status can also be attained through knowledge of a second, high-status language. The cultural enrichment that additional languages confer has in all times and in all places been limited to the few rather than available to the many. Modern education movements have concentrated on teaching the vernacular to the masses—that is a primary purpose of schools from the United States to Nigeria. But worldwide, English as a second language is reserved for elites, just as languages other than English have been reserved for the few in this country. The United States has gone further, believing in its pride that languages other than English should either be stamped out or considered of no consequence even as an enrichment for elites.[16] Most other peoples, by force or by election, accommodate to our pride by learning our language.

Language defines class and ethnic boundaries within countries, whether by means of the high-status English of elite British public schools, or the European languages taught to the rich in Latin American countries,[17] or the distinctions between high- and low-status Arabic in North Africa.[18] In the United States, distinctions of class and status are supposed to be rubbed out by public school, which teaches a single universal English to all. On the surface, this looks like a highly democratic process. Yet Americanization through the language taught in school falls differentially on different Americans.

The language teachings of school primarily provide drill exercises in grammar, syntax, diction, spelling, and pronunciation. Such teaching ignores the complex social and cultural webs in which language actually functions, which are not reducible to simple grammar and vocabulary drills. The teachings of school cultivate a strong bias against all languages and usages other than standard English. The cultural contexts of most schoolchildren, including those whose mother tongue is English, become by definition low status, and the bias against other languages categorizes competent users of other languages as low status.

Such attitudes are not limited to the United States. No English-speaking nation anywhere has shown any great enthusiasm for its citizens acquiring language facility beyond English.[19] But the United States goes further. Language fluency in English, although consistently described as a primary purpose of schooling, is taught neither to speakers of other languages nor to native speakers of English. We perceive language as utilitarian and we fuss over correctness, but we deeply distrust anything fancy, highly wrought, extensive, or even fun, and strictly limit clever rhetoric to clergymen infected by the turns and tropes of biblical English. Americans do not love English, an understandable attitude to the national language of the rejected parent nation. Language play and multiple language facility belong to societies with leisured classes, but not to ours. Such attitudes did not prevail among our eighteenth-century political founders, but grew up in the increasingly xenophobic nineteenth and twentieth centuries. The pattern of school in the past forty years has seen the dismantling of meaning, rhythm, context, and beauty from the language drilled in school. We have sought to separate children from their mother tongues and to atomize English into ugly nonsense. Succeeding in these efforts, we have alienated a significant portion of our population in the process.

Accent on
Legislating Language

A͟t no time in America's history did we all speak English.[20] In the early years
of our federation large numbers spoke German and some, Dutch; then the
Louisiana Purchase and the Treaty of Guadalupe-Hidalgo annexed large
numbers of first French and later Spanish speakers. Among our earliest
pieces of language legislation was the 1790 Uniform Rule of Naturalization
law which required applicants for citizenship to establish a term of residence,
proof of good character, knowledge of American history, and understanding
of English.[21] But in 1795 the massive presence of the German-speaking populace led to a proposal that all federal laws be printed in German as well as
English. This proposal failed to pass by only one vote.[22] *The Articles of Confederation* were published in German.[23] The German language continued to
be a major presence not only in Pennsylvania, but also in the expanding West
throughout the nineteenth century. The first pedagogical book published in
America was a 1770 Mennonite text written in German, *Schulordnung*. More
than half of the midwestern high schools formed between 1860 and 1900
conducted all instruction in German.[24] Ohio's public schools required
instruction in German as late as 1903, but by 1919, at the height of the anti-
German reaction of World War I, that state banned the use of German
absolutely.

Americans at war had started the habit of turning against the language of
their enemy during the Revolution. Some felt such animosity toward the
British that they recommended replacing English with some other national
language. Suggestions for the new language variously included German
(because German-speaking immigrants were the largest immigrant group in
the latter half of the eighteenth century); Hebrew (because of its status as a
sacred tongue, and because many immigrants of all nationalities believed
themselves to be establishing a new Eden on these shores); French (because of

our revolutionary friendship with France and because French was a high-prestige language throughout Europe); and Spanish (because of the dominance of that language throughout the rest of the hemisphere). The supporters of Hebrew as a national language had to rest content with its requirement at universities and its continued use as the language for Harvard's commencement addresses through 1817.[25] Various German speakers nevertheless continued to hope for some time to establish a German-language state.[26]

American schools not only had to choose their modern language of instruction, they also had to struggle with old ideas that equated "grammar" with the study of classical languages. American academies, like European upper schools, wrapped their curricula around Latin and Greek. Franklin's 1755 proposals for an English curriculum were ahead of their time. Some of our oldest preparatory schools, like Phillips Exeter, introduced side-by-side classical and English curricula (1818), a pattern followed by most of the other American academies. Entrance to the universities continued to require substantial skill in the classical languages throughout the nineteenth century. At the time of the Revolution, college entrants had to be able to compose Latin prose and read the Gospels in Greek. Not until 1875 did any university require knowledge of a modern language other than English, although professorships in modern languages had existed in the late eighteenth century. French did not become a regular offering in high schools until after 1900.[27] Until then, knowledge of modern languages was assumed to be something you picked up on your own rather than labored over in school.

Quite the contrary: in the nineteenth century, school became a place where speakers of other languages were meant to be assimilated and where the poor were meant to learn the English-language habits of the middle class. Yet many publicly supported schools functioned entirely in other languages or offered bilingual programs. Some one million school children in Cincinnati received instruction in German and English from 1839 to 1919, and the Ohio law that permitted this inspired a similar bilingual French program in Louisiana after the Purchase. Half the St. Louis population took part in German-based instruction by 1860, and 80 percent by 1880. Other groups in that city protested, however—the Irish, Jews, and French feeling excluded. In 1887 they seized control of the school board and ended the German hegemony there; Louisville and St. Paul ended their exclusive schooling in German at about the same time.[28]

The population of California remained half Mexican in descent until the Gold Rush of 1849 tipped the balance toward English speakers. In two years the entire population of the territory went from 15,000 to 95,000, and by 1850 the old legislation requiring publication of laws in Spanish as well as English was abandoned. No linguistic accommodation was made for the Chinese immigrants, however, who had gone from a few dozen in 1849 to 25,000 by 1851. New Mexico, a U.S. territory after 1848, was primarily Spanish and Native American, and offered bilingual education in Spanish and English from the start. After 1884, all-Spanish public schools were authorized, but again Anglo migration to New Mexico changed the balance and by 1891 schools were being required to teach English.[29] New Mexico has always, however, retained its commitment to Spanish, and today is an "English Plus" state that encourages all teachers to be bilingual and all students to study more than one language.

Language instruction in American schools until the last few decades assumed that students would pick up English as best they could, through submersion in the language and culture of middle-class, English-speaking teachers. School stressed correct pronunciation and the amelioration of foreign accents and lower-class speech habits. McGuffey's textbooks and the heavy school emphasis on declamation treated speakers of other languages and the native-born poor alike.[30] Children were to acquire middle-class English at the expense of whatever linguistic habits they brought with them to school.

Immigrant groups who from the start realized that the assimilationist purposes of school precluded the maintenance of ethnic culture and language often set up private schools to do so. Such schools ranged from full-time cultural immersion programs to after-school or weekend supplements, often focused on sacred language learning along with the culture and history of the ethnic group, much as Hasidic day schools or supplementary afternoon Hebrew schools do today. But most private efforts to teach foreign languages have generally been as ineffectual as those of the public schools.[31]

U.S. language policy, beginning with those early attempts first to stamp out British English and then to require English of all new citizens, has continued throughout our history to vacillate and to contradict itself. The federal government first recruited settlers to the West by using the minority languages of the newest immigrants, but then refused to confer statehood on territories that lacked English-speaking majorities.[32] Swedes, Norwegians, and Germans were enticed to the rural West by the Homestead Act of 1862; the Irish tended to settle in the cities.[33] Public schools in the West and Northwest were often de facto conducted in other languages. Until the 1880s, public schools were a new idea still in formative stages. Once public schools were well established, along with the state and district bureaucracies set up to run them, they resisted linguistic accommodations. Post-1880 immigrants like the Italians, Jews, Poles, and Slavs never received instruction in public school in their own languages. They were submerged, sink or swim, in middle-class English instruction.[34] This was the period when nationalism, racism, and the wholesale creation of Americanism was at its peak. No language concessions were to be made for immigrants again until the 1960s.

After the 1880s the modern foreign languages became elitist studies in the new, two-track high schools, limited to successful, English-speaking students.[35] Language facility was to be eliminated from the curricula for the poor and the immigrant in elementary school. Once reduced to inarticulateness in any language, they were tracked into "vocational" education in high school if they managed to stick with it that long. English-speaking, middle-class students, meanwhile, learned no second languages until high school, at which point a smattering of French was offered and an abrupt submersion in Shakespeare.

The new immigrants went to city high schools much less frequently than their native English-speaking contemporaries at the turn of the century. While their drop-out rate probably had as much to do with poverty as with cultural and linguistic alienation from school,[36] we must remember that after 1880, and especially after 1905, school did not work well for anyone who was poor. The refusal to accommodate new immigrants with instruction in their language has generally meant that twentieth-century immigrants have had to find alternative routes to the middle class on their own or through group self-help before their children and grandchildren could find themselves comfortable in school. And for many, particularly people of color, neither economic success nor English as a mother tongue has helped.

Political power has been the key to groups' abilities to introduce their languages into schools. The San Francisco schools had a long and tawdry history of denying language access to the politically weak and only admitting their languages onto school property under duress. In 1917 the San Francisco system "taught German in eight primary schools, Italian in six, French in four, and Spanish in two."[37] The Spanish-speaking people of Mexican descent who had been a majority fifty years earlier had been thoroughly marginalized.

Public schools were silent on the subject of Native American languages until very recently. Until 1871, Native Americans ran their own schools or attended mission schools, which were soon replaced by government schools. In 1879 boarding schools were established by the U.S. government with the purpose of segregating Native American children from their families, languages, customs, and culture. The children in these schools were forbidden to use their mother tongues or to engage in native artistic or religious practices. This policy of destroying what remained of Native American culture merely administered the coup de grâce to an already decimated population, which had by then lost most of its homelands, been forcibly removed to alien territory, and lumped together with unrelated tribes.[38]

Just when tracking removed foreign-language instruction from the reach of new immigrants and people of color, foreign language for enrichment of the white middle class was at its all-time high in public schools. In 1900 half of all high school students took Latin for college entrance or preparation for the professions, and in 1910 another 34 percent were studying modern foreign languages. This increased to 36 percent in 1915, when of the modern languages German was the most popular (24 percent) followed by French as a distant second (9 percent); only 3 percent studied low-status Spanish by choice.[39] World War I nearly eliminated German from all schools and consequently greatly reduced foreign language study. After that, American schools at one and the same time refused to teach non–English speaking students in their native languages and offered French in high school only to the privileged. Since foreign language was a college entrance requirement, this policy maintained social stratification by reserving access to college for the Anglophone middle class.

As a result of such tracking policies, just as high school enrollments increased and diversified, the proportion of students studying foreign languages for enrichment and college entrance decreased. By 1934 fewer than 20 percent of secondary students were enrolled in foreign language classes, by 1948 only 14 percent; yet all the while high school was enrolling more and more of the nation's young people. Despite the embarrassing inability of our soldiery to communicate with our allies in World War II,[40] various policies continued to disregard the foreign language facility of new citizens. The 1950 Internal Security Act required that new citizens be able to read and write English, a far more stringent requirement than had prevailed. The 1906 Nationality Act required only a speaking ability in English.[41] Ironically, America's emergence from isolationist policies and transformation into a global power in the two world wars was in both cases quickly followed by ever stronger restrictions on language use by its own and would-be citizens.

A law requiring literacy in English was first proposed in 1897 and vetoed by Grover Cleveland; the same requirement was passed over Wilson's veto in 1917 at the start of America's involvement in the First World War. Between 1917 and 1923 the states removed statutes that had tolerated instruction in school in languages other than English; in some cases states even forbade the teaching of foreign languages for any purpose. By then, Americans realized that schools could not act as the major vehicles for teaching English to immigrants anyway, since the vast majority of them were beyond compulsory school attendance age.[42] Public funding for church-related schools ended in the 1920s, greatly reducing public support for language education other than English, which had flourished in private institutions.[43]

World War I brought with it not only fear and hatred of foreign languages, but also love of psychological testing. The army's use of I.Q. tests on a massive scale was transformed in the 1920s into a civilian exercise enabling schools to "scientifically" track desirables and undesirables toward their separate fates. Until World War I, cultural theory in America was based on a belief that each nationality inherited separate behavioral characteristics. After World War I, I.Q. tests were available to prove "innate intelligence." Some new immigrants, tested in English, were declared feeble-minded; some children of immigrants, tested in English, were declared retarded.[44] The tests had become a powerful tool for declaring the debilitating effects of other languages and for shunting undesirables away from the opportunities touted by education.

From the turn of the century until the early 1920s, schools had been engaged in a campaign designed to "Americanize" by insisting on English acquisition, as if the language alone would by definition transform immigrants. In the Southwest, the campaign was aimed at Americans of Mexican descent. But those people had resided there for many generations—revealing that the program was fundamentally designed to eliminate alternative language and culture. The U.S. Bureau of Education's "Americanization through Education" national conferences in 1917 and 1918 not only emphasized the need for the children of immigrants to learn English in school but even called for compulsory attendance at night schools for their parents.[45] By 1923, thirty-four of the forty-eight states had declared that English must be the only language of instruction in school.[46] A Supreme Court ruling in 1923 established that Nebraska's law requiring instruction in English was constitutional, but the state's prohibition against ethnic groups teaching second languages privately was not.[47] The norm up until World War I had been bilingual education; by the early 1920s, legislation had changed that norm to create an America whose schools were overwhelmingly English only. Restrictive immigration laws of 1921 and 1924 reflected American nativist fears.[48] Once languages other than English had disappeared from public schools, we began to believe in an English-only myth we had just created.

Language as a definition of a people, like religion as a definition, has its complexities and vexations. The collapse of the Old World order in the First

World War dispersed the old empires held together by European monarchies and left the world floundering in conflicting definitions of nationhood, ethnicity, and language. The American response was to withdraw into itself. We were all Americans as long as we all spoke English, and school was going to focus on social conformity for everyone. Our foray into global politics had exposed us to dangers to our integrity that we would fend off by pretending they didn't exist—either abroad or at home.

Our populace turned away from the foreign with revulsion just as America was declaring itself a world power. School became a place where language was despised rather than prized, with the result that the next generation of soldiers sailed and flew off to World War II in Europe and the Pacific with even less language facility than the doughboys of World War I. The onset of the Cold War brought with it yet another set of contradictory U.S. policies regarding language. Language facility became critical to our national defense, yet speakers of other languages were seen as culturally deprived. New psychological theories in the 1950s suggested that speakers of minority languages should no longer be seen as inherently, genetically inferior and incapable, but as sufferers from cultural deprivation.[49] The ironies of seeing children with different languages and cultures as lacking something rather than having something, albeit something different, were lost on a public that at the same time began to worry that we lacked the language skills necessary to compete in the global standoff between the politically and economically opposed superpowers.

By the 1960s, the deprivation theory that labeled our minority cultures as suffering from a lack of white, middle-class language and culture informed President Johnson's War on Poverty, and especially its attempt to intervene at early ages with the culture of poverty.[50] The children of the poor were perceived as having no culture, or a culture interfering with the preferred school culture. In 1958, however, the National Defense Education Act funded language programs for those who already participated in English, middle-class culture—creating for them by 1960 elementary instruction programs in foreign languages in every state in the Union. So while the federal government waged war on the languages spoken by the poor, it simultaneously spent money to instill those languages in the middle class. Not because of the absurdity of all of this, but for lack of continued federal attention, within a decade these fledgling elementary foreign language programs had mostly disappeared.[51]

The confusion of the early 1960s was exacerbated by the start of a new era of bilingual education. In 1963 an elementary school in Dade County, Florida, instituted a bilingual program for its middle-class Cuban and Anglo children, where half the day's instruction was in Spanish and half in English for all children. Originally funded by the Ford Foundation, the program soon attracted federal interest. Government weighed in with massive support for bilingual programs throughout Dade County. Significantly, since that time bilingual programs have developed very different goals. Bilingual education fundamentally became a way of separating Spanish speakers from other children in special programs. Spanish speakers alone of all minority language groups in the history of the United States were to be educated in public schools separately from native English speakers until they had acquired enough English to assimilate.[52]

In the 1963 experimental school, the purpose had been to maintain the Cuban culture and language for the Cubans and to introduce that culture to Anglos while also introducing Anglo culture to Cubans. Both groups were meant to end up happily bilingual and bicultural. As the idea was later interpreted in schools and programs for the poor, however, maintenance of language and culture for Hispanics or acquisition of Hispanic culture by Anglos disappeared in favor of using bilingual funding to Americanize Hispanics and move them as quickly as possible into English. The key difference in treatment between those first experimental Cubans and later Hispanics would seem to be class.

By the late 1960s, the Civil Rights movement had brought to the fore many Spanish-speaking Americans who demanded language rights in school as a civil right, and it was in that context that the 1968 enactment of Title VII of the Elementary and Secondary Education Act, known as the Bilingual Education Act, developed.[53] Spanish speakers were being treated differently in schools from all other post–World War I speakers of minority languages partly because at least in Puerto Rico, the West, and the Southwest many were involuntarily absorbed by U.S. takeovers of erstwhile Mexican and Spanish territories.[54] Many others, such as Puerto Ricans migrating to northeastern cities, could not with any honesty be described as immigrants either. The Bilingual Education Act did extend language rights in schools to all language groups; but with Hispanic children in mind, it resulted in a tendency to isolate or segregate minority-language children from the majority inside each school. English speakers were required by law to be present in bilingual classes, but only on a voluntary basis. Few chose to do so. Bilingual classes ended up consisting mostly of Spanish-speaking or other language minority children alone.[55] And, of course, the ever-ready testers were always there to make sure Spanish speakers did appear in the isolated classes specially prepared for them.

The history of federal policies of the past two decades is confusing to follow because they developed along two different tracks. The first, deriving from Title VII of the 1968 Elementary and Secondary Education Act, seeks to provide financial compensation to schools that need to offer special instruction for students with limited English proficiency. The second track has to do with the civil rights of students who have had unequal access to education because of language differences. The same education offered to all but inaccessible to some because of their inability to understand the language of instruction was deemed a violation of civil rights, corrected by Title VI of the 1970 Civil Rights Act. This ordained that school districts with five percent or more of their enrollments of minority national origins must take affirmative action to remedy the inequity.[56]

In addition to these two separate federal policies, individual states have also enacted bilingual laws of their own. In the late 1960s the Boston public schools had discovered that as many as half the school-aged Hispanic children in the city had not registered for school at all. The Massachusetts legislation of 1972 was the first state law requiring bilingual instruction and the first "transitional" law. Transitional approaches state that the purpose of bilingual education is not to maintain the language or culture of the child, but to move the child as quickly as possible into English.[57] Such laws perceive English acquisition as a replacement for the native language.

The Bilingual Education Act of 1974, however, superseding the 1968 act, extended the application of its provisions beyond low-income children. The initial act had tied bilingualism to poverty; the new act still, however, primarily saw its beneficiaries as deprived and in need of quick transition to English.[58] The education policies were boosted by a 1974 case, *Lau* v. *Nichols*, brought on behalf of Chinese-speaking students in San Francisco. The Supreme Court ruled that the schools must provide equal linguistic access to these students under the Fourteenth Amendment.[59] The *Lau* v. *Nichols* case led to a series of interpretations of the court decision, known as the "Lau Remedies." This list of things schools could do to comply stressed transitional programs and a focus on English.[60] Within the space of a little more than a decade, *bilingual* had changed from meaning programs like those of the nineteenth century (that maintained two languages and cultures throughout schooling) to programs in which the minority language speakers were segregated from the majority for a period of time until they were speaking English, at which point they would enter the mainstream language and culture wholesale and all other language usage would cease. *Bilingual* had come to mean "Anglification of non-English speakers." The law called "bilingual" thus operates *against* bilingualism.[61]

All of the laws and remedies of the 1960s and 1970s resulted in a policy toward language that does the minimum necessary to acknowledge the existence of speakers of other languages. In the words of one commentator, these rulings are "parsimonious" about equity.[62] Only when the courts agreed that minority language speakers sitting in classrooms where English was the sole language of instruction in fact lacked access to that instruction did the schools grudgingly acquiesce to doing something about it. From about 1880 until the 1970s, for nearly one hundred years, children were simply flung into English-speaking classrooms and left to sink or swim. Those children, now grown, can often be heard to protest that they managed just fine and that no special bilingual programs should be offered for new immigrants when for most of the nation's immigrants in the past none was deemed necessary. The reality is that most immigrant children dropped out, in 1880 as in 1930 and in 1960, leaving it to the next generation of American-born to learn English and to succeed in school. Dropping out of a schooling they could not understand, the first generation has established itself through ward politics, group solidarity, small business operations, and crime.[63] Their children, usually English speakers from birth, have derived some benefit from school and, if their parents have gained enough economic security, have gone on to enter the middle classes. School itself, however, has not typically provided the entrance ticket, but the barrier until the family has succeeded by other means. Exceptions to this pattern include many Chinese, whose isolation in their own communities perpetuates Chinese language and culture beyond one generation; the various Hispanic groups who find that English and educational attainment do not necessarily change their economic status; and African-Americans, who perceive a society ranged against them. Social rewards for taking on the language of power is a worldwide phenomenon, but one that works unevenly when factors such as race, religion, and ethnicity interfere.

The 1960s and 1970s saw a global revival of ethnicity, the point of which elsewhere as well as in the United States was protest against the alienating ways and means of modern society.[64] People felt their individualism and autonomy were increasingly threatened by faceless government, business, school, mass entertainment, mass marketing, and the obliteration of the uniqueness of place as the landscape was transformed into an overriding sameness. In a sense this *was* the accomplishment of an American culture undifferentiated here and threatening to homogenize cultural differences abroad. The ethnic protest against assimilation into a whitewashing mainstream gave rise to an ethnic heritage revival in the United States, to strong support for bilingual education, and to the beginning of the end of the myth of the melting pot.

This in turn gave rise to a reaction as many Americans began to fear that the United States would become Balkanized by ethnic differences. By

1978, the federal enthusiasm for bilingual education was already waning. As President Carter said, "I want English taught, not ethnic culture."[65] Ironically, the same individual found himself creating the President's Commission on Foreign Language and International Studies in that same year, which in the name of the 1975 Helsinki East-West accords advocated that everyone needed to learn other languages and cultures. We were as a nation scandalously ignorant about such matters, they said.[66]

While this President's Commission was calling for massive programs to enhance our knowledge of other languages and cultures, school superintendents were balking at the laws requiring bilingual instruction, and studies were claiming that bilingual education programs were ineffective anyway. The 1978 reauthorization of the bilingual act weakened the requirements, backing off native language maintenance. By the time President Reagan entered office on a campaign promise to reduce government intervention into private life, true bilingualism was nearly dead.[67]

One of Reagan's first acts in office was to remove pending legislation on the Lau remedies, effectively leaving schools with no guidelines on how to serve needy students. Reagan's secretary of education tried to support bilingual education, but the American Federation of Teachers, the American Legion, and "U.S. English," a group founded in 1983 to legislate English as our official national language, took stands against it.[68] Nebraska had been the first state to pass an English Only law, as early as 1923; but the majority of states who joined in (sixteen to date) did so after 1981.[69] Such laws have been considered in forty-four states and municipalities. California, Colorado, and Florida have passed English Only legislation in the teeth of large non–English speaking populations; these states are sure to face court tests.[70] Twenty states defeated similar legislation between 1987 and 1989.[71] In contrast, New Mexico resolved in 1989 that all its citizens should learn English plus another language; Hawaii decided in 1978 to designate English and Hawaiian as co-equal official languages, and Louisiana in 1974 asserted the preservation and promotion of minority languages and cultures.[72] These latter states are proud of their history and their linguistic and cultural inheritance. The English Only states, most of which are in a solid block in the South, now have policies that may ultimately hold little or no importance for daily life. But "U.S. English" and the conservative federal education officials of the 1980s found a large part of the nation in agreement with their ideas. Although the Bilingual Education Act continued to be renewed despite such opposition, and despite claims that children were better off immersed in English in school, by 1984 the act allowed English Only programs to be funded by the Bilingual Education Act. In a 1985 speech to the

Congress, the secretary of education claimed that any purpose other than attaining English fluency was outside the scope of "bilingual" education.[73] At present, 25 percent of the money for "bilingual" education is used for monolingual English.

The controversy over bilingual education continues, but here are some well-known facts. Teachers know that keeping children in school is better than letting them drop out. They also know that children are more likely to stay in school if their instruction is conducted in a language they understand. Success in school has as much to do with wealth—and failure with poverty—as it has to do with the language the child brings to school.[74] Reagan agreed with Teddy Roosevelt that multilingualism is fundamentally un-American, but the Reagan era saw a larger proportion of the population speaking mother tongues other than English than Teddy Roosevelt's pre–World War I period. Despite this, fully 85 percent of the U.S. population speaks English as the mother tongue and approximately 95 percent of the population has acquired spoken English. Schooling or no schooling, Hispanics as well as all previous speakers of other languages become English speakers by the second or third generation. Hispanics continue to *seem* not to have acquired English only because fresh immigration continues to infuse new Spanish speakers into the United States all the while second and third generation Hispanic-American residents, like all other language groups, do attain English at the usual rate.[75] Who we are as Americans seems to depend on what we speak. This close association between language and nationality, an identification that has vexed us from the start, is one that has been legislated largely in vain.

Speaking American

❦

Linguistic nationalism was and is essentially about the language of public education and official use.

ERIC J. HOBSBAWM,
NATIONS AND NATIONALISM SINCE 1780

Worldwide there are some four thousand different languages, but only 160 nations. The idea that everyone in any country should speak only one language is therefore absurdly at odds with linguistic realities.[76] Despite U.S. and global histories of multilingualism, English has prevailed as the national tongue without any specific federal legislation to make it so. Because from time immemorial language has been the link between a people and godliness, each language group has always associated its own language with sanctity and religious beliefs. In the United States, "language becomes part of secular religion, binding society together and mobilizing it to face whatever its challenges are taken to be."[77] Ethnicity and language, however, are not supposed to be definitions of a democratic nation, so by a sleight of hand, English as an ethnicity disappears. The English are perceived as non-ethnic, therefore as legitimately national rather than ethnic group-specific. Only minority languages and ethnicities are seen as separatist and therefore destroyers of the national integrity. Minority groups long for a sense of authenticity of their own, sometimes associating this with language and often with "revivals" of customs and beliefs that are pure fabrications. The creation of authenticity through invented customs and rituals has more to do with genuine emotional needs than with logic or historical accuracy. Kwanza is an American invention, not an African festival, yet it fulfills the need for a binding ritual among disparate African-Americans. American flag rituals were invented in the late nineteenth century for a comparable purpose.

Language loyalty movements such as those of Hispanics, Native Americans, Hasidim, and so on, assist groups that have been violently dislocated from their roots to regain links to each other and to shift power balances in their favor. These self-help movements via language revival, whether in the Baltics or in America, are attacked by those in power as "divisive," "Balkanizing," and atavistic.[78] (The English Only movement is also a language loyalty movement; witness the emotional conviction with which it is associated.) Language minority movements are perceived as anti-modern, seeking to wrest control from the central power and to convert monolithic homogenizing modernity into a more personal set of community ties and identities. Central authorities fear such movements, yet language and ethnicity revivals, which have surfaced periodically throughout our history, have done no damage to American integrity at any time. Schools established by ethnic communities to maintain ethnic culture and language have always done so within a context of mainstreaming the children of those who established them. Ethnic schools in fact *Americanize* children.[79] No example of this could be more clear than the Catholic schools of our country, which have taught an intense American patriotism from the start, despite their origins in a revulsion against the enforced Protestant Americanization of the public schools.

Ethnic schools most often have taught a religious language or a language no longer in active use in the ethnic community. And when they have taught school subjects in the mother tongue, children of illiterate parents have done far better in school than their counterparts who have attended schools where English immersion predominates.[80]

Fears of bilingualism and of minority bids for ethnic culture in schools are as irrational as the longings for ethnic authenticity they attack.[81] Forcing the issue one way or another is done only at the expense of the children themselves. The dominant language in America, and increasingly in the world, is the English that all minorities want access to—for the power and success that cannot come without it. Power and success may be possible within minority language communities that boast international connections (for example, Chinese communities), but *American* success is still only possible with acquisition of English. Conservative defenders of English Only in our schools and of quick transitions to English see their beliefs as nonpartisan, but such beliefs strengthen the position of those in power. At a time when decent jobs for the unskilled were plentiful, non-English speakers suffered little; but as such jobs have grown scarce, English has become a major gatekeeper to the economy. The amount and nature of the English taught in school makes less difference for economic success than the nature and number of available jobs.[82]

Everywhere in the world, continued residence in a place where a different language predominates has meant that eventually people shift to the dominant language and lose the mother tongue, whether or not some bilingualism also continues. This takes from two to three generations, depending on economic incentive and degree of access to the dominant language. Voluntary migrants shift their language faster than those who have been annexed or colonized. Continued access to the mother tongue through new immigration or use of written materials of high cultural or religious prestige may also help retain the mother tongue.[83] But the shift is inevitable, as we have consistently seen in the United States, school or no school.

National languages are always to some extent artificial—imposed afterthoughts or late developments, rather than foundations for nations. National myths tell the story otherwise, but nations are created first, languages selected or simply evolved after. The choice of language is arbitrary, not foreordained.[84] Early American discomfort with English is testimony to this pattern. In the France of 1789, only 50 percent of the populace spoke French and only 12 to 13 percent spoke it according to Parisian ideas of purity. The Italy of unification in 1860 contained a populace of which only 2.5 percent were Italian speakers. The German unification movement rallied around the language of the theater, the French revolution around the language of a literary elite;[85] American independence around the pamphleteers. The whole idea of forming modern nations in the period from the seventeenth to the twentieth centuries depended heavily on the unifying effects of reading the Bible in the modern vernacular languages. Such readers, at first a small group, gained power through their link to a particular form of the vernacular as expressed in the newly sacred biblical translations. National languages often inconvenience the majority in many other countries as well as this one. The choice of high-status Hebrew over low-status Yiddish as the national language of Israel, for instance, imposed a language nobody spoke on the entire population.[86]

After the 1860s, censuses in European countries began asking citizens language questions and basing "nationality" on their answers.[87] For the first time, place of birth gave way to language as a key determinant of nationality—and led to minority groups being stigmatized as subversive of national purposes. Jews who spoke Yiddish and Gypsies who spoke Romansch are examples. The Romantic idea that a people could be defined by the purity of their language ultimately came to mean that "impurities" should be eliminated. The romanticizing cult of "the people" who bore the pure, simple, uncorrupted language of the forebears was carried out in the nineteenth century, as now, by intellectuals in love with their theories and their research, looking for a vehicle for self-promotion through revival of the folk, with themselves as spokespersons on behalf of the folk. Such movements serve useful purposes in providing access to power for minority groups in the United States, just as the invention and cultivation of "American" customs in the late nineteenth century consolidated the power of those who could trace their ancestry to British colonial times.

The links between nationalism, purity of language, and racism were forged from 1870 to 1918, fed by nineteenth-century "scientific" proofs of racial and linguistic hierarchies derived from Darwin. By 1900 race, nationality, and language were fused concepts, and all three were perceived as *inherited*. The national language was de facto imposed by government clerks and school teachers on all who wanted access to public services and, therefore, power.[88] The resistance of bureaucrats to languages other than English results from their own incapacity in languages other than English as much as from their belief that English is morally good for the people with whom they deal.

The English Only movement has found resonance among these officials and among many other Americans alarmed by large numbers of new immigrants from Latin America and Asia. Asian immigrants recently began appearing in parts of America where little heterogeneity of population had been seen before, as new post-Vietnam policies sprinkled them liberally around the country. The immigrant speakers of different and non-European languages became, by the 1980s, the problem not just of New York City or San Francisco, but of rural Wisconsin and Missouri alike. The movement to exclude languages other than English from all public life begins to look like a revival of virulent nationalism in the face of exotic immigration. English Only advocates claim for themselves the need to preserve national unity and see other language efforts as separatist and conducive to ethnic rebellion, whereas ethnic groups fighting to maintain their languages in public life claim that the English Only movement alienates and polarizes their groups and increases their unrest.[89]

Before 1980 only three states had declared English their official language; by 1988 only three states had not yet considered such a law.[90] The attitude that multilingualism is a sign of being un-American seems pervasive in our country. But white, native speakers of English are not guaranteed economic success as a result of their linguistic capacity, and language cannot help us define our Americanness without risk of either racism or absurdity—we see English spoken all around the world without defining all English speakers as members of one nation. The languages to be taught in school can neither make us a nation nor hinder us from becoming "American." But language policy in school can define an Americanness that excludes or stigmatizes some Americans.

A Tongue-tied Nation

Language as taught in school—whether English for native speakers, bilingual programs meant to assist speakers of other languages to acquire English, or enrichment programs to introduce other languages to native speakers of English—has been taught so badly that schooling has done as much to obscure communication as to further it. Over the past half-century the reading industry grew up to create English language programs that, as we have seen, have left large parts of the population disconnected from complex language. The basal readers have been accompanied by workbooks where children complete silly exercises and answer dumb questions, and teacher's manuals have provided so much step-by-step assistance in framing lessons that they are "teacher-proof," meaning that the teacher becomes merely the agency through which the book conducts the class.

These books, published in complicated series, are usually adopted by schools wholesale; single publishers sell books to entire schools and districts for all elementary grades at once. Basals are four-color and expensive, especially considering that the workbooks are used up by each student and must be replaced. The basals are edited by committees and largely written by educators. They are overwhelmingly devoted to prose fiction, but contain little or nothing by recognized writers. Children whose only exposure to reading and language comes through these books and worksheets associate reading with boredom and misery. Children who find alternative books at home and elsewhere associate school reading with perplexity, trivia, and misery. Basal readers dominate the schoolroom through grade six and now threaten to invade our new "middle" school structure, since middle schools are increasingly taught by elementary-trained teachers who often depend inordinately on textbook approaches to language and literature.

Basal readers lay out a universe in which the purpose of reading is to answer questions posed by somebody else; they therefore enforce a Puritanical, "practical" attitude towards reading that consigns it to a purely functional place. Basal readers create an artificial, manufactured language that no real speaker or writer ever used, so that children confronted with this language find themselves as puzzled by it as if it were an unknown tongue.

At "reading level five," the Merrill *Step Up* basal asks children to read aloud the following:

A Good Plan

On a sunny day, Tom said to Dot, "I have a plan for today. I think I will dig a pit to set this plant in. Then when the plant gets big, we can have the plums from it."

"What a good plan, Tom!" said Dot. "I'll help you dig. Let's plant it next to the kitchen."

"Yes," said Tom, "let's get going."

When Tom bent to dig, he said, "Dot, I must be getting plump. I can't bend much to do this digging."

"That's OK," said Dot, "we'll get it dug."[91]

If you try to read this aloud, it becomes immediately apparent that the passage is neither idiomatically nor rhythmically English. No one except the advisors listed on the title page—"Former District Language Arts Supervisor," "Director of Edutec Unlimited [sic]," and a "former Assistant Director of Reading"—has ever in the history of the language written or spoken like this.

Children confronting language in print for the first time in their lives, moreover, are offered the following in the first basal of the Merrill series:

Is a cat on a mat?
A cat is on a mat.
Is the cat fat?
Is the cat Nat?
The cat on the mat is Nat.[92]

The teacher's manual urges her to "discuss the story." After the first line, the teacher is to ask the children entrusted to her care, "What is the first thing you want to know?" Surely any self-respecting child's answer must be, "When's recess?" The fat cat Nat goes on having stimulating adventures of this kind for pages and pages—weeks and weeks of first grade.

When basals do reprint the work of recognized writers, they eliminate everything from the writing that makes it linguistically interesting. Kipling's camel with its "great big lolliping humph" gets changed to "a great big humph." Zealous editors take out the lovely words, the good storytelling, the conflict at the heart of storytelling, the voice of the narrator. What's left is repetitive, pointless, and dull.[93] It's also dishonest to fob off some "language skills" supervisor's bowdlerization of a real writer's work as if it were the original. Nowhere in basals can one find a warning label that alerts children to the fact that they are not reading Kipling but a travesty in Kipling's name. Reformers of school readers aren't much better. A reading series prepared by E. D. Hirsch, the first title of which is *What Every First-Grader Should Know*, presents versions of Aesop and Grimm with no indication anywhere in the books as to the sources of the texts presented, translations, or editions used. Citing textual sources is basic to honest scholarship and to reprinting conventions. Searching out authentic, lively, and sound texts as the basis for the reading we offer children in school should be the first order of business for any textbook editor.

Contemporary basal readers also contain selections that look like poetry but were chosen for their moral rather than their music. In one basal reader Lee Bennett Hopkins's "Girls Can, Too!" attempts to render a dialogue between a taunting boy who boasts that boys can "leap off a wall" and the narrator, a girl who proves her equality by telling us, "Then I leaped off the wall."[94] The line is unidiomatic, whether it is meant to convey children's speech or not, and fails to convey the act of leaping in its language. A line conveying the speaker's triumph needs to be triumphal, an effect readily achieved by at least one student poet (who is discussed more fully in the final part of this book), who renders the lines

> i wud laugh jump leap
> up and touch the stars

The lack of punctuation urges forward the three stressed verbs at the end of the first line and emphasizes the uplifting motion in the placement of *up* at the beginning of the second line, raising the cadence throughout. The writer, a tenth-grader when she wrote these lines, has an acute ear and a natural sense of poetry's ability to render action in words.

There's a simple, straightforward purpose for reading just about any kind of writing: to find out what happens next. Awkward, unidiomatic language, questions that reek of the falsehood of the schoolroom, wrenched rhymes and rhythms masquerading as poetry—fail to serve this purpose. A schooling that depends on basals for instruction in language dismembers reading, disembowels form, disengages minds, and destroys the very capacity to learn.

Our public school record is just as dismal in other languages as it is in English. Poor teaching characterizes language instruction across the board. Although the Soviet Union's enforced language policy in Russian backfired, the Soviets were remarkably successful in teaching second and third languages (in second and third alphabets) to those privileged to attend its "English" schools. In these, English began in the second year of school (age eight or nine) and proceeded in small classes for five or six hours a week. At the secondary level, classes were as small as half a dozen students. Teachers in such schools were fluent speakers of English. When I asked Soviet teachers how they managed to teach so successfully, they answered, "It's no problem." The schools and the nation had a commitment to language instruction that they carried out regardless of costs.

The United States banished second languages from the elementary schools after the turn of the century. Later the excuse often given was that children were too young or unready for languages until the middle teens. The fact that all children happily and without harm pick up their mother tongue in early childhood and bilinguals usually move easily between two or more languages at tender ages has not altered that negative opinion about young children's capacity for language. By leaving language acquisition to the teen years, we ask our adolescents to make language mistakes in public precisely at the time of their greatest desire to conform to their peers and their time of greatest social anxiety. And like so much else that happens in school, we equate language knowledge with memorization of vocabulary lists. The foreign language programs for elementary schools (FLES) that flourished briefly in the 1960s have all but disappeared. They, like much American second-language instruction, were taught by unskilled teachers, were based on rote memory and repetition, and then as now provided too little class time to accomplish much.[95] Elementary foreign language in affluent districts now follows the pattern of much schooling, offering an "introduction" to language for a couple of hours a week or less. Children learn to count to twenty in a second language by the end of a year's such "introduction."

Bilingual education fares much the same. Only 11 percent of the eligible children currently receive it. Over half the schools that provide bilingual programs offer no content instruction in the students' native language, so they lurch from a transition English class to a math or science or history class in which no transition assistance is available.[96] Average use of the mother tongue in bilingual classes was found to be only 8 percent of class time in one study. Other studies have shown the teachers of bilingual programs to be less fluent in the languages of their students than the students themselves, and instruction is therefore filled with talk about superficial symbols of culture—tacos, piñatas, and so on—instead of serious discussions of any cultural depth. There are few bilingual teacher-training programs and few trained teachers available. Classes get taken by untrained teachers' aides instead.[97] The attitude that "bilingual" equals "Hispanic" has led to absurdities where speakers of wildly disparate languages, such as Chinese, Vietnamese, and Tagalog, are lumped together in one class. Since no shared language can prevail, the so-called bilingual instruction ends up as English only instruction.[98] The result of all of this is that the full burden of learning English is left to the minority-language child.[99]

The brief resurgence of second language learning in the 1960s, due in part to the National Defense Education Act, was also a response to the unprecedented number of children of G.I. Bill, college-educated parents. The baby boomers wanted to attend college in the 1960s and needed language credits for admission. Ironically, students whose native tongue wasn't English were never given second language credit for learning English in school, and were thereby unable to use either their first or their second language to fulfill college admissions requirements. This Catch-22 for bilinguals served to bar access to college for many a fluent speaker, while native speakers of English could squeak by with the seat-time spent in minimal foreign language classes.[100] For these latter students, a smattering of French or Spanish or Latin for a couple of years in high school has been taught as if covering the textbook in a given time were the equivalent of learning a language. The textbook has become the curriculum—the object of the course.[101] Grammar substitutes for facility here just as it does in the English basals. Foreign languages are often taught backward from the way we learn our native tongues. In school, we start with grammar, stay with that until we wear down the learner, then proceed to reading and writing.[102] Speaking is rare, except to ask students to fill in a blank "what" question. Most of the talk in the classroom comes from the teacher, and far too much of that is in English rather than the language being studied. Any given student probably uses the spoken language to the extent of one or two words per class.

Second-language instructional theories have changed over the years and contradicted each other. The memorization of grammar plus translation had been the method used for classical language learning from the eighteenth century on, and prevailed with modern languages as well until the 1950s. This method depends on highly literate students whose entrée to language comes through printed texts. In the 1950s, the "audio-lingual" method was introduced, based on psychologist B. F. Skinner's stimulus-response theory of behavior: show a rat a green light often enough and it will learn to press the lever to get a pellet of food. Applied to language learning, this theory suggested that language was a habit you learned through repetition. Based on an oral approach, it stressed endless repetitions. Noam Chomsky's linguistic theories of the late 1950s showed up this model of language as ridiculously simplistic. A series of more recent theories and methods have followed, stressing sometimes immersion in the new language, submersion (where less skilled speakers are placed in classes with skilled speakers), and methods that try to build on students' cognitive knowledge base.[103] Whether designed for speakers of English or of minority languages, these methods at best had a poor showing for the years devoted to them. Our high school graduates arrive in college generally unable to use a second language, needing remediation in English exposition, haltingly able to use English well (whether native speakers or not), stumblers and stammerers in their native tongue and tongue-tied in all others. The 1958 National Defense Education Act (NDEA) was America's major response to Sputnik. Our aim was to try to catch up in the science, math, and languages at which the Soviets clearly excelled. Our national security depended on it. But not even national security scares were seemingly enough to spur us on to do a better job at teaching languages. For all the NDEA flurry, little improvement in language learning occurred. We did make it to the moon, where our first American footstep was recorded around the world in an astonishingly awkward, unclear phrase. We did the science and math poetically; we tripped on the language.

A Paucity of Language

~~~~~~~~~~

Still little understood by the linguists, cognitive scientists, anthropologists, and neuroscientists hard at work on its complexities, language seems to involve an enormously complex set of interactions and reverberations among an infinite number of variables. Among these relationships, the web of circumstances relating language and class is one we need to be keenly aware of. The success of English learning for the Cubans in the 1963 Dade County bilingual school experiment had as much to do with their middle-class status as the program's teaching efficacy.[104] Similarly, the failure rates for other Hispanics in school, while certainly not helped by poor teaching practices, are greatly influenced not just by poverty but also by negative attitudes to poverty found in school.

In the twenties, U.S. health authorities assumed "that working-class immigrants did not know how to bathe, take care of children, or prepare food";[105] curricula developed at that time sought to instill proper American attitudes towards these areas of life. Language was just another dirty or improper manifestation of the behavior of poverty. Until as recently as the 1960s, use of one's mother tongue on school property, including playgrounds, was actively punished. Native American and Spanish children were regularly beaten whenever they lapsed into native languages.[106]

Schools equated fluency in English with logical thought, thereby assuming speakers who weren't fluent to be irrational.[107] Many minority groups seem to agree, rejecting logic as somehow a cold "linearity" peculiar to Anglos and believing soulfulness and emotional warmth peculiar only to other ethnicities. The irony of this belief is that the so-called logic of English was a fabrication of grammarians who only achieved its semblance after various fruitless attempts to fit unruly English into the grammatical patterns of Latin. If Latin had a subjunctive and an infinitive form for its verbs, then English was made to have these too. For centuries the majority of school time has been spent in the futile exercise of learning logical grammar for English and requiring schoolchildren to memorize it—despite children's knowing full well that this was like the stepsisters' vain efforts to fit their ungainly feet into Cinderella's dainty glass slipper. English grammar is a messy combination of half-lost West Teutonic forms of old verbs (what used to be called "irregular" forms like "am," "was," "been") with an overlay of Norman French from the period after the Norman Conquest, plus earlier Danish and Celtic, plus the exuberance of worldwide speakers and writers since the Norman Conquest who happily adopt, invent, and accommodate the language to suit their momentary needs.

School teaching wished desperately to form a link between the revered classical languages and English, partly out of the myth of inheritance of classical virtues and partly because when modern English did become a subject of school study no other grammar models than those of the classical languages existed. Jonathan Swift—whose bowdlerized *Gulliver's Travels,* a satire on English politics, has unaccountably become a children's book—also wrote a scatological satire "proving" that Hebrew, Greek, and Latin derived from English: his 1765 "Discourse to Prove the Antiquity of the English Tongue."[108] Nevertheless, the grammarians went on with their busy work of making English look like Latin. English has thus been taught to native speakers in schools for two centuries as if it were Latin and as if it were primarily a written affair. And minorities associate correctness in deadly grammar exercises with school's belief in the superiority of standard English to all other language forms.

Luckily the writing process movement begun in the 1974 Bay Area Writing Project and now flourishing throughout the country abandons these foolish teachings in favor of language practice. The writing process advocated by many of our teachers today eschews the worksheets in favor of developing student fluency through writing for the student's own purposes. Part of the new "whole language movement," writing-process approaches, when married to new understandings of reading, are highly effective teaching methods. Teachers are coming to realize that reading to children and giving children multiple opportunities to read books they already know and love are effective ways of learning to read. Real writers teach word meanings by the contexts in which they embed words. The control of meaning is a transaction between the child and the text. Wholistic approaches to language such as these put the power of language control into the hands of the child, who constructs his own meanings as he goes.[109] When applied to learning English as a second language, whole language approaches are equally powerful. One high school student put it succinctly when he described his own learning in a portfolio entry: "Before I was in Vietnam so the teacher memorize and summarize in the book and he just write on the black board and we copied down and just memorize just like machines. So now I learn from taking notes by myself."[110]

The writing process movement, though promising, is unevenly available and not yet as well developed as it needs to be. The poorer you are, the more likely to suffer from grammar drills and the imposed controls of managed textbooks. The I.Q. tests beloved of schools and psychologists disproportionately steer minority language children and African-Americans into special education and vocational tracks where drill and worksheets still prevail. The complexity of language is such that it is impossible to create a culture-free or class-free test that uses language.[111] A landmark case brought in 1970 in California established a ruling that all such placement tests had to be culturally relevant to the child being tested and that all children then marking time in classes for the retarded had to be re-tested.[112] Large numbers were immediately reclassified as not retarded, but simply as speakers of limited English ability. Test development, however, lags behind court decisions. We seem not yet to have sufficient or useful means of finding out how best to serve children who differ from the norm. Tests to discover students' language needs should be culturally relevant and as close to natural contexts for language use as possible.[113]

Researchers seem to agree that poverty is the single most important obstacle to educational success.[114] The schools' confusion of language issues with deprivation of knowledge, identification of bilingualism with poverty, and abhorrence of the cultures of those who are poor, result in practices that institutionally slam the door in the face of those who would enter the world of learning.

Second languages taught in U.S. schools today, still primarily the European Spanish, French, German, and Latin of yore, are perceived as having high-class status. The Spanish of the Americas, however, was always a low-status language to Americans who learned contempt of Spain in school. It entered high school curricula slowly and not to any extent until well into the twentieth century. French, however, has grown in prestige as German has declined. Some years ago I developed a series of intensive summer institutes for urban teachers of foreign languages that included one on "Francophone French." The idea was to introduce teachers to the rich culture, literature, theater, arts, and traditions of French-speaking West African and Caribbean nations. I hoped teachers would come away from these institutes familiar with books and films, poets and dramatists, who were both black and producers of a Francophone culture that would appeal to a largely black urban school populace. One teacher—a department head of great power in the district because she regularly headed curriculum development committees—

was heard to snort afterward that she had no intention of teaching the "vulgar patois" spoken outside of Paris. For her, as for most French teachers schooled in the arrogance of the superiority of Parisian French, anything other than Académie Française French is low-status and therefore unfit for school.

Class snobbery in language teaching harks back to long-abandoned theories of correctness in language. Language teachers learn in college to feel superior to those who are less able linguists, and teach accordingly. Spanish teachers wrapped up in Castilian purities look down on the "street" Spanish of the Puerto Rican or Mexican. Northern New Mexican Hispanics, long-settled descendants of Spaniards, also look down on more recently established southern New Mexicans. With arrogance the staple of foreign language classrooms, anyone not fully secure in his sense of belonging is sure to be flushed out. Foreign language learning becomes a matter for a small elite, while the largest number of speakers of other tongues ever to attend American schools are stigmatized by a fearful middle class, feeling under siege from below. The middle-class teachers of foreign languages reflect the insecurities of the middle class worldwide, which sees itself losing place, prestige, and wealth in the face of overwhelming poverty.[115] As a nation we seem to be shutting the door on that poverty and on access to the good life we but tenuously hold in the face of so much misery. Just as we turn away from our own urban disintegration, we narrow the opportunity for school to help make a difference. Offering foreign languages only after children prove their facility in school English is the final arbiter of class status. Fewer and fewer of our children ever get a chance to try.

Devalued Families

❧

Language teaching in school separates children of the poor from their families. Perhaps the earliest legislation dedicated to linguistic and cultural assimilation of a despised minority group occurred in 1609, during the reign of the first Stuart, James I, who joined his Scottish crown with England. The law removed Scottish children from their Highland, Gaelic-speaking homes to the Lowlands nearer the English border where they could be schooled to feel ashamed of their origins.[116] Similar policies infected Bureau of Indian Affairs schooling in the United States. Children were sometimes kidnapped and carried off to the BIA boarding schools; if they ran away, they were recaptured and forcibly returned.

Physical removal from family and the cultural community of origin is only the most extreme mechanism for separating children from their home culture. More subtle methods prevail in schools where children are taught to feel that the way they (and their parents) speak is low status. One of the purposes of school is to create national, general loyalties, if necessary at the expense of family and group loyalties.

The standard of English enforced in school represents a moral order. Those whose English usage departs from that norm are therefore perceived as immoral. Language standards become "a dike against a sea of moral turpitude which threatens to engulf the social, and hence the moral, order."[117] Speaking "properly" becomes a civic virtue; speaking "improperly" is perceived as a threat to the nation.

The transformation of children's language use into middle-class language use first blames parents for children's language habits, then demands that parents allow school to detach their children from the family through language. School encourages children to speak standard English at home, whether that is the custom or not.[118] Among Hispanics and African-Americans, a few of the talented in every heavily minority school find themselves specially trained for educational achievement. Teachers will put in extra time for such students, working on their manners, pronunciation, vocabulary, and grooming, until they look and sound as middle American as possible.[119] Such school attitudes toward the manners and language habits of the poor effectively separate children from their cultural contexts, so that now to be educationally successful is to be charged with "racelessness" by one's ethnic brethren.

Standard English has come to be associated with race, and school has gone far to encourage that idea. African-Americans now seem as prone to thinking language an aspect of race as did turn-of-the-century white racists. One bilingual teacher arguing against programs that maintain the mother tongue in the schools says that educators should expand the mind, not teach the informal, non-standard language of the home.[120] Contempt for the language of the home has even surfaced among Puerto Rican parents who have demanded that the Spanish used in bilingual classes be the Castilian, high-culture language of classical Spanish literature, not the everyday language of Puerto Rico. The equivalent in English would be for us to insist that school teach children to speak Shakespeare's English.

I am not suggesting that school should disregard teaching standard English. I am suggesting that it should not be necessary first to destroy children's respect for their parents in order to do so. Bilingual programs as now constituted seem to have disrespect for the culture of origin built into them. One writer on the subject seems quite pleased with the idea of promoting intergenerational conflict, finding this a "natural phenomenon."[121] But such punitive attitudes to the culture of origin effectively debar students from learning.

The opposite approach welcomes the child into learning by according respect to her culture. A teacher at a largely Hispanic urban high school once organized a special course for students on contemporary Hispanic poetry. With a small grant she was able to invite a few poets to come to the school to give readings of their work. The readings were scheduled for the fifth period of the day, and anyone who wished could obtain an excuse from other classes to attend. The large library was jammed every time, not because the students wanted to cut their other classes, but because they came to listen. Not a sound, not even a breath disturbed the attention of the several hundred students. After the readings those students asked some of the best questions I have ever heard at a poetry reading—questions that demonstrated a profound understanding of the poetry and desire to know why certain poetic choices of language, form, or theme had been made. These were neither textbook nor teacher questions; they were real questions about real poetry. Through the course and the readings, Hispanic students encountered themselves in school for the first time, and their own culture as one valued by school. They encountered contemporaries who had made poetry out of street Spanish. About halfway through the year, the biggest, toughest, roughest student of all sidled up to a visiting poet after everyone had left for the day, with a thick wad of manuscript in his hands. He asked the poet if she would please read his work. He had been a closet poet for years, afraid until then to admit it to anyone. Soon student poets were popping up everywhere. They asked for a literary magazine for the school so they could publish their work. Not since the school had ceased to be majority Anglo had anyone thought it worthwhile having a literary magazine; no one had thought these Hispanic students had any language.

Teaching children in *their* language—whatever that language may be—is essential for the early years of school. It's the starting place for communication with children. Respecting children's language and encouraging them to speak, read, and write frequently and in their own words is the start of literacy for all. Offering students opportunities to encounter each other's language as well as the language of real poets and real writers early, often, and continuously will enable them to become real writers in turn. The joy of language that is highly non-standard is what Dr. Seuss' wonderful nonsense is all about; the illogicality of English and poking fun at prissy school teachers is at the heart of the fun in *Alice in Wonderland;* creating new words and new ways of using old ones is what real poetry always does; delighting in catching the rhythms and cadences of real speech is what makes theater. The poets practice subversion of school standards. Maybe that's why the real poets don't turn up in the basals.

The power of poetic language is a kind of civil disobedience, but school is there to confine within boundaries the rules that poets regularly break. School therefore dismantles language into exercises where only one correct word, already known to fit, is allowed. We treat language as if it were a coloring book where skies may only be blue, never red, and grass must be green, never violet; all colors must stay strictly within the lines. Yes, we must first learn traditions in order to learn how to transcend them to new visions. But we can't even get access to the traditions if our starting point excludes the students' traditions.

For years our presidents told us they believed in the family, yet that belief seems to hold only for model families, not for those of the poor. Bilingual education policy certainly hastens disruption of families when children end up speaking only English at home because school has disregarded and even stigmatized the mother tongue.[122] Schools try to supplant families and then blame parents for the children's failures. We know that children can easily gain literacy in their mother tongue, after which a transition to a second language and English literacy is achievable with much greater ease. Such a program would accomplish English goals without disrupting or denigrating family life. But our policies toward immigrant children end up leaving them uncertain and uncomfortable in the new language and culture and illiterate and uncomfortable with the language of the home.[123] We must also remember that some of our immigrants are refugees of war-torn Cambodia and Nicaragua, children whose prior lives were lived in prison camps, in flight from guerrillas, in a chaos that may have meant they never attended school at all before arriving here at the age of ten or twelve or sixteen. We affront such students when we seek to strip them of what little of their cultural origins remains after the violence of their transplantation to our shores.

Every learner of English has a different cultural context for such learning. Chinese families stress respect for adults, which helps Chinese children in adult-directed classrooms. Rural Italians emphasize family learning and sometimes see formal schooling as harmful. Poles who experienced Russian-dominated schools at home distrust state schools here.[124] Hawaiians expect unsupervised children to take charge of many tasks at home; schools full of teacher-directed and constantly supervised activities alienate such children. Native American children are taught by parents to remain silent in the presence of elders, but schools expect them to speak up. An endless list of such clashes between parental and school upbringing could be cited here. While these are certainly generalizations, they do serve to remind us that language and cultural clashes between home and school are pervasive and, while no longer as violent as kidnapping, can be as subtle as a smile. Teachers often take for insolence the smile of embarrassment of an African-American child.

Recent moves toward self-determination through schooling by and for minorities promise to narrow some of the distance between home and school. Such is the case among an increasing number of BIA and other Native American schools that use native languages to preserve their culture;[125] such is also the case in a number of urban school districts where particular minorities are not only the majority of the school population but also of the teaching staff and administration. Self-determination might mean that the school's interference between child and parent is reduced; it might also mean that the same middle-class antagonism to the poor continues to prevail and to stigmatize the poor. Racial or ethnic similarities among teachers and their students won't automatically overcome the class differences that are equally endemic between a black or Hispanic middle-class teacher and her poor charges. Where class differences do not exist, however, and where school districts take the hard road of devising curricula rich in language opportunities, self-determination should make a great contribution to schooling. That hard road is highly unlikely, however, as long as budgets are tight, time is entirely taken with the relentless effort to cover subjects, and basals are prepackaged and ready to go, complete with machine-scorable tests to match. Under such circumstances, what poor, overburdened school district will take the time and enormous effort to retrain teachers, develop new curricula, transform classrooms, and explore the riches and beauties and powers of language?

Freely Spoken

~~~

Reforming schools to teach language more effectively would have to occur in the face of pervasive anti-language sentiment in the United States. We have a habit of requiring not just fluency, but fluency without an accent. In the nineteenth century, German speakers were thought to be dangerously unassimilated; in the twentieth century we shifted our fears first to Eastern Europeans and then to Hispanics. Language legislation is used as if it were a weapon against the speakers of other languages and we hardly bother to hide the racism at the heart of it.[126] Only Spanish in New Mexico, Hawaiian in Hawaii, and French in Louisiana are both protected and supported by legislation. English is believed to be the equivalent of democracy and freedom—to learn English is supposedly to adopt the language of democracy; those who don't learn it are perceived as subversive by virtue of their speech.[127]

English is not loved, however. Schools teach only the plain language of economic success Americans seem to want.[128] Although nineteenth-century schools reveled in biblical, political, and literary rhetoric, our scientific age seems to believe that verbal pyrotechnics are out of place for modern Americans. Only the Reverend Jesse Jackson and occasional southern politicians manage to get away with biblical (that is, Renaissance) English. Our basal readers actively teach ugly language to children, and no one seems to consider that nearly all the other materials children read in school also treat the language shabbily—in history, science, and math books as well as English readers. The pleasures of reading—what education theorist Paolo Freire calls the sensuality of reading—is foreign to American schools. Freire also says, "The scientist is not obliged, just because he or she is a scientist, to write ugly."[129] America shrinks back from such an effete idea, which somehow doesn't seem to suit our rugged self-image.

Our anti-language beliefs and English Only movement reflect a near-hysteria over the condition of English here and abroad. But worldwide 316 million people speak English as their first language and another 300 million speak it as a second language. More than 60 of the world's 160 countries recognize English as an official language.[130] Hysteria would more properly belong with speakers of the countless "small" languages, like Dutch and Hungarian, that are dying out on all continents. Eleven of the world's four thousand languages are now spoken by 70 percent of the world's population.[131] No statistics tell us how well foreigners learn English before they arrive here; but Americans stoutly resist learning other languages before they go abroad. The ugly American is still the rule abroad, embarrassingly unwilling to notice differences of language and civility. In the words of one writer, we are "devoutly monolingual."[132] The 1978 President's Commission on foreign languages talked about "our vital interests" and "dangerously inadequate understanding of world affairs," but their warnings fell on deaf ears. As long as we see ourselves Americanizing the world with our culture and business, our golden arches and Coke, we will continue to believe it's the world's desire for *our* language and culture that will prevail.

Yet intellectual development has always been an international affair. The very mark of education has always meant knowledge of other languages, travel to study under foreign masters of reknown, and the ability to participate in the international community of scientists and scholars. We can only learn new things from each other. It is time to recognize that the intellectual development of our children depends on conceiving of education not merely as a national enterprise, but as an invitation to a much larger world of understanding.

America could learn to love language in school, but only if real language is permitted. Schools fear the power of speech to break the bounds of bureaucratic rules and restrictions, to speak the truth in the face of controlling perceptions of reality. In their passion for control, schools impose forms on the language that, like that gruesome basal *Reader* passage on digging a pit, substitute obscure grammatical purposes for a real language of grace and meaning. One teacher has pointed out that the basal *Readers* focus on skills " 'that don't really exist except in the minds of textbook designers.' "[133] If the books teach what doesn't exist and control the grammar and the discourse of school, then our classrooms resemble in highly disturbing ways places that exert totalitarian control. Language remains the possession of the school and its processes, and children remain linguistically the dispossessed.[134]

Attempts to repress or impose language, either by disdaining children's usage or insisting on school usage, always backfire. The Soviets proscribed only one of the USSR's many ethnic languages: Yiddish. The ban did not prevent two million people from using it.[135] The proscription of Native American languages in the United States has very nearly destroyed the viability of those languages, but has also created a strong backlash among

Native American communities determined to preserve and transmit their languages. Language *is* culture. Freedom in America must include the freedom to be, which is dependent on the freedom to speak. A new law enacted in 1990 finally permits Native American languages as mediums of instruction in BIA schools, citing freedom in its wording.[136]

Conflict arises not from the freedom to use language, but from its suppression. France, the country that is most chauvinistic about its language, has no legislation requiring its usage. Two hundred years of efforts to impose Parisian French on the French populace have failed. In some countries that do have official languages, such as India, Nigeria, and Uganda, less than half the population speaks the legislated tongues. The British have no official language. The British administration and courts have, over the centuries, variously used Latin and French in their official transactions.[137] Queen Elizabeth I used French in her official letters, and the majority of written documents of all kinds in Shakespeare's age, whether for political, scientific, literary, poetic, personal, or business purposes, were composed in Latin by courtiers, writers, philosophers, merchants, and private citizens.[138]

In our own times, language has become less richly tapestried than in the past for many reasons. One linguist suggests that the stark utilitarianism of modern American English has to do with the high status of science and technology since the Treaty of Versailles and the correspondingly low status of belles lettres.[139] The twentieth-century attitude to the language of science equates starkness with utility. This is an aberration from past practice; witness two of the greatest science writers of the last century, Charles Darwin and William James, who managed at once to be precise, complex, and pleasurable to read.

Our times have knocked the pleasure out and, by so doing, rendered scientific writing opaque to the rest of us. In the eighteenth century, Newton's optics and mathematics inspired a flurry of poetry. Our times have separated the language of science from both the language of poetry and the language of the people, and yet inspired us to want everyone to write like high-status scientists. Because science has discovered so many new phenomena, an enormous new vocabulary has had to be constructed to describe them. For the most part, that vocabulary (medical and biotechnological terminology in particular) has been constructed out of Latin and Greek root words. The physicists have indulged in some linguistic fun, giving new subatomic particles "charm," "spin," and in one case borrowing a coinage from Joyce's *Finnegans Wake*: the *quark*. Computer scientists creating whole new worlds of language could have had more fun, but perhaps refrained partly because they have often worked within the confines of corporate life, where linguistic play is not generally well received.

The preponderance of Latin and Greek in science vocabulary and the resulting length and complexity of compound scientific words have resulted in scientific language that looks opaque to the uninitiated. People outside of the scientific community, wishing to elevate their occupations to the higher status of science, have consequently elaborated scientific-looking jargons of their own. This is as true for educators as for other social sciences, in a bid to convince the world that their practices are rigorous; *utilize* replaces *use* in educationese whenever possible. But jargon that just looks scientific serves as a smokescreen for imprecision and thoughtlessness in other fields.

Scientific language and modernity are believed to go hand in hand. The modernity of the nation demands conformities to language that restrict freedom, erase the bumps of individuality, and control the differences. Individuality of voice, however, may depend on the nurturing of smaller groups. Historian Ali Mazrui has written an interesting book on the English-speaking nations of Africa, pointing out that English will soon become an Africanized language. Since English usage is increasing among many growing African populations, Mazrui calculates that within a half-century the majority of world English speakers will be black. When such writers as Chinua Achebe, not a native speaker of English, take on English and make of it a West African language, the language becomes a powerful mechanism for self-determination. Mazrui also suggests that the dominance of English as a lingua franca in Europe is a more telling linguistic conquest than its spread to other continents. Overcoming the chauvinism of the centuries-old political disputes of that continent, English is a pliable tool, transformed by its users and transforming other languages in turn.[140]

The power to speak freely ought to be our most basic concern in school. Instead we teach a fearful language, one that eliminates options rather than providing them. We reduce children's choices to use their home language, to offer alternative answers to questions, to construct complex arguments of their own, and to have fun with words. We hasten to remove foreign languages from our midst despite the fact that "the average language-minority child entering kindergarten has a higher level of language mastery than the average graduate of the intensive and expensive 47-week Defense Language Institute program."[141] While former Secretary of Education Bennett wanted foreign languages taught to halt a shrinking American influence in the world, his successor, Lamar Alexander, allowed a major federal plan for improving education to go forward without any mention of foreign languages at all.[142] Many writers suggest that instead of transforming monolingual speakers of other languages into monolingual speakers of English, two-way bilingual programs would be in everyone's best interests.[143] Second languages do not interfere with ability in native languages if instruction is carried out positively—not as remediation, compensation, or substitution, but based on recognition of the riches the child already has and willingness to add to them.

Many people believe that children should master English before they try to learn another tongue. We know, however, that languages don't come in serial form, one after the other. To delay second languages to the teen years is often to preclude second language learning. The early years are the years when language learning comes most naturally and enthusiastically. The business community ought to be able to help, since it is commercially interested in maintaining second languages in advertising and television to target specific markets and laments, along with government, Americans' lack of ability in languages when working abroad. Yet when allied with government to suggest massive new school reforms, business has been equally silent on the question of language.[144] The policy change we need is a simple one—to view language facility as an asset, no matter how acquired.[145] Such a shift would immediately and by a single stroke assert the value of many of the nation's poor, whose patriotism could, paradoxically, be expressed by and in their native tongues.

The Council of Europe sees English as a valuable and recommended second language for all, and has recently generated new recommendations for English in all European schools in the context of new rules of freedom for all nations.[146] The freedom comes not from the particular choice of language, as if freedom resided in English, but from the general addition of language. Herder believed that many languages are necessary for the maintenance of our humanity. Senator Paul Simon has said that skill in many languages opens the door to civilization, to power, sophistication, ease, and grace of interchange in all circumstances. Such grace should be our desire for all our people, not just for a few. The "higher order thinking" many business and education leaders want from our schools can only occur if the language in which to conduct it is ready to hand. A multilingual society would be the symbol of its multiparty, multilateral political framework.[147]

Ours is a nation that lives in tribal formations. Immigrants arrived on these shores whole villages at a time and sought out residences in village patterns here. Brooklyn's and Chicago's neighborhoods and farm districts in Minnesota and Wisconsin reveal alike the tribal patterns of the past. Voluntary segregation continues to create ghettos and barrios, and discrimination in the workplace repeats the pattern of housing in the countryside and in small-town America as in the cities. The current transnational labor migrations on unprecedented scales repeat this pattern worldwide. The result is a new territoriality whose basic unit is the local, community unit drawn on ethnic lines.

Such communities are generally self-supporting and self-enhancing, developing American versions of old customs, cultural heritage, and language habits. The tribal, territorial instinct has its ugly side when border clashes erupt over control of the land, as in the Canarsie section of Brooklyn, and its positive side, as border dwellers grope their way toward understanding each other. Native Americans are trying to assert the equal status of all languages, including theirs, and to assert their place on tribal lands. The land and the language equally create cultural identity.[148] Schools become a part of territorial struggles as village borders shift. This reality is stronger and perhaps ultimately will prove more fruitful for all if we acknowledge that language cannot be legislated and controlled without damaging our capacity to think. We should simply accept the reality that 4,000 languages cannot and will not result in 160 monolingual nations.[149] Our multilingual nation is not only a fact, it is an end to be desired.

Our nation has long been built. The unifying, nation-building role of school is no longer so urgently needed. Only paranoia would suggest that English is in the least danger in our country. But massive worldwide migration and the concomitant rise of worldwide fundamentalism strike fear into many a comfortable American. Fundamentalists yearn for certainties and absolutes in a time of social disruption and massive change. In our nation-building phase we were intolerant of multiple traditions, seeking to forge a uniform culture of our very own. Now, as our American century draws to a close, we see American fundamentalist movements rising to create out of whole cloth new "traditions" that will strengthen tribal ties.[150] The minority group that called itself the "moral majority" sought to impose its traditions on all; the federal government in league with business wanted a return to the absolutes of traditional schooling. Language as it is actually used by all Americans, however, suggests that single answers to questions and single meanings or interpretations are never possible, even in highly controlled societies.

Multiple answers to multiple questions are the key to a multicultural, multilateral society. As Amy Tan has shown in The Joy Luck Club, the children of immigrants become Americans readily enough, but draw on scraps of their parents' cultures to form a dynamic new Americanism.[151] School efforts to restrict language end up with a generation of young people who escape through other media. If we truly want to woo back the disaffected to language, then language must be freely placed in the hands of the people to do with it as they will.

V

MAPPING CULTURE

If white people are pleased, we are glad.
If they are not, it doesn't matter.
LANGSTON HUGHES

The warm touch of cheeks,
interior of houses, and particular human lives
of which the chronicles make no mention.
CZESLAW MILOSZ

Introduction

~~~

In Milwaukee, Detroit, and Washington, D.C., school boards announce the creation of special public schools whose Afrocentric curriculum is designed to make a difference in the achievement of African-American boys. The Bureau of Indian Affairs relaxes its strictures on the language of instruction, and Native American nations turn BIA schools into extensions of communal life. Miami schools host student-written dramatic musicals celebrating Caribbean cultures. Baton Rouge schools pledge a new curriculum that will include Cajun as well as Spanish, Native American, and Anglo heritages. Denver schools take a look at the five cultures of the West; Connecticut schools revise American history to explore the Great Migration of African-Americans.

At the grassroots level, America seems headed for regionally and locally distinctive curricula in history, literature, and the arts that accommodate the distinctive heritages and ethnic composition of their populations. At the federal and state level, however, government seems headed for a single, national curriculum enabling students in Miami to be measured against those in Taos, Portland, Detroit, and Bangor. George Bush, the patrician Episcopal president who never attended a public school, wanted the public schools to "break the mold" to become competitive internationally as the best remedy for our failing American economy. He allied himself with big business in this quest. Districts struggling to raise test scores, lower the drop-out rate, and convince taxpayers to support public schooling try to be responsive to vociferous community demands for an education that is meaningful for their children. The universities, leading the way into turmoil, engage in a debate that seems to pit the heart and soul of the Western world against the heart and soul of racial and ethnic groups, making for juicy national news headlines. *Multicultural* becomes a code word inspiring divisive and angry ideological brawling on podiums, in classrooms, and in school-board meetings around the country.

The debate generally polarizes around two positions. *Multicultural reformers* and *traditionalists* are the terms I shall use to describe the major opponents in the debate. The most radical multiculturalists have given up tinkering with the system as it now exists, believing that nothing short of a total transformation of both the society and the schools that bolster the status quo is in order. The most staunch of the traditionalists, however, are unwilling to budge an inch on a system they believe made this country great. Their position calls for strengthening traditional education rather than changing its fundamental organization. Note that some traditionalists are equally radical reformers, since they feel schools have to restore a curriculum they consider to have faltered. A constellation of other reformers maintain a variety of positions between these two extremes, in the belief that schools are capable of positive renewal.

Traditionalists in universities and among educators, federal officials, and business leaders continue to urge that the civic religion of the United States should remain our fundamental American myth. This belief states that civic, public virtue and the common weal depends on individual virtue and accomplishment. For traditionalists, each individual student should receive an education that prepares her as a moral being who will strive for her own success and, through it, the success of the nation. The individual will, if well educated, subsume personal good in the common good on those occasions when his moral understanding so dictates.

Multiculturalists approach education very differently. Since group solidarity has been the key to minority success, many feel that collective action should subsume personal interests and that the enhancement of group interests will be good for the nation. Collective action desegregated American schools and college faculties, created academic departments to study ethnicity and feminism at universities, and challenged the easy and often unconscious racisms and other prejudices of our society. Since the group and its collective political action have been the most effective remedy of recent decades for what minorities have seen as endemic, institutionalized racism in our country, those now in leadership positions as professors, superintendents, school-board members, and newly vocal community representatives disdain the traditionalists' myths of individual achievement in favor of collective action.

In the many writings on multicultural education I have reviewed, the traditionalist's belief in the individual and the multicultural reformer's belief in the collective arise from such different philosophical frameworks that they fail to engage dialogue. Middle-of-the-road reformers, equally troubled by this difference in belief systems, are confused as to how to reconcile the two very different models of education that emerge from the clash of mythologies. Because the fundamental assumptions of each of the most extreme views differ so markedly, there is a tendency for each to dismiss the beliefs and proposals of the other wholesale. Traditionalists find the work of some multiculturalists based on shoddy and untenable research; the multiculturalists accuse traditionalists of an unwillingness even to listen to alternative points of view. Traditionalists call on reasoned debate and critical scholarship to bear witness to the value of their position; radical multiculturalists sometimes dismiss reason as yet another formulation of an alien culture, imposed on their work.

The degree to which the multicultural education debate has become an unseemly brawl—with charges of racism and hegemony from one side and countercharges that the United States is in imminent danger of totalitarianism or disintegration from the other—is a measure of the degree to which this debate touches on our most deeply held beliefs about who we are and how we become Americans.

A Little More History

~~~

As we have seen, history, literature, and language, the subjects most heatedly debated in the current culture wars, were for the most part fashioned to promote social and civic behaviors at odds with the nature of the disciplines themselves. They were at best indifferent to the diverse cultures of the majority of students and at worst disdainful of many of their cultural attributes. We will briefly review a little more public-school history to see how various populations entered into public schooling and the conflicts they encountered between the promise offered by the civic religion and the realities of the curriculum.

Such conflicts have always been a feature of public life in particular locales, but the current multicultural debate has reached a national scale for several reasons. The unprecedented federal leadership in education over the past twelve years was accelerated by the creation of a cabinet-level secretariat during the Carter administration, changing the dynamic of what had previously been exclusively a state-level mandate. At the same time, increasing economic and political strength and a dedication to self-determination have empowered relatively large numbers of minorities of all kinds, many of whom have gained positions from which their rejection of the paternalism that prevailed for two centuries can be heard.

Lacking ethnicity, language, or birthplace as common denominators, the early Republic's definition of the American people depended solely on a commonly held ideology, a set of values and beliefs about government and the way in which each American should take part in government. This self-conscious and radical departure from the way nationality was at that time determined in every other nation-state immediately fixed attention on the need for a highly educated, moral citizenry. Education would enable disparate Americans to put the good of their common destiny above narrow self-interest and at the same time keep a watchful eye on government to prevent its corruption. The ideal American would be the independent-minded yeoman-farmer described by Michel-Guillaume Jean de Crèvecoeur in his

Letters from an American Farmer (1782), a vision of the American into which all would be assimilated.[1]

As we have seen, the idea of a common schooling for all Americans was crucial to the capacity of its citizens to become ideal democrats, but as the common schools took shape the national identity forged there during the course of the nineteenth century was appropriated by those Anglo-Saxon Protestants—the Horace Manns and Noah Websters and Presbyterian ministers—who led the common school movement, defined the curriculum, wrote the textbooks, and served as schoolteachers. The first half of the nineteenth century saw the forging of a nominally "nonsectarian" ideology that generalized the Protestant ethic. The later part of the century reduced world culture to Anglo-Saxon culture; the twentieth century worked at socializing disparate Americans to conformity of belief in a triumphal America that disregarded or discarded differences from the norm. In the process, the eighteenth-century idea that nationalism would transcend the old loyalties to divine authorities and monarchies, each citizen becoming instead a monarch of reason in his own right, was discarded in favor of a Romantic nationalism that inculcated a new set of irrational patriotic beliefs. Meanwhile, the American way to success has never been accomplished through the schools alone for any ethnic group, whether we look at southern Europeans at the beginning of the twentieth century or Hispanics and African-Americans now. Yet economic and political success is what the school's civic religion has claimed to provide all along, and most Americans continue to believe this despite massive evidence to the contrary.

People of color were excluded from the promise from the start. Until 1865, except for a handful of schools for free blacks in the North, public schools did not admit African-Americans. Native Americans and Hispanics were forcibly schooled to discard their heritage and adopt the generalized curriculum. For most of this nation's history, moreover, people of color were not expected to succeed in school. Most of the talk of common schools and democracy in education until the 1950s ignored race, assuming it to be a continuing condition of American life.[2] The *Plessy* v. *Ferguson* decision of 1896 provided a legal basis for "separate but equal" education for minorities that prevailed until the 1954 *Brown* v. *Board of Education* decision reversed it.

Twentieth-century school policies developed with the express purpose of suppressing alternative behaviors in school, including the use of other languages. From the 1920s on, scientific mental testing supported beliefs that some people would never learn very much anyway and never assimilate properly. Louis Terman, one of the earliest champions of I.Q. testing, was a confirmed racist who believed that Nordic and Alpine peoples were mentally superior to all others and therefore better Americans.[3]

Always it has been the common schools' overt exclusion or denigration of minority culture that has created collective reaction and protest, whether this involved Catholic dissent in the 1840s or the many minority protests of today. The Missouri Synod of Lutheran schools, Chicago's Eastern European schools, and even Jewish schools were initially set up in the United States to transmit language and culture rather than just religion and to preserve a sense of community in a land where rugged individualism was less productive for the latest immigrants than communal action in the face of discrimination and a tough struggle for survival.[4] The Anglo-Saxon social elites also set up schools for themselves to preserve their culture and ethnic identity. After 1880, institutions like Choate, Andover, and Exeter modeled themselves on British public schools whose overt task was the preparation of imperial masters. Long blatantly segregationist, such (ethnic) schools have rarely been charged with separatism or disloyalty, since they incarnate the American ideal.[5]

American public schools have repeatedly attempted to dissolve communal ties among all groups except those who arrived at school already conforming to America's assimilationist ideal. Massive Japanese protests in 1905–07 against exclusion from San Francisco schools ended only when President Theodore Roosevelt intervened and a "gentlemen's agreement" resulted in segregated admission for these children. When a 1947 court outlawed segregation in Texas, the schools reclassified Hispanic children as "white" and "integrated" them into previously all-black schools. Bilingual education since the 1960s has tended to segregate many non-Anglo children within school buildings.[6] Throughout this sorry history, segregation persisted until collective action forced the issue to change the system.

Although the redress of wrongs has primarily succeeded only as a result of collective action, the dominant group is likely to charge that this collective action is "separatist," or disloyal and hence un-American. Yet the Japanese in 1905 in San Francisco or African-Americans in 1990 in Milwaukee share the same passionate desire to participate in America through its common schools, and hence to participate in democracy. It is important to realize that today's controversies are part of a continuing series of group actions against the assumptions and strictures of school that began when the first large and organized group, the Catholics of the 1840s—who wished heartily to become Americans but could not accept wholesale the beliefs taught in public schools—insisted on their democratic rights.

After the Civil War, black school enrollments equaled or exceeded white working-class school enrollments. In Booker T. Washington's famous words, blacks then made up a "whole race trying to go to school." But school led nowhere for educated blacks. Elementary schools serving blacks failed to link to high schools, and an elementary education led to the same unskilled jobs as no school at all. So did high school and even college for those who struggled through. The only professions in which blacks succeeded, the ministry and teaching, were until recently the primary end of advanced study for most African-Americans.[7] Somewhere between *Brown* v. *Board of Education* and now, the race that had gone to school for a century to no effect began to suspect that the myth of the civic religion whitewashed systemic racism. White immigrants had to wait two and three generations before they began to be successful in school; perhaps if we count from 1954, African-American school success ought to begin with the generation currently in kindergarten.

Many writers are careful to point out that differences in school success for different groups seem to depend on cultural attitudes toward school. The Japanese protest of 1905–07 revealed a deep commitment to school that these immigrants brought with them. According to historians, "The Japanese may have been America's best-educated immigrant group; over 90 percent of arriving immigrants [from 1900 to 1920] were literate in Japanese and averaged eight years of schooling, considerably above the educational attainment of the average American at the time."[8] Nineteenth-century German immigrants saw public school as an essential part of their culture— after all, the organization of state schools began with Frederick the Great. Both present-day Japan and Germany continue to place formal schooling at the center of cultural development. Jews, excluded from state schools in Eastern Europe, saw their acceptance in U.S. public schools as a redress of past wrongs. African-Americans and Mexicans believed school would do this for them, too, but after many generations they have yet to attain the promised success.

Matching Curriculum
to Students

~~~

The first attempts to diversify curriculum actually began as early as the 1940s and 1950s, when an "intercultural" movement sought to explain away differences among people. The thrust of intercultural education was that discrimination and racism arose out of ignorance. The answer to ignorance was education, which would create interracial harmony. (The idea that getting to know each other better will do away with divisiveness pervades much multicultural theory and practice today.[9]) The intercultural movement was basically paternalistic toward minority cultures, seeing them merely as versions of the mainstream and subordinate to it.[10] In the late 1960s and early 1970s radical ethnicity arose and then settled into searches for roots and a sentimental identification with ethnic heritages of all kinds, from "black is beautiful" to school programs where the ethnicity of the month prevailed in orgies of Chinese food and Mexican piñatas. As recently as 1980, a major article on ethnicity in education could state "The new ethnicity may well be similar to the return to religion: an important intensification of sentiment and identification that poses no threat to accepted patterns of conduct and participation."[11]

Ethnicity, race, and related issues, however, increasingly radicalized throughout the 1980s, burst into national news in 1990 with renewed vigor. The benign sentiment of ethnicity of the 1970s resided in ghettos in the curriculum. There were special projects on the Holocaust, Black History month, brown faces in illustrated textbooks, mentions of Harriet Tubman, and "contributions" sections stitched onto traditional histories, but school still told the same basic stories with the same protagonists and the same plot lines it had of old.[12] African-American children still dropped out too often, although the 1980s saw a steady rise in their SAT scores, attendance, and graduation rates. Hispanic and Native American children still lagged behind whites on these measures.

During the 1980s many state and district superintendents instructed schools to go beyond the add-ons to the curriculum; it was time, they said "to weave multicultural perspectives into the entire fabric of the American story."[13] *Weaving* and *infusing* were the operative words for the mid-eighties. Both are interesting metaphors that seem to say there's a basic medium—a warp, or a volume of liquid—into which the new multiculturalism should enter as the woof or the tincture. Neither suggests starting all over again with a completely reconceived curriculum. In New York State, however, a committee appointed by Commissioner Thomas Sobol of the Board of Regents looked at the social studies curriculum of the state and found it deeply racist. The committee's report and its strong language echoed the deeply felt anger in many a heart in the late 1980s at the entire education system.

As the anger swelled, federal education leaders dismissed what was happening at state and local levels, calling instead for an end to the disruptive intrusion of all these special studies and a return to a traditional common core of learning for all. Many a multiculturalist and traditionalist began the decade amicably enough, but ended it entrenched in radically opposed positions. Meanwhile, the president and governors got together for an unprecedented education summit in September 1989, to emerge with a pledge to renew education nationally. A year later their plan allied itself with big business leaders in a joint pledge that there were to be five national core subjects: English, math, history, geography, and science; that all children should arrive at school ready to learn; that the United States would lead in international science and math competitiveness; and that parents would choose schools freely on the basis of merit. Having taken on at the national level an education that had always before been designed and conducted by the states and local communities, the "America 2000" plan blithely announced that the private sector, allied to federal leadership, would carry it out.

This national plan seemed unaware of the tensions tearing at our schools and our beliefs. The contenders for power over the curriculum have simultaneously begun to put their own new plans in place in urban and rural schools throughout the nation, with little regard for the "America 2000" plan. Luckily, a democracy depends on differences of opinion and the free marketplace of ideas. The radical critique of American schools has had its ugly racist side, but has also forced some traditionalists to explain and defend their hitherto unexamined positions on the fact of diversity in our country and its conflict with the uniformity of our schools. While few entrenched believers in either camp are willing to understand the terms used by the other, at least the debate has emerged into the open and it is acknowledged on all sides that there is a problem that needs to be addressed.

Who are the debators and what positions do they take? To employ the metaphors used by the contenders themselves, there's a common core of knowledge out there, familiarity with which provides access to "the club" of power and success in America—this according to E. D. Hirsch, a professor of English and suddenly popular writer on "cultural literacy." For Diane Ravitch, former assistant secretary of education and a major education historian, there's a common heritage we should all learn, rooted in Western culture, but contributed to by non-Western folk—new members are welcome to the club; for the most part the club rules should remain the same as always, or even be reinforced. Nigerian-born John Ogbu, an anthropologist, says it should be possible for minorities to learn to play the club game successfully without having simultaneously to give up membership in the old neighborhood solidarity—play by the club rules when there, play by your own rules at home. Afrocentrists such as Molefi Asante would like to change the club rules, perhaps excluding the old members. Extreme radicals, such as Gerald Pine and Asa Hilliard, aim to change the game as well, and the society that has clubs in the first place. None of these theories and the educational experiments generated by them is as yet wholly satisfactory—usually because of failure to address perspectives other than its own, or because it approaches a highly complex set of issues superficially.

Whose Religion?

～✦～

America's deep religiosity has permeated public education since the start, despite our rocky history of attempts to separate church and state. Traditional school teachings, which in the past clustered around religious teachings, have given rise to a "civic religion" in the present. Much of these teachings are offered as a matter of faith and have successfully taken hold as a set of beliefs forming the foundation of most people's understanding of America. In this sense, traditional schooling resembles a faith. Afrocentrism also seeks to construct a set of beliefs about America, but from an African rather than northern European perspective.

With its roots in centuries of covert, enslaved culture, Afrocentrism in the 1990s draws heavily on the spirituality and faith that sustained earlier generations, and in many senses resembles a religion more than a philosophy or a theory. Afrocentrism's explicators, most of whom are academics, take inspiration from the Black Power movement of the 1960s and from a deeper tradition in the African-American culture of group solidarity and protest that goes back through colonial and pre-colonial times. Lawrence Cremin, in his 1980 history, *American Education,* showed that during slavery, southern owners and southern states forbade formal education. Owners provided the lessons of slavery, and encouraged only those preachings and dicta designed to reinforce slavery. The enslaved Africans developed their own informal curriculum, however, whose purpose was to maintain human dignity, traditions, and links with the past, and to undermine the slave curriculum. According to historian John W. Blassingame in his 1979 book, *The Slave Community,* the culture that developed in the slave quarters was a culture of dissent. Song, story, dance, superstition, and even religion, all developed outside the control of the white owner, and in protest against his purposes. Carter Woodson's classic 1933 book, *The Mis-Education of the Negro,* told the even sorrier tale of education since Reconstruction. A highly skilled race of artisans lost their knowledge for want of work, and schooling taught them nothing but to despise themselves. Woodson in 1933 was already saying that the Greeks had been influenced by Africa, and that Africans "first domesticated the sheep, goat, and cow, developed the idea of trial by jury, produced the first stringed instruments . . . and [discovered] iron," none of which is taught in school. A white curriculum is taught, and when black teachers teach it, they are acting white. Woodson called for an education and a curriculum by and for blacks, since white education perpetuates a slavery of the mind. African philosophies, he insisted, are as valuable as those of the Greeks. Instead of European history and literature, blacks should study African traditions, amalgamating with them Western math, science, languages, and English composition, so as to forge a new set of capacities specific to their group.

Blassingame and Woodson between them traced two themes that have come to figure largely in present-day Afrocentrism: the culture and curriculum of dissent and self-determination. Muted by the nonviolent Civil Rights movement, the themes re-emerged aggressively in the mid-sixties Black Power movement. The establishment of separate black studies departments in universities during the 1970s created an opportunity to study this history, to contribute to it, and to emerge in the eighties with the Afrocentric idea.

In presentations on Afrocentrism, academic proponents of the movement equate race with African continental origins, both of which are then equated with a single culture through the "pan-African" idea. Pan-Africanism seeks to amalgamate group solidarity for all African-Americans through identification with generalized beliefs and allegiance. Features of the movement most often emphasized are the glorious ancient past of Egypt, which is reclaimed for black Africa; the Egyptian origins of high civilization later adapted by the West; and selected high points of other African civilizations, such as Yoruba mathematics and the cultural riches of Benin. While for the most part pharaonic Egypt reigns supreme as the orientation for African culture, rituals, and ceremonies, deep respect for ancestors and other cultural manifestations of unity with the people and the past draw on a variety of other African traditions, including sub-Saharan ones.

Throughout this book I have tried to show that the conventionally established set of beliefs about American democracy constitute more faith than practice; moreover, as they have been promulgated in public schools, they have been taught dogmatically. The story of democracy, as advocated by traditionalists, is inherently a Whiggish story of political and economic progress based on wide acceptance of middle-class manners, beliefs, and mores; success, in its terms, is based on economic growth for the country and hence its individuals. These beliefs, of fundamentally northern European, Protestant origin, ignore the brown and black and yellow and red citizens who have been here for many generations without benefiting materially from the mainstream economy. These beliefs also ignore the other possible models for success that are suggested by such movements as Afrocentrism and radical feminism, models that have more to do with the sense of self, family, and community than with economic well-being. Indeed, the alliance of "family values" with many well-placed defenders of the status quo is usually connected closely with a schooling that sticks to the old political, economic, and biographical history, a patriotism that verges on jingoism, and the Protestant economic virtues of thrift, hard work, and self-discipline. This story slights what ethnic-studies specialist Ronald Takaki points out as the history of the legal denial of participation in democracy for Americans of color and female Americans until well into this century. If you were Asian, from 1874 until 1924 you were excluded from American citizenship and from owning land in most western and southwestern states; if you were black or female or Native American you suffered absolute exclusion from democratic participation for much of this nation's history, and when you finally won citizenship you saw it undermined by Jim Crow, by land deals and water-rights exclusions and employment practices and social discrimination that kept you effectively out of the democratic as well as the economic development of the post–World War II society.[14]

Who is an American, and how is that image taught in school? I would argue that the answer has more to do with religion, and the model of civil religion, than most Americans realize. Traditionalist beliefs, including the Protestant faith, the Bible, the Judeo-Christian, Graeco-Roman, democratic beliefs—all are equally mythologies. There is no question that these are magnificent mythologies, or that they are worth living by and dying for. But they are nonetheless mythologies. And much of what is taught in school concerning these traditions is taught as a belief system fundamental to American culture. For the traditionalists who blithely ignore the exclusion of so many good Americans from the nation's active political and economic history, the democratic story is still the best story that can be told. For them, secure in their own full participation in this saga, there is no distinction between individual identity and national. The cultural identity of the individual matches closely the national identity with no intervening group-identity ties. For Catholics who did see a major distinction, the response was to set up their own schools to teach the group culture, as distinct from the national culture of the public schools. Jews and Asians have by and large not done this, but maintain their own community, neighborhood, or religious institutions to reinforce group culture while taking fairly skeptical advantage of the public schools. For these latter groups, and indeed, for all successful minorities, the national culture as taught in public school and the group culture are maintained as two separate worlds that the individual negotiates, often appreciating and acknowledging the beliefs of school, but doing so intellectually and not as a matter of faith or self-identity. The challenge currently being posed by Afrocentrism (and by many other dissenting ideas as well) is that maintenance of the group culture should be available in public school rather than in some other, private institution, precisely because public school does teach faith in one group's culture already, a culture that is as impossible a fit for Afrocentrists as for, say, Catholics.

Since Stokely Carmichael's revolutionary declaration of Black Power in 1966, "go slow" has been replaced by a powerful new dynamic in American politics. Group after group coalesced around new alliances that left the old identification between the individual and the nation in the dust, taking advantage of the democratic process to create change aggressively, particularly in the social realm. And since school—far more than work, neighborhood, sports, or any social activity—remains the primary meeting ground of the races in an otherwise racially and ethnically segregated America, the power of group politics has been played out primarily in education. Groups demanding bilingual education or ethnic studies or gay-Lesbian approaches to curriculum are making headway in schools and on campuses across the nation. Each group demands changes in curriculum that often, like Afrocentrism, seek to glorify the past and preserve the sanctity of the people. In doing so they differ little from the Puritans who settled on our own shores to educate their children and ultimately all Americans to believe themselves a holy people with a holy cause.

The religious cause of the traditionalists has been furthered by the texts and tropes and structures of school as well as by the curriculum. Because of schoolbooks' habits of "mentioning" second-hand a list of major writers and thinkers and events in Western history, generations of school children have grown up with precisely the sort of list mentality advocated by E. D. Hirsch, Jr., and standardized curricula: we've been teaching our children to recognize names as if they were saints in a Western Civ hagiography. In such a vocabulary-list, fill-in-the-blank, recognition curriculum, many Americans have been schooled to memorize great names without having had to tussle with the works and ideas they created.

The Enlightenment rationalism so esteemed as the focus for traditional curricula is now itself the object of attack.[15] Afrocentrists basically agree with traditionalists that schooling in America is a matter of enlisting the young in a secular Church Militant, but propose an alternate set of beliefs more comfortable for African-Americans. "The Movement," a phrase used by leaders in the field,[16] gathered strength at the Second National Conference on the Infusion of African and African-American Content in the School Curriculum in Atlanta (October–November, 1990), where incantatory rituals prevailed. An alternative hagiography was intoned, listing the major figures of the Movement's ancestors ("Marcus!" "Malcolm!" "Elijah Mohammed!").[17] An African enstoolment ceremony honoring the elder of the faith, John Henrik Clark, followed. A workshop leader in Washington, D.C., has elementary school-children gather in a circle, breathe in and out, invoke ancestors (Malcolm X, Carter Woodson, Mary McLeod Bethune), and pray. She tells them that *Amen* is an "ancient African word for God Almighty."[18] Gospel singing has appeared in many a school, introduced as an important expression of African-American culture. Hieroglyphics are being taught to schoolchildren so they can study their ancestral texts, much in the way that Jews teach their children Hebrew or Catholic priests study Latin or Greek.

Meanwhile the traditionalists claim that the matter of school is universal and not particular, that the values and beliefs of school are secular and democratic, and that the foundation texts of democracy should become the foundation texts of school. *The Federalist Papers* seems to have taken on a special value to the conservative alliance between labor and government in their efforts to clarify this position.[19] But the *Federalist Papers* proclaim that "Providence [had] been pleased to give this one connected country to one united people—a people descended from the same ancestors, speaking the same language, professing the same religion, attached to the same principles of government, very similar manners and customs."[20] The religious foundation of our understanding of America is there to be seen in the most prized text of those who would defend the traditional American faith. Quite a few traditionalists have noted the religiosity of the Afrocentrist movement, while failing to mention their own. Andrew Sullivan in *The New Republic* refers to the Atlanta conference's audience responses as a "litany of faith";[21] Stephen H. Balch, president of the National Association of Scholars, says advocates of multicultural education behave more like "a religious sect" than like academics;[22] Diane Ravitch takes to task their "filiopietism," their "fundamentalist" notions, and describes them as "true believers;"[23] a writer for the *Washington Times* notes that the new Egyptology of Afrocentrism has become "gospel";[24] Gilbert Sewall refers to the Afrocentric "hagiography";[25] and John Taylor describes Afrocentrists and all counter-culture groups as equivalent to "Christian Fundamentalists."[26] As a counterpoint to these charges we must also note that the prominent Afrocentrist Asa Hilliard believes the traditional canon of literature to belong in "sectarian religion [rather than in] a scientific and democratic school and society. Curriculum catechism [is] propaganda [not] truth." The canon is "cultural indoctrination."[27]

At the same time, Hilliard refers again and again to the need to teach "the truth." This constant reference to "the truth," more than any other aspect of the Afrocentrist movement, suggests its religious character. Absolute truth is a matter of religion, whereas provisional truth is the child of rational inquiry. Post-Enlightenment science and history opted for provisional, rather than God-given, truths. Such inquiry posits hypotheses, holding them to be useful descriptions of nature or the past only so long as the weight of evidence supports them. Rationalists are interested in teaching students methods of investigation, argumentation, critical capacity to search out and review evidence, and so on. Rationalists search for, but never arrive at, truth. It's interesting that Afrocentrists do not simply want their new evidence added to or used to modify old evidence concerning, say, the origins of Western thought or the glories of the African heritage. They wish instead to replace what they see as one consistent body of beliefs (the Eurocentric) with another (the Afrocentric). Afrocentrists see the civic religion taught in school as an untrue faith.

As we saw in "History Lesson," Egypt has been perceived as the foundation civilization, not only of the West, but of the former USSR as well; Egypt seems as moveable on the imperial maps of the world as Poland. Afrocentrism's view of Egypt is actually very much in keeping with the nineteenth-century Romanticism on which American schools were founded. As Egypt features in Afrocentric school teachings, however, there is less of straightforward historical lineage than of ritual.[28] And as we have seen, ritual also prevails in traditional teachings about the West.

This deep embedding of religion in our schools and in new alternative curricula as well exposes the deep and equally embedded religiosity of mainstream schooling, supposedly free of doctrine. To believers, this embedding is often invisible. According to education historian Larry Cuban, "The fabric of beliefs shared by the American public and its officials—that public schooling could improve not just individuals and groups but the entire nation politically, socially, and economically—has been labelled by some observers as a civic religion. The British political scientist Denis Brogan referred to the public schools as 'the formally established national church of the United States.' "[29] Those brought up to believe in the civic religion equate their own identities with the national myths. Those who have not been able to believe in those myths, in contrast, see no threat either to their personal integrity or to their country's in proposing alternative myths. Defenders of the traditional faith do see such a threat, and issue grave warnings that the very fabric of the country is thereby in danger. *Their* group is in fact under threat.

And so traditionalists arm themselves for a revived assertion of "common culture" and "the common core of learning," unaware that the charge of religiosity can equally apply to themselves.[30] "Excellence," "intrinsic worth," and so on are criteria of a belief system and an aesthetic that are neither value-free, objective, nor ethnically neutral. In some ways both traditionalists and Afrocentrists equally reject secular rationalism. And while the contending forces on both sides gather their troops, let's consider what the rest of us should do—and particularly, what teachers and other educators not yet involved in the battle might do.

As a practical matter, each of us must examine closely our own beliefs and the makeup of our faith. Then we must decide whether public schools in America are to continue primarily as vehicles for moral and social development or as centers for the intellectual development of our children. Afrocentrists and fundamentalists of all stripes say that this distinction is impossible, since the moral is implied by every choice that is made of what to teach, how to teach, and how to assess (put value on) the results of our work. Traditionalists equally proclaim the moral basis for American public education. Both leave the rest of us floundering with the monumental differences in belief systems of these contending groups. Indeed, if Afrocentrism is to prevail in certain public school systems, there is no reason why Catholic education cannot equally prevail in some, or Islam in yet others.

Religion has permeated American schools since their nineteenth-century origins[31] and continues today in the form of civic religion. American schooling, as the Afrocentrists have rightly noted (and Catholics and Jews before them), seeks to indoctrinate beliefs painful or impossible to many, many good Americans. We would like to oblige with belief, but we find our consciences just won't allow it. Should new religious impulses take the place of the old in public school? As long as it is perceived that traditionalists are allowed to get away with their religion, others gaining newly powerful voices in school management and control will try to instill their alternate doctrines.

Afrocentrists have opened up a fascinating and difficult set of questions concerning the ways in which "culture" and faith are intertwined. Rather than criticize either Afrocentrism or any other belief system (which it is not open to nonbelievers to do), perhaps we can shift to the difficult discussion of how church and school can possibly be separate, and how and whether schools can function in light of the profound religiosity of our country.

Schools do have a function in building nations, and faith does play a major role in building nationalism. But faith is highly problematic for modern nations. In one sense, beliefs are tribal, representing groups too small to satisfy the size and scope of the modern nation. In another, major faiths are transnational, too big to define single nations. As a result, nations look for substitute religions akin to America's, represented by flags and cult heroes and other icons of invented ritual, to satisfy religious urges and needs.[32] The Afrocentric critique of the American civic religion as exemplified in school history and literature constitutes serious dissent based on a perceived exclusion from participation in the promises of its faith. The terms in which this debate are carried out do not have to do with history, but with a thoroughly American, ecumenical religiosity. As Irving Kristol has pointed out, American religiosity's civic dimension has little to do with theology, but everything to do with irrational belief.[33] Why, then, should Afrocentric missionaries be put to a proof that is not required of traditionalist ecumenical missionaries? And why should such proof be required when, in our American schools, "for the last thirty years educators have evaded, denied, or underestimated [religion as] an impelling historical force?"[34]

Finally, we must remember that one of the fundamental tenets of American democracy, the idea of liberty, draws its origins not just from Greek thinking, but also from that of St. Paul. The Greeks defined liberty in terms of the ability to participate in civic life; St. Paul defined freedom within the confines of submission to the will of God. American ideas of freedom within the context of this Christian overlay on the secular Greek idea constitute a portion of the problem I have outlined in this part. Some of what traditionalists wish to teach in school includes the American version of liberty "under God"—the Pauline and hence the Christian definition. Paradoxically, modern European definitions of liberty are not so circumscribed. The question of what to teach in American schools indeed opens up for inspection these profoundly challenging issues. It is time we all worked on this together as Americans.[35]

Alternative Views

In a classic volume of 1936, *The Study of Man*, Ralph Linton described the average American getting up in the morning:

> On his way to breakfast he stops to buy a paper, paying for it with coins, an ancient Lydian invention. At the restaurant a whole new series of borrowed elements confronts him. His plate is made of a form of pottery invented in China. His knife is of steel, an alloy first made in southern India, his fork a medieval Italian invention, and his spoon a derivative of a Roman original.
>
> . . .
>
> He reads the news of the day, imprinted in characters invented by the ancient Semites upon a material invented in China by a process invented in Germany. As he absorbs the accounts of foreign troubles he will, if he is a good conservative citizen, thank a Hebrew deity in an Indo-European language that he is 100 per cent American.[36]

The ancient Egyptian use of papyrus also brings Africans into an intimate and essential relationship to the literacy of modern, democratic humankind. American culture, social structures, and politics derive from multiple sources. It is unnecessary to invent these origins, but it is necessary to teach them accurately, fully, and honestly.

National pride has tended to obscure such multiple origins, however, preferring to think ahistorically as well as parochially. It is not much of an improvement on patriotism to believe that somehow all these "contributions" add up to a special apotheosis in America. When Afrocentrists complain that they're taught to believe white folk invented everything worth having, they are pointing to one of the superiority myths of America. Our politics and economics are constantly touted in school and public life as "the best in the world," our products the most superior, our way of life the envy of the globe. Since we imagine the world eager to become American, we feel justified in our pride.

Despite the existence of powerful historical, literary, artistic, and philosophical evidence plentifully available to construct a powerful multicultural and international curriculum, too many multicultural theorists are content to proceed from the writers' own belief systems rather than from genuinely enlightened research. We need to know much more about ourselves than we do. We need to shake off easy assumptions and do the harder work of finding out who Americans are and how Americans of all kinds perceive the world and their place in it. What are their hopes for their children? Those hopes should form the basis of curriculum building, but curriculum cannot depend only on hope. It must also be based on freely researched inquiry into those subjects we want our children to know. As it stands, writers other than Afrocentrists advocating multicultural education tend to create theory with little reference to precise cultural phenomena, while traditionalists prefer to mention only those aspects of American society that "tell the democratic story." The multiculturalists too often avoid the specifics of history, literature, art, and politics, while the traditionalists' position looks too often like simple flag-waving.

Many multicultural advocates point out that the melting pot theory that held sway in America for well over a century has been thoroughly debunked. People retain many marks of their culture of origin by choice and have other marks thrust upon them by a dominant culture that refuses to assimilate minority habits. Yet schools continue to operate on an assimilationist model: a standard curriculum for all, an insistence on gaining English at the expense of the native language, and a lack of interest in varying individual needs. "Anglo-conformity remains the effective policy of almost all of this country's public schools, and promises a unified nation as well as equal opportunity for disadvantaged immigrant students. Neither promise should be [believed]."[37] Traditionalists sometimes seem oblivious to the fact that school culture does reflect white, middle-class, Protestant culture in an infinite number of subtle ways as well as in its basic forms and structures. What the multiculturalists miss, however, is that the culture of school imposes a way of being that is equally useless to all students, Anglo or otherwise. Instead of offering Western culture to students, the culture of school more often withholds it—from everyone.

A different and more powerful American education has been described for us most succinctly not by politicians, educators, or social scientists, but by artists and writers with transcendent visions. James Baldwin as early as 1963 called for a teaching that would liberate blacks and whites alike. "To lie about one aspect of anybody's history, [is to] lie about it all," he said. The stories taught in school, such as the foundation myths, are untenable. "So many people really appear to believe that the country was founded by a band of heroes who wanted to be free. That happens not to be true." The version that Baldwin offers instead reminds us that some Europeans had to leave Europe for reasons of hunger, poverty, and crime. "Those who were making it in England, for example, did not get on the *Mayflower*." Baldwin wants school to teach an American history that is "longer, larger, more various, more beautiful, and more terrible than anything anyone has ever said about it," so that black and white children can see how large the world is and that it belongs to them.[38]

Liberty is also the theme of writer Michelle Cliff, who speaks of the liberation that came to her as a writer when she began to use her native patois in combination with the King's English taught in school to shape a powerful new language.[39] Baldwin and Cliff are urging education to allow a child to take history and language into her own hands to shape them anew. Writers like these have the most important things to tell us about how education needs to change, because they keep their focus on specific aspects of culture—particular moments in history and particular purposes for writing. They keep their eyes clearly on the purposes of school—the empowerment of children through language and history, science, and math, and the capacity to do and to be in a world larger than the merely national, the tribally occupational, the gender- or group-bound ethos. This process may begin with patois, but its ends are transcendent.

Carlos Fuentes tells that official versions of history he studied in U.S. public schools spoke of a string of American military victories, while at home his father gave him Mexican books in which he read a litany of defeats. Living and writing in Chile later in life, he felt, like the poet Pablo Neruda, that the Spaniards may have conquered and ruled, but had left their verbal gold to the natives to spend freely. Similarly, he is able to acknowledge both that the English created an empire and that it was a democratic one. Fuentes lives and writes in the borderland where he can use all these paradoxes to create, moving from the particular to the general, the ethnic to the epochal, the local to the universal. It isn't a matter of particularists in deadly battle with the generalists; both the particular and the transcendent are essential to everyone, and especially so for the artist. All history is a history of cultural encounters. In learning that history—of the victory and defeat that simultaneously describe each encounter—we learn that "there were no privileged centers of culture, race or politics; that nothing should be left out of literature, because our time is a time of deadly reduction." To reduce, to ignore, or to forget is to lose the possibility for creativity and understanding—to circumscribe a world in an isolated and inert perfection.[40]

One can teach hieroglyphs to children as I saw them being taught in one inner-city school, as some kind of mantra for getting in touch with one's holy ancestors. Or one can teach them as a history teacher did in another, very different classroom; there, students trying to understand how writing first came into being tried to compose messages to each other using hieroglyphic symbols, reeds, ink, and papyrus. They discussed the economics of papyrus versus clay tablets as a medium for writing. Then they engaged in an exercise wherein they were to invent pictographic forms to convey messages to each other. One tenth-grade boy, who does not yet know how to read, managed to compose a symbolic system that conveyed a written message to his classmates. He was finally on the road to participation in literate culture. The lesson became an occasion wherein the students could work their way to the inside of other places, other times, and other people, at the same time arriving at new understandings of themselves and their own relations to literacy.

The borderlands where conflicts arise are also the source of creativity and life for Baldwin, for Cliff, for Fuentes, and for many others, who speak movingly against the kind of control over conflict that traditionalists prefer.[41] The fuss over multiculturalism in the schools may ultimately be about fear of losing control, or fear of the results if too many children have access to the power to know and to create that a multicultural education might give them.

Fuentes's words about the loss of privilege for any one culture fall on deaf ears for too many, whether multiculturalists or traditionalists. David Mura thinks "the wish for superiority is simply the reverse side of feeling inferior, not its cure." Real liberation involves accepting some fault and blame,[42] and, one would like to add, some humility—a feature of true scholarship that is too often absent from this debate. The offenses of the past loom so large to so many minorities, and the assumptions of truth to so many traditionalists, that self-aggrandizement takes over the language and the purposes of the discussion; everyone remains stuck in either a particular vision or a generalist defense, blind to what Fuentes saw as the need to negotiate both.

Practical Solutions

In the view of multicultural advocates, school imposes one culture at the expense of discrediting others, but in the view of conservatives the culture of school seems to transmit universals. Traditionalists think school has a common culture that should be accessible to all, and multicultural critiques see school as political oppression. School rewards behavior that conforms to the dominant group and marginalizes or discounts ways of knowing important to the solidarity of subordinate groups, such as the high value placed on academic knowledge and the low value placed on achievement in manual tasks. I would suggest that, to remedy this, we need mediators who can operate well in both realms—border dwellers who can negotiate between the worker and those in power.

John Goodlad, a leading education reformer, believes that equity and access to knowledge depend on transforming the teacher-student relationship, the elimination of the academic-tracking and social-sorting mechanisms of school, and the development of school as a nurturing place that yet doesn't lose sight of its fundamental academic purpose. In his 1990 *Access to Knowledge*, Goodlad sees teachers as the mediators, or border dwellers, between the cultures of the students and that of the larger society. In that larger society, Goodlad thinks, self-interest has overwhelmed devotion to the common weal among the powerful and the comfortable. He wants a new kind of common school—one that may indeed have different kinds of curricula for different children, but where all curricula are of equal value, and where all can learn to practice democracy to improve the commonweal.

Such schools may very well exist already somewhere in the United States, which has seen unprecedented experimentation in thousands of classrooms in the past decade—all designed to begin with the knowledge students bring to school from home and proceed to new knowledge from that base. Traditional education told students that what they already knew was false, useless, or unworthy. The new approaches teach that there can be no knowing without building on what is already known. The mere presence in school of Hispanic poetry radically alters a Hispanic student's perception of both self and school. His native language is no longer trash—it's an opportunity for knowing, perceiving, and creating. School is no longer alienating. This does not mean that the student learns no English poetry; it means that Spanish poetry is a route by which the student engages in school as a whole, English poetry included. Nor is Spanish poetry superseded by English. Both cohabit as points of access to knowledge and to the power of language.

Learning local history does not preclude learning national history. It *is* national history, seen from a local perspective. A child who reads the letters William Penn wrote to his ten-year-old daughter—the actual letters, photocopied from the originals, rather than summaries prepared by educational bureaucrats—has an opportunity to raise historical questions of her own and to begin acting like a historian. Her ability to ask such questions and to figure out how one would answer them gives her access to the purposes of history as a whole. There's a fifth-grade teacher in Philadelphia who does this with her class regularly. The students notice Penn's concern for his daughter's religious and intellectual education and his descriptions of life in the wilds of the new colony. They get one man's view of seventeenth-century colonial life, as adapted for the eyes of an English Quaker girl. By learning to see these perspectives, the assumptions and limitations of both writer and implied reader become clear to the students. These fifth-graders emerge from the exercise able to read historical documents critically.

School can be a place where children are given the basic tools and materials of history so they can learn how to learn at a sophisticated level. Children who are given poetry to read are learning how to read and to love reading. It makes no difference whether the poet is white or black or Hispanic—as long as the child wants to read more. If it helps for the child to encounter poetry that uses familiar language and syntax—not "easy" language, but familiar language—then teachers should by all means begin there. The criteria for poetic choices should have less to do with moral lessons or national agendas than with engagement with rich and complex language and the wish to inspire children to read.

Thousands of classrooms all over the country are currently trying such experiments.[43] But these are only thousands in a country with nearly three million classrooms. The experiments came about because a few principals here and a few foundations there were willing to let teachers transcend the boundaries, to see what they would do based on their many years of experience teaching diverse children. Teachers given such opportunities have based their new work not on theories so much as on their own instincts and practical knowledge. Many teachers turned to the arts as a way of enticing children to school learning. The subject might be history or science or even math, but the place they started was the arts.

In an elementary school in New Mexico the staff agreed to involve the entire school in a year-long exploration of Southwest architecture. The children visited ancient sites and contemporary pueblos, old missions and churches, read creation stories from several cultures, and decided to transform their flat-roofed, modern school building, with its cinder-block corridors, into a museum of architectural styles. With a mile of brown paper, some glitter, and paint, the older children refashioned a set of exit doors to a dull hallway into the facade of a Spanish mission; the middle group so altered the entrance to the school library that to enter it was to enter a pueblo. But genius was reserved for the youngest children. The kindergarten and first grade created a model of an entire pueblo on the floor of their corridor, to a scale based on a fundamental unit of early childhood construction: the two-inch-square graham cracker. Not only did the children learn the history of pueblo architecture, the purposes and meanings of the styles of the various buildings, but they also learned how to figure ratios, and estimate how many boxes of graham crackers (walls), how many of Triscuits (corrugated roofs), and how many of pretzel sticks (ladders) they would need to complete their project.

The results were magnificent. The children began with a particular piece of a particular culture and followed its traces to learn history, architecture, and mathematics of real sophistication in the process. They beautified and personalized their school building. They worked together to accomplish a complex, long-range goal. And they learned important elements of New Mexican history that brought them together through the study of diverse cultures.

In a high school in San Francisco, the English as a Second Language teacher confronts twenty students whose mother tongues come from ten different language groups; the six Chinese Americans in the class speak mutually unintelligible dialects. He pairs off all the students to write each other's biography in English. Each student interviews his or her partner, writes a few pages, has the subject of the biography read and criticize the writing, rewrites, has a second editing session, and polishes the work off for presentation to the class as a whole. Throughout the process, the students themselves create a social context and purpose for using English. What they are studying is highly particular and uncanonical, of course, but the process of speaking and writing English on a topic unfamiliar to them—someone else's life—is a complex exercise in learning not only to use the language but also to enter into the literary purposes of school. Perhaps after a year or so of such work they will be ready to pick up the canonical books in English, having acquired enough skill to read them.

A high-school English teacher in an alternative program for failing teenagers testifies to an assemblage of federal agency heads and chief executives of multinational corporations. The chair of the National Endowment for the Arts and the National Endowment for the Humanities, the secretary of the Smithsonian Institution, the director of the National Gallery of Art, the Librarian of Congress, the CEOs and former CEOs of Mobil Oil, Time-Life, and a dozen other companies sit ranged around enormous tables. The teacher, carrying a canvas bag jammed with student papers, reads from a piece of writing that a girl in her class had prepared in September. The writing is choked, chaotic; the writer grabs words at random, forcing them into a string of fragmentary sentences that starts nowhere in particular and trails off with nothing accomplished. The teacher tells her distinguished auditors about acquiring books written by black women writers for her class. She tells about getting the students to read Toni Morrison. She tells about her students' astonishment at their capacity to read Morrison's prose. She reads from another piece of writing the same student did in February. It has a glow. The girl's writing is confident and fluent; she has something to say. She has found her voice, and she uses it intelligibly to share what she knows with the reader.

The teacher's auditors are pleased and impressed. But the Librarian of Congress is worried. He asks, "Does this mean that you are substituting Toni Morrison for Dickens, Chaucer, Shakespeare?" The teacher replies that she has to get her students to trust her. If they don't trust her, they won't read anything at all. Toni Morrison was their gateway to trust in the teacher, the school, and the curriculum of the school. They may now be willing to explore Shakespeare, a required part of the school district curriculum for tenth grade. The Librarian of Congress was still unsatisfied. He asked again, "Didn't the Toni Morrison work take up time better devoted to Shakespeare?" The teacher replied, "Who are we to say that Toni Morrison is worth less than Shakespeare? Look what Toni Morrison did for my student. She gave her a voice she could write with." Unimpressed, or still worried about the traditional curriculum, the Librarian of Congress returned to the charge. The teacher responded, "I assure you, as we speak now, my class back home is reading Shakespeare with the substitute teacher who's minding them while I sit here in Washington and talk to you. Toni Morrison helped them to do it." The Librarian of Congress was not convinced, but the chairman of the meeting ended the discussion there. The teacher shoved the students' papers back into her bag and took the train home, marking a wad of essays all the way.

In a school in Miami fractious with racial hatreds, where six different kinds of Caribbean and Central American students rub each other raw in daily and hourly conflicts, a team of four teachers have encouraged some Haitian students, usually considered the outcasts of this school, to study their culture. Students have written plays, songs, poems, and stories; practiced singing and dancing and performing the music of their homeland; sewed costumes; and created a two-hour revue to put on for the entire school. The audience comes to jeer, but leaves singing, chanting, exhilarated. The poetry and song and the dramatic sketches tell about anguish for a native land in turmoil; about family conflict when the children partake wholeheartedly of American youth culture while parents worry about abandoned traditions; of the joys and the agonies of trying to reconcile a love of America with a love of home; these are thoroughly American children, despite the French patois. They take the stage with poise and dignity. They put on a ripping good show, every word of which they've written themselves. The audience loves what they see, not because the writers are their friends, but because what the performers have written and produced merits joyous and serious attention. A school of several thousand young people leaves the auditorium united in the spirit of the arts they shared that day. They have all learned about being a Haitian in America. They have all learned about America.

These stories, and hundreds more that I could tell, speak of efforts here and there around the country to trust our teachers to devise curricula in the arts and humanities with the explicit purpose of exploring multicultural issues. Every one of these examples resulted from a partnership agreement between public schools and other agencies, such as state humanities councils or local private agencies whose purpose is to stimulate support for public education in large cities. Every one benefited from the stimulus of grants from private and public foundations. Every one agreed to trust the teachers; in every one the teachers agreed to trust the students. In every one the students became the makers of the curriculum, beginning with the study of something particular to their own personal circumstances and culture of origin. In every one they used the particular as a route to the curriculum of the school—the reading and writing, history and art that provide the students with something far more important than a list of facts laboriously memorized and quickly forgotten. Above all, in these experiments students who had been disaffected by school, whose attendance had been poor, and whose standardized-test scores claimed they were ill-educated, proved their capacity to achieve at high and complex levels. They have learned how to enter into the world of school through their own creative acts and thereby to become Americans.

Every one of these attempts to work out a multicultural education also has its weaknesses. At best, these and dozens or even hundreds more I could cite are no more than a cottage industry, struggling to take shape in the confines of the bureaucratic education system that threatens at every turn to crush them in its machinery. Sometimes teachers have silly ideas and carry them out in the name of the humanities. Sometimes they just substitute new material for old in a traditional, authoritarian manner that yields no more learning than the old material. Sometimes teachers miss opportunities to help students make connections because their own knowledge of history or art or language is sketchy or uneven. Sometimes teachers are afraid to try their own wings, and sometimes they are so boxed in by the walls of the corridors they have dwelt in for so long, they no longer know how to see over the top.

More damaging, however, are soft and fuzzy notions about study that result in fluff rather than serious multicultural education. Many new curricula are based on the belief that students will learn to like each other better just because they know more about each other intellectually. I have seen projects where eating Chinese food substituted for the harder work of learning languages or history. I am worried about projects that are founded on assimilationist purposes for language learning, and even more worried about facile social science theory being substituted for tough thinking about how to engage young people, how to transform the curriculum, and how to make the changes stick. Finally, I am tired of hearing about "culture" and hungry to learn about a new poem, a piece of history I didn't know before, a specific work of art.

The success stories, such as those I've sketched here, all share a specificity about the objects of study and a toughness that is instructive for us. What makes their results valuable has as much to do with the work invested by students as with any property of the objects of study that might be labeled "intrinsic." The pueblo becomes important not just because it represents a feature of American history and culture, but because it becomes a product of the students' hands, minds, and hearts. The students' investment of effort and time makes the objects of study into subjects. It makes the material a possession of the students; it makes the curriculum their own.

Education as Quest

⟋⟍⟋

A liberal education neither begins with a priori assertions nor ends with truth.[44] Too many traditionalists and multiculturalists alike, however, mistake assertion for fact, the quest for provisional truth for absolute truth. The purpose of any learning is to revise what one already knows, to adjust the old to the new, to accommodate the current study with what one has acknowledged in the past, and to extend outward into the fearful unknown, trusting in the guidance of the teacher.

The tensions between new and old, fact and judgment, are necessary to learning. To learn only what is comforting is simply to reinforce what one already knows, to risk turning mere knowledge into belief that will resist new knowing in future. To discard everything one already knows to chase after the chimeras of the new is to lose one's way in trackless swamps from which there may be no escape. To accept the tensions, the friction of true learning is not, however, always to seek happy, mindless compromise, consistency, or even clarity of thought or belief. Sometimes we must be content with not knowing, but not knowing requires us to keep at the task of learning in the hope that clarity will eventually present itself.

Like the rest of the Western world, the United States has continuously secularized its social institutions since their founding in the eighteenth and nineteenth centuries. The secularization of school, like the secularization of science and of daily life, has defined our modernity and frightened many of our people. The tensions between modernity and traditional life find their fullest expression in school, where parents' hopes for their children's welfare confront an undemanding and comforting K–8 curriculum and a 9–12 curriculum that pretends to take the child out into the modern, secular world. Parents' wishes constrain the society's to some extent, but the society also constrains parental control. The school necessarily takes the child away from the warm embrace of the family and asks the child to take her place in a colder world, where love is not the purpose of learning or its reward, and where reason prevails over the yearnings of the heart.[45]

Teachers trying to overcome the disparities between home and school, the cultures of their students and the culture of the curriculum, the demands of the society and the indifference of the young, characteristically turn to interdisciplinary approaches that they hope will bridge the gaps. They often do so because, trapped themselves in the corridors of the mind created by school subjects, school departments, and their own educations, they see no other way to break out of the confines set up by these disparities. What teachers are doing when they try interdisciplinary experiments is to restructure the idea of "knowledge"—of what this branch of knowledge, social studies or language arts or reading, is or ought to be. Western philosophers have been struggling with the structure of knowledge—epistemology—for 2,500 years. A social studies teacher in one large city puts the problem succinctly, basing his entire world history course on the question, "How do we know what we know?" It could just as well be the foundation of the entire curriculum. The person who needs to ask the question, however, is not just the teacher, but the student.

One of the ways we know comes from faith. One comes from reason. And one comes from experience. None of these ways of knowing can possibly be allowed to dominate school. If faith dominates—whether the faith of traditionalists or of any kind of fundamentalism—it will preclude knowing by reason and by experience. Faith will get in the way of the child who is told he is an immigrant if he is not, and equally get in the way of the child told he is descended of people who invented philosophy if he is not. If reason dominates, it will be put to the test of experience and on occasion found wanting. If experience dominates, it will sometimes preclude the learning of much that faith alone produces—much of the beauty and the best hopes and wishes of humanity.

In the name of faith, or reason, or experience, much evil has been wrought in the world at various times and by all peoples. We will perpetuate these evils if we allow faith, or reason, or experience to dominate in our schools. Does it then follow necessarily that our schools would abandon the faith that created this country, or reduce all truth to relativism, or allow our children to emerge from school unaffected if we permit faith, reason, and experience to interact in school? Karl Popper, a great philosopher of our times, taught us to understand that if all truths are ultimately relative, some absolute truth will reside in the discourse between relative truths.[46] The multicultural debate will become valuable and necessary as we watch the various debaters learn to create a truth that comes into being only if and when they can cease talking past each other and truly engage in dialogue. It is our job to help all American students take an active part in this business of constructing their own interpretations of the evidence and marshaling the arguments of the debate for themselves. Education for a diverse democracy must claim this as one of its major ends.

VI

LIFE ON THE BORDER

Frontiers

~~~~~

The human species has a couple of million years of tribal experience behind it and only a few hundred years of nation-state experience. Our own democracy has just celebrated its second century, but our public schools have had less than one full generation of experience trying to address themselves to the task of educating the entire population that finds itself within our borders. We should not be terribly surprised, therefore, to find ourselves behaving tribally over the question of who possesses the knowledge that defines our Americanness. Tribal fears seem to dominate much of the discussion—fear of the other, the alien, taking over or intruding his ideas on ours; fear of the general populace learning too much and getting out of hand; fear of new and different forms of knowledge and ways of knowing; fear of losing our national integrity; fear of losing cultural integrity. All of these together constitute a single great fear, the fear of the terra incognita outside the tribal boundaries, whether one defines that boundary as a cultural enclave within the political border or as the nation itself.

Traditionalists and multicultural reformers alike tend to want to define school as the place where the nation-state is described for the rising generation and their patriotic beliefs formed. So many of the arguments, however—about individualism versus group allegiance, preservation of multiple cultures versus national identity, political and ideological commonalities versus ethnic differences—set up seemingly adversarial positions, theories, and assumptions that leave the debators on opposite sides of unbridgeable chasms of thought. What is needed is a larger vision, one that sees past the chasms or views them from so far above that they shrink in importance. Or we need a vision that sees the differences not as barriers but as opportunities. Such larger visions are the point of the arts and humanities.

Most of the defenders of traditional curriculum are people whose own personal success derives from a firm belief in and facility with the Western liberal arts tradition of learning. Most of the multicultural reformers are successful social scientists who have learned how to negotiate the terms of traditional education, but choose to try to construct new beliefs that don't leave people of color in the intellectual dust. There is also a third group of writers, some not American-born, who have had opportunities to live and learn in more than one cultural context. These are the border dwellers—the successful bilinguals, artists, and philosophers who move with grace and ease from language to language, from culture to culture, using and glorying in all the riches that their multifarious experiences have blessed them with. These are the fearless, because these are the ones who have crossed the borders, leapt the chasms and, having landed safely on the other side, found themselves able to imagine new territories of the mind and heart. They know that my knowing is not a matter of loss to you; that my beliefs do not make me less an American than you; that my having *more*—language, literature, history—doesn't diminish either of us, but increases our collective understanding and thereby makes America, too, a larger place.

Working against this enlargement of the territory of the mind, however, is that intractable American resistance to the intellect as a corrupt, Old World habit, coupled with distaste for worldliness and a belief in the frontiersman mentality that prefers guns to books, entertainment to scholarship, relaxation to endeavor. Working against this enlargement of the territory of the mind is the global dominance of Anglo-American language, popular culture, and Western economics and political organization, at odds with a world of people dislocated from ancient lands, cultures, languages and local political ties. Those who fear commercialism, abroad as well as here in the United States, react with fundamentalism to the evils of capitalism and the global Western culture. The poor, whose only heritage is the ills of the Western world, remember or imagine a golden age when their ancestors were at peace with nature and the gods, when language, custom, and politics were in harmony. To sit at the top of a society that trumpets the virtues of its beliefs is to believe in their universality. To sit at the bottom of such a society is to disbelieve that those virtues are universal. But to move freely across the boundaries is to see an America that is quite a different place, never before explored; it is to create new habitations from the multiple inheritances of the old.

National boundaries are only one kind of imagined, bordered territory, and the most recently imagined of all. National borders overlay many much older boundaries, including those separating languages, ethnicities, and religions. The emergence of the idea of nation took place first in the context of a European struggle to establish and define religious territory. The American national definition of territory grew out of a rejection of supranational Catholicism and in the context of Protestant national self-determination.

Catholic children ended up in schools of their own, since the boundaries between nationalism and religion could not successfully be negotiated within a Protestant, state school system. Language boundaries fail to coincide with national boundaries everywhere in the world. America and the American culture, envied by all the world, is nevertheless an English-speaking culture. All Americans eventually acquire English, perhaps by the second or third generation, but acquire it nonetheless—a plain-spoken, practical English with no frills, yet one that functions as a global lingua franca.

The greatest boundaries, however, are to be found wherever black and white, ethnicity and ethnicity, live in separate neighborhoods, worship in separate churches, work at different tasks, and isolate themselves in separate social clubs. Boundaries of race and ethnicity are ubiquitous, confirmed countless times each day by every citizen. Stick to your own kind; 'tis kind to be kin; blood is thicker than water; take care of your own. Ali Mazrui recently wrote a book reminding us that the borderlands of ethnicity, religion, and other cultural habitudes hold, by their overwhelming weight of history, far stronger ties on people than the very young idea of nation.[1]

Meanwhile, American popular culture crosses national boundaries with such ease that fundamentalists and traditionalists worldwide have become seriously alarmed. This popular culture, however dominant it appears to the world, is the true creation of a culturally democratic society, made up of four parts African-American music to one part denim jeans and an emphasis on youth, casual attitudes to traditional restrictions of any kind, and a democracy of social relations. American popular culture means modernity to the world, a challenge to tradition, an easy social interaction that disregards differences of language, religion, race, and even class. The cultural democracy of popular music and its place in the lives of young people worldwide has accomplished a shared worldliness that no theory of educational pluralism has been able to even imagine—a shared culture that is truly the creation and possession of all the people.

But popular culture doesn't get taught in school. School teaches a culture of preservation, not of creation; it teaches of the past, not of the present or future; of an elite, not of the many; of a text-centered world, not a musical one; of the political leaders, not of the cultural makers. That is perhaps what school needs to go on doing as long as it is necessary to instill in young people a sense of where we've been and how we got here. The trick is to instill this message of the past in a way that will not forestall the future. We need to know where we've been, but we also need to learn where we're going. It is this forward-looking idea of school as a preparation for creativity that gets lost in traditionalist thinking, whereas it is the sense of where we've been that gets lost in some discussions of multicultural reform. In neither approach does the child get a chance to have any say about constructing his own culture.

The fearless border dwellers are those who have no difficulty living in both past and future. The border is the place where teachers and students ought to dwell. That is the solution to the conundrum we set ourselves when we imagined this nation as a democratic one. For us as Americans it is not enough to learn only of verities from the past, nor is it enough to dwell exclusively in the present. Either place alone is lifeless. It is in the border transaction that the future is born—the frontier of the mind that can be explored best by the schoolchildren of America.

Borders seem insuperable only to those who see it as their business to defend them against both the threats from without and within. To traditionalists, the liberal arts subjects exist in departments—places where the rules for study are carefully defined and the students circumscribed by disciplines. Traditional high-school education in this country abandons the unity of the elementary classroom for a model where students move from subject to subject, classroom to classroom, teacher to teacher, whenever the bell rings. Traditional education considers each subject as if it were a separate corridor to be traveled from first grade to twelfth, with accidental encounters between subjects as they may occasionally intersect over the course of the years. The student is expected to make the broader connections on her own, not only among the separate subjects, but also between the whole of the matter of school and the whole of the matter of her life.

The boundaries school creates between the subjects and between school and life, however, seem to have grown so strict that few students see any possibility of making such connections. We all know of students perfectly capable of calculating batting averages but incapable of learning how fractions work in school; we know of students who hate school reading but love stories; we know of the teacher who sends third-graders to a library to do "research" on animal behavior instead of home to record observations of their pets. We also know that teachers everywhere in this country are aware of the artificiality of the boundaries school creates among the subjects and between school and "life," as if life stops at 9:00 A.M. and starts again only after 3:00 P.M.

Many teachers have begun to work to overcome these boundaries. In the early 1980s the Ford Foundation encouraged the creation of public education booster organizations in dozens of cities and towns throughout the nation. These "Public Education Funds" usually began their work by raising money from the private sector to offer small grants to teachers. These "mini-grants," of a few hundred dollars apiece, were available through applications that asked teachers to try out in their classrooms new ideas that they believed would benefit their children's learning. Teachers in cities large and small served by the Public Education Funds responded with energy and enthusiasm. Most teachers had never in their careers been given an opportunity to try something positive on their own. In Philadelphia's mini-grant program I found that when teachers were given an opportunity to invent their own solutions to education problems, they immediately crossed the borders. Most applications for mini-grants that I read (and I read several thousand over a period of eight years) crossed disciplinary boundaries. Teachers wanted to get out of their long, boxed-in corridors, to help children see over the top, to leap to new places where literature spoke to history and drawing spoke to science and science spoke to writing and mathematics spoke to art. One teacher, knowing the students in her Spanish class loved to watch soap operas, required them to follow an Argentine soap opera broadcast on a local television station, write something about each episode every day, and discuss it in Spanish in school. She added the study of the history of opera to the mix and eventually had a class of enthusiasts ready to mount their own original opera in Spanish.

Another teacher, preparing her class of first-graders for a museum trip, not only told them about the art they would see, but also had them draw maps depicting the route the bus would take and record data on five different kinds of graphs measuring how many cookies they would have to sell to pay for the trip. The class chose a particular artist to study, learning about his work and life as well as discussing his reasons for his artistic choices. One of my favorite works of art came out of that class and hangs on my office wall as I write. It's a picture of a house, with grass and sky and trees. The house is pink, yellow, green, and blue. But instead of using a strip of blue at the top of the paper to represent sky and an equal strip of green at the bottom to represent grass, this six-year-old child, inspired by Van Gogh, has filled the entire sky and earth with undulating waves and pools of color—blue, green, red, yellow. She has taken the conventions of school art (one inch of blue at the top, one of green at the bottom) and the language of Van Gogh's brilliant waves of color and, using both conventions, painted herself into a new way of seeing sky and landscape.

Grants helped countless other teachers work with the arts to forge connections between students' interests and school. They taught reading by getting children involved with poetry; they taught history by getting students acquainted with the arts of the past. The teachers who attempted all of these experiments had turned their experience of students over many years into an opportunity to climb out of the corridor curriculum. Sometimes their efforts were superficial, a problem with interdisciplinary study often raised by traditional scholars.[2] Traditionalists insist that there's a way of thinking peculiar to each discipline that needs to be learned first and thoroughly before one is ready to make connections with results drawn from other disciplines. Unfortunately, the structure of education is such that the more one progresses in one discipline, the less language one has in common with other disciplines, and the less capacity to reach or even perceive possibilities for connection. Schools throughout America do generally offer American history and American literature in the eleventh grade, yet few departments of English and social studies can manage to sit down together to find common ground across their disciplinary borders. In elementary schools, one has the absurd situation of "reading" and "writing" as subjects separate from "social studies," "science," and "arithmetic," with the result that these are genuinely believed to exist as separate subjects or disciplines. Such corridors of thought give rise to the newest subject in school, sometimes called "higher order thinking" which is sometimes offered as if it, too, were a subject on its own. But the teachers with whom I have worked for a decade have struggled to overcome this atomized curriculum by creating connections among school subjects whenever they could.

Too often the world of learning sees knowledge as if it were territory subject to possession—knowledge as a preserve of the scholar or of a privileged class. Knowledge as a secret, priestly domain that by its nature can only be known to the few must, to preserve its integrity, be kept apart from the culture of the masses. Western education, deriving in large part from a text-centered study of Holy Writ that was, until the Reformation, the preserve of the clergy, continues to maintain this hierarchial exclusiveness in the structures as well as the teachings of school and university. We continue to withhold knowledge despite the democratizing influence of a Reformation that sought to put the words of the holy texts directly into the hands of the people. It is on the boundary between the priestcraft of knowledge and the democracy of literacy that school suffers warfare. The priestly preservers worry over the vulgarization of the sacred preserve; the masses protest against the existence of the preserve. One group believes that unless school knowledge is kept unsullied by popular culture it will be trampled by an unknowing herd; the other group is enraged by the arrogance of this attitude.[3]

Good teachers know something that goes well beyond this territorial dispute. Their students come to school in possession of popular cultures of many kinds. The teachers' job is to find a way of transmitting the culture of the school, which simply cannot be done unless a way of crossing the boundaries can be found. Teachers must begin with the contexts for learning and the content of knowledge their students already have—not to teach or even to reinforce those contexts and that knowledge, but to form a common culture in the classroom that will be modified by what school teaches. The result is a transaction between the cultures of the children and the culture of school. The dispute over multiculturalism is over whether that transaction should result only in modifying the children or whether it might also result in modifying the culture of school.

Let's go back to that classroom of thirty African-Americans from whom the teacher wanted a piece of rote memorization: "We are a nation of *what?*" "We are a nation of immigrants," chirped many of the children. But at the back of the room one boy's eyes narrowed. I sensed serious disagreement with what was being taught. The teacher missed or ignored that silent protest.

In other classes that I have observed, something very different happened. In such classes rote memorization is not the goal; rather, thirty fifth-graders plus an adult get together to talk about American history in such a way as to create a new understanding of themselves as Americans. The teacher says, " 'We are a nation of immigrants' is a statement often used to define America." Then he invites the class to consider the extent to which that is a good definition and the reasons for its appeal. The point of this lesson is to supersede the definition, understanding its historical importance but moving on to better ways of defining America that include the children in the classroom. In such classrooms there would be an opportunity to begin to talk about the subject that lies at the heart of American history, which is how we are to reconcile our democratic ideology with our history of inequity, slavery, and racism. Not all of history or culture is a matter of race; but no study of American history or culture should dare to attempt to describe itself as free of the matter of race. Those thirty African-American children are the subject of the classroom. They are the purpose of the classroom—the culmination as we have it of American civilization. Teaching American history means engaging those children in a discussion of who they are or might become as Americans. When and if they learn to reconcile their own role in American history, something new will appear on the scene. Then American history will be a living, breathing subject because the children make it so.

Many Afrocentrists disbelieve that such a reconciliation is either possible or desirable. The search for a glorious past in Africa seems to say that not enough glory will ever attach to the history of Africans in America. But their solution also disregards learning as a transaction. It sets up new border patrols on territory, claiming Egypt for all of black Africa, seeking to return myth for myth, border for border, glory for glory. Afrocentrism plays by the old, traditional rules. It encourages belief and faith as the underpinnings of knowledge, which remains a form of worship. Perhaps faith is a prerequisite to acquiring knowledge of any kind. Our models of scholarship are so intricately bound up with religious purposes—Protestants needing to read the Bible, Jews to study Talmud, Muslims to live by the Koran—that we cannot often transcend our religiosity to find other entry points for study. Faith is the mode of knowing that pervades American society. Repeated in school as a way of knowing—whether by traditionalists or by Afrocentrics—faith creates barriers against the unfaithful. The teacher has three choices: to go on preaching the old faith and allowing the boy at the back of the room to narrow his eyes and grow up angry with a school that preaches lies; to preach a different faith, such as Afrocentrism; or to conduct class as if it were a place where new knowledge gets made in the transactions between kids, ideas, texts, and the matter of America.

When traditionalists insist that the primary purpose of school is to teach the democratic ideology we hold in common and the origins of it, we remember that the rule of law is not alone a sufficient description of America. The remedy of the law declared the end of segregation, yet decades later we still await a moral remedy for the continuing injustices of schools that exclude the poor from access to learning. Molefi Asante, the originator of the Afrocentric idea, has reminded us of the distinction between a *society* common to all, and the different *cultures* that it contains.[4] Schools that would restrict themselves to teaching only the commonly held virtues of the society's ideology would quickly find themselves repeating the old myths, making up new ones, or fudging the morality.

Another border mentality exists over the ideological importance of individual will as opposed to the common weal, or autonomy as opposed to civic virtue. Traditionalists often oppose the study of groups. The individual, they assert, is what America is about. All this group collectivity (not their term, but it's what they mean) is un-American. Political philosophers have labored to find a middle ground wherein school becomes a place to learn autonomy and individualism at the same time as one learns to put the greater good of the whole above self-interest.[5]

Missing from all of these is a clear understanding that minority groups have found a commonweal in political units *within* the nation to supersede the good of the individual. Such groups see the idea of autonomy and individualism as code words for an imperfect status quo; traditionalists see group action of this kind as separatism. Now as in the past, nationalism and cultural or ethnic group solidarity are seen as incommensurable loyalties by traditionalists even though the entire history of the country has been built on group loyalties and self-help among kith and kind. Schools are themselves the territory being fought over in this battle. Should either ideology prevail and the winners take all, or will we emerge as we have in the past with some schools becoming the preserve of various minorities while most remain the preserve of the majority white, Protestant group?

Culture/culture

~~~

Oh, let America be America again
The land that never has been yet—

LANGSTON HUGHES

I was brought up in a home where *culture* was pronounced with a capital C. Cultured people were those who had a highly developed knowledge of the Western world's aristocratic ways—they knew the languages and literatures of many nations, they moved with social grace and ease among many people. To bask in the presence of a cultured person was to engage with the history, the poetry, the music, and the ideas of the world.

This mistaken notion that "our" ways are culture whereas "other" ways are primitive or savage or barbarian is a tribal habit of mind shared by peoples all over the globe. In many languages, words for the speakers of one's own language denote civilization; words for speakers of other languages denote barbarism. *Barbaros* is a Greek word invoking the uncivilized babble of those who don't speak Greek; but such designations can be found among Chinese, African, and Native-American languages as well.

Anthropologists in the nineteenth century set out to discover living people who displayed a "primitive" state of human development, with the idea of giving Westerners insights into what they themselves might have been like in prehistory. But anthropology has long abandoned this tribal view of the world, realizing that cultures aren't high or low, civilized or barbarian, despite our habits of so portraying them. In the process, culture became redefined as something in the possession of all human beings, not just the preserve of the few. The discipline of anthropology changed radically, from Western imperial study of the rest of the world as objects to a discipline seeking to understand human culture in a much broader sense. It changed to find what it is that we share as a species, and to learn how those universals are differently interpreted among different peoples. And then it changed again, to become a discipline that rests content with learning how to interpret the phenomena of cultures in all their particularity and rich individualism.

The entire debate about multiculturalism in our schools has been conducted largely without any reference to what anthropologists might tell us about what culture is and how it works. The founder of modern American anthropology, Franz Boas, insisted very early in this century that no national or racial group possessed superiority over any other, that race does not determine behavior, and that no group is "pure" or uninfluenced by others. Throughout our century anthropologists have argued against the myth of trying to create a single American identity. There never was one and there never will be one. All Americans need to grow up negotiating multiple identities.[6] Similarly, anthropologists' understanding of *culture* has failed to guide either the proponents or opponents of multiculturalism in their slack usage of this notoriously slippery term. One of our greatest anthropologists, Clifford Geertz, recognized that in observing human behavior the writer's ethnocentricity is unavoidable, but perhaps irrelevant. The subject of anthropology is neither the "other" nor oneself. It is the conversation between us wherein we both attempt to understand each other's meaning.

According to Geertz, we are not only social animals but symbolic ones. What distinguishes human beings from the rest of the animal kingdom is that the human animal lives entangled in symbolic webs of meaning. These symbols are not confined just to such obvious symbol systems as language, costume, religious rituals—they are our entire way of life. All "human behavior is . . . symbolic action."[7] The anthropologist's task is to learn how to converse with unfamiliar symbolic behavior; that is what "interpretation" of a different culture means. Geertz suggests that "understanding a people's culture exposes their normalness without reducing their particularity. . . . It renders them accessible . . . it dissolves their opacity." When the anthropologist writes a description of her understanding of a group of people, she is interpreting, and therefore she is also creating something. And to create in writing is to be engaged in the business of fiction.[8]

School curricula are fictions that seek to interpret the society—to write a narrative descriptive of the society. Curricula are fashioned, made-up accounts of who we and the world are and how things came to be that way. When the fictions we tell in school are opaque to many of the children there, it is because the fictions of school fail to interpret the symbolic worlds of the children in the classroom. Then the symbolic web of school and the symbolic web of the child fail to converse. School ought to be able to prepare the child to converse with ease with many different webs of meaning—to enhance and enlarge the languages and symbol systems at the child's command. But we have seen school operate to restrict the conversation instead, to reduce the numbers of conversations to which the child has access instead of increasing them.

Anthropologists have been rather in the habit of studying "typical" villages and generalizing from these studies to the society at large. Geertz teaches us that to do so mistakes the *place* of study for the *object* of study. "Anthropologists don't study villages; . . . they study *in* villages." The purpose of study is the specific circumstance, not a generalization. It is an illusion to go on seeking what human nature is in general, exclusive of cultural differences and particular circumstances. Human beings are the product of their particular cultural webs, which differ enormously from place to place and time to time. The human being cannot be contemplated apart from his customs; the customs are the creature. Just so, we cannot separate ourselves from our ethnocentricity, despite that word having become a term of moral abuse. There simply are no specific beliefs and practices that human beings universally agree on. Conversely, "it may be in the cultural particularities of the people—in their oddities—that some of the most instructive revelations of what it is to be generically human are to be found." But, I hear you protest, is that not to give up the idea of some human phenomena being morally superior, more valuable than others? Is that not to be a relativist, to see every cultural phenomenon as equal in value to every other one? Geertz dismisses such panic as a "false bogey." The point is that it doesn't matter what you study in anthropology as long as you study enough phenomena so that you can begin to synthesize an interpretation of what you've seen.[9] The analogy to school is a simple one. If the object is for children to learn to read poetry, one poem is not "better than" another for that purpose. Many poems, however, are necessary.

Education is complex for the human animal because her social, symbolic systems concern so many facets of life that learning to negotiate them takes up an inordinate amount of that life. "There is no such thing as a human nature independent of culture," and that culture is never general, but always expressed "through highly particular forms." Culture is "the link between what men are intrinsically capable of becoming and what they actually, one by one, in fact become. Becoming human is becoming individual, and we become individual under the guidance of cultural patterns, historically created systems of meaning in terms of which we give form, order, point and direction to our lives."[10] The link between what the individual is generically capable of becoming and what he actually becomes through specific cultural performances is where education needs to conduct its transactions. The scientist seeks major revelations through the specific occurrence of peculiarities and oddities. The panda's thumb, the aberrant radio wave from a particular stellar source, the appearance of singularities in subatomic particles—all of these are major clues to meaning. So it is with culture. The singularities are all of equal value to interpreting human existence, and the particular cultures are all of equal usefulness in making sense of the universe. To that extent, the study of each singularity is of equal usefulness to the study of any other.

Geertz addresses, moreover, the problem of nationalism and its effects on different cultures. In establishing the forms and rituals of the nation state either one group's particular culture is mined for the national language and symbols, or else a generalized symbol system is chosen. When the particular symbols of one group are chosen, they will seem "natural" for some, but uncomfortable for those whose symbols were excluded. When national symbols are invented, no one feels an emotional affinity with them. The tensions that result from the discordance between national symbols and those of the subgroups whose symbols are absent from the national realm is a discordance of meaning and understanding.[11] One of the discordances that arises is between those who consider the national symbols finished and complete and those who consider them to be still in the making. The former hang on to traditional symbols and feel any changes threaten a "natural" order, whereas the latter see themselves as still building the nation and recognize the national symbols as essentially artifices that can be changed.

In much of the world, nation building is still a mark of modernity. To participate is to join that larger, global world; to be left out of the national symbols is to be threatened with the loss of a larger world. But at the same time, modernity in the rest of the world is mass culture, undifferentiated Americanism, loss of traditional cultural definition, absorption, and invisibility. In a sense, within the United States minorities are protesting an internal colonialism that has sought to assimilate them into a mass culture whose symbolic forms do not seem to include them. Their protest is one against the loss of the particular cultural markers that distinguish us each from each; against routine, against a faceless culture that some perceive as bloodless as well.[12]

Traditionalists who deplore particularism seem blind to the difference between their comfortable symbol system and the symbol systems of minorities—simply fail to see that minorities (and often women) experience profound discontinuities between the national models and symbols and the particular symbolic webs of kith and kin. Yet for the state to succeed in binding loyalty, it must seem to represent the individual in all its acts and appear to its citizens as in natural continuity with the people. When the state fails to do so, it loses its symbolic legitimacy, and the symbolic legitimacy of the primordial ties reassert their importance. It is fair to say that minority groups in the United States are not themselves "separatist," but that the national symbols as taught in school appear to them to be tattered artifices. The failure to keep the ties that bind us intact is a failure of the original choice of symbols for the commonweal. Nobody disputes the rule of law or democracy—these remain fundamental beliefs of most multicultural reformers as well as traditionalists. It's in the rest of the stories taught in school—the stories of history, literature, and language in particular—that the discordance arises, as we have seen throughout this book.

If particular cultures are precisely our ways of expressing our humanity, then transactions or conversations between and among particular cultures should in part constitute the discourse of school. School could then become the place where we study each other in order to create interpretations of highly complex and fascinating symbol systems. Those conversations would give rise to understandings of what is not just generically American, but generically human.

New culture studies have increasingly turned to transnational and diasporan topics. Globally, we are in a period of tremendous social upheaval, with whole populations on the move as development, ethnic strife, and new national boundaries dislocate traditional means of subsistence. As borders and populations shift, more and more interest is devoted to study of those borders: the interfaces between North and South, between modern cities and traditional countryside, between the arts and literatures of the literate and those of custom and tradition, between the local and the national. Culture studies increasingly work "toward the contested *edges* of cultures, nations, identities."[13]

Within the United States, the Great Migration of southern blacks to northern cities and the middle-class flight from those cities, the new immigration of Asian and Latin American peoples, and the economic changes that have disrupted and minimized the possibility for unskilled labor in this country have profoundly altered the territory of school. The contested edges of these internal diasporas have to do with our acceptance of the necessity to keep all the children in school as long as possible. But to do so, we can no longer extend the fictions of elementary school into the high school the way we did after desegregation. Then the attitude toward the poor and people of color was to lament their cultural deprivation and to remediate them endlessly. Students spent four, five, and six years on the same atomized curricula, completing worksheets on the same topic in tenth grade that had failed to engage them in fifth or sixth or seventh. They dropped out, and rightly so. But now we want them to stay. To repeat the "nation of immigrants" story, or speak of U.S. triumphalism, or impose manufactured prose written by a committee of language skills teachers that fails to convey the authentic voices of writers or elicit the new voices of students—to go on doing these things is to go on insisting on opaque symbols and to leave the children out of the conversation.

To shift our attention from the central Western civilization story to the edges is not to diminish the Western story in the least. It is to give students and teachers access to that story—to begin the conversation in such a way that students can join in it. To shift our attention in this fashion is to recognize, acknowledge, include, and honor the cultures of the children as a part of the discourse of school, rather than to dismiss them as either nonexistent or undesirable. It is to say that both the child's culture and the school's are equally valid symbolic systems, equally functional in interpreting aspects of the world. The child needs to know the things that will enable her to converse in cultural settings beyond the neighborhood and family culture; the school needs to know the things that will enable it to converse with the child. The classroom, with its diverse children, is a place where many kinds of conversations need to occur. The teacher is the interpreter of each to each, of the child's world to the worlds the school can give access to, and of the world beyond the school and its neighborhood to the child. Most importantly, the classroom is where the children engage in conversations with books and maps, pictures and music, dances and plants, mathematics and theater— *with each other*. The classroom needs to have an edge to it, to dislodge the mind from comfort and complacency, to make it tough and urgent. All of that can only take place if it is first and foremost a safe and trusting place, where children and teachers alike know that they venture into the borderland together, joined in an enterprise to enter "the land that never has been yet."

The Art of Teaching

❦

The teachers who took their grant money to buy art supplies for their students, introduce poetry readings, escort children to see plays and dance, or put on an original opera knew that the arts are fundamental symbolic systems with an immediacy that enables students to enter into educated discourse. In the history of every language, poetry long precedes prose as a major vehicle for telling stories, for chronicling history, for celebrating worship, for explaining natural phenomena, for describing political systems—indeed, for all the major transactions of social and public life. Poetry is the link, in literate societies, between oral and written traditions. Poetry provides mnemonic devices enabling the speaker and listener alike to find the metaphors that most strikingly interpret the world, and to repeat and review what has already been said, the better to remember it—to keep the furniture of the discourse in the rooms in which it belongs.

Prose, however, is where we begin with small children in school, and prose dominates our reading and writing instruction. Prose is the most abstracted, least metaphorical, furthest-from-oral language that we have. All children must learn how to work with prose, but it makes little sense to begin school that way. One of the simplest ways of moving from the child's preliterate, oral culture to the prosy culture of school would be to focus heavily on poetry in the earliest school years. The late and greatly lamented Dr. Seuss, with his nonsensical repetitions of sounds, his wacky drawings, his gentle morality, and his light humor; Langston Hughes with his inside-out metaphors, his spare, lilting rhythms, his penetrating compactness—one could list dozens of wonderful poets whose work could be read aloud, read again, savored, memorized, read for oneself, read with a friend, read while sitting on the teacher's lap, until reading became the place first and foremost where cultures came together for a conversation.

Poetry and the other arts, however, are perceived entirely differently by traditionalists and radical reformers. The former get rather dewy-eyed about poetry, believing it's somehow a comforting, complacent sort of thing to have around. And that's certainly true if the poetry chosen is of the "O Captain, My Captain" or "God's in his Heaven,/All's right with the world" variety. Multicultural reformers, on the other hand, seem to think that poetry is politically unsettling, that its job is to roust one out of torpor and into action, a battle cry of the oppressed. Poetry certainly seems to thrive in places where direct dissent is forbidden; witness the uses of metaphor by Eastern European writers during the Cold War slyly to undermine the totalitarian regime. School poems—those carefully chosen bits and pieces of allowable Whitman, James Russell Lowell, Longfellow, Frost, Sandberg, Pope, Browning, Milton, Shakespeare—are too often the nice but rather dull bits of American and British writing. Satire, sharpness, and the unsettling have been carefully avoided. Too many pressure groups would undoubtedly get upset if poetry stopped being something safely dead and began to shape living thought in school.

The arts live on the margins, the place we want our classrooms to inhabit if those classrooms are truly designed to stimulate conversation. One could, as we have for the past century and a half, continue to choose works that mirror the moral instruction we wish to deliver. Or we could do what the teachers with small grants did—search out living poets and other artists as well as those of the past who have an edge to their voices; select the works that make us uneasy, that use new metaphors, that take us to unexpected places.

The arts are not holy relics to be kept in secret places out of children's reach.[14] The arts are tough, not soft; the arts are disciplined, not a free-for-all. Not every string of words on paper is a poem; few language-skills supervisors are poets. There's no reason at all to invent bad poetry for school use or to fob children off with poetasting in place of art. Children know better. They know when it's not worth their time and attention. The invention of poetry should also be part of the child's task, because then the child will be searching for the metaphors that allow him to converse. School culture will cease to be something imposed by school on children and begin to be something created by children for themselves and for the interactions school makes possible among them.

The inner-city high-school teacher who described her course on black women writers brings an array of novelists, essayists, and poets into her curriculum. Students who have never before willingly read literature find themselves hooked when they begin to explore this literary tradition, its themes, its language, and its immediacy for their lives. Students who have never written very much or very well also find themselves encouraged to keep journals, write essays, and even to try their hands at poetry. Terron M. Kane was a tenth-grader when she wrote "To P.J. (2 yrs old who sed write a poem for me in Portland Oregon)."

> if i cudever write a
> poem as beatiful as u
> little 2 yr old brotha
> i wud laugh jump leap
> up and tuch the stars
> cuz u be the poem i try for
> each time i pick up a pen and paper
> u and morani and mungu
> be our blue black stars that
> will shine on our lives and
> makes us finally be.
> if i cud ever write a poem as beatiful
> as u little 2 yr old brotha
> poerty wud go out of business.

There's a beatitude in such writing. It's a place from which an individual student begins to connect the personal with a larger world.

If the human animal is defined as a symbol-making creature, then symbolic forms that start with the child's capacity for utterance will have an immediate appeal. Rather then alienating the child, school will be a place that invites the child's collusion in its creation. Such an approach can and must include the poetry of many cultures from the start, while not in the least neglecting Western culture—currently as neglected as it can be, while we attempt to deflect children with manufactured prose. Real poetry would introduce Western culture together with other cultures. It will not ask students to read in order to answer textbook questions. It will ask students to read in order to find out what happens next, to answer their own questions, to lead to new ones, and to discover forms of discourse that can be shared with the whole class. In that sharing comes a common culture—a culture partly derived from the poets and partly derived from the students. That is why we still, in our technological age, need to gather children together in classrooms with live teachers rather than issue each of them a book list, computer, and modem and let them study at home. The classroom gathering is a necessity if children are going to learn to interpret, and to converse, and ultimately to create a shared, common culture. The essential point of school is that its symbol-making is a public, social act that defines what it is to learn to be human. The classroom is the common ground where the individual cultures of the children give rise to the community of culture that they create. And that's what America will become. The business of America isn't business; the business of America is finding out what America might become. Education is the American battleground, since America depends on what the children make of it in school.

The arts are the way in to school and to what American culture can become. They are a major vehicle toward achieving conversations among children of diverse backgrounds. That is not to say that those backgrounds will become merged or assimilated into the common culture of school, but that they will be interpretable each to each in the shared culture of school. Children will learn to negotiate many different forms of discourse in school; that is why the subjects need to intersect but also maintain their integrity. The arts may be a way in to reading, and even to history on occasion, for children who enter school preliterate. Mathematics, science, geography, all have their characteristic methods for perceiving, exploring, and recording meaning. All are languages, symbolic systems. None are finished products to be seen only from a distance, or simply vocabulary lists to be memorized, but methods and traditions allowing each of us to extend our own interpretations of phenomena into the world.

If children are to learn the languages of these disciplines, they must use those languages in school. Students must become the active partners to historical, scientific, and mathematical transactions as much as they are to poetic conversations. That does not mean children should be expected to reinvent Boyle's experiments or the Second Law of Thermodynamics in the classroom. It does mean that the way in to history or science requires us to *begin* with the contexts the children bring to school, and then to demand that our students extend themselves outward to new contexts.

The children bring with them evidences of a historical past. One can begin as one group of teachers did when a small grant gave them resources to study the history of their elementary school, which was about to celebrate its one-hundredth anniversary. The teachers began by having children construct a map of the neighborhood of the school as it is now, marking on it the local shops, the houses, the abandoned factories, the municipal facilities, parks, community gardens, wasteland, and offices to be found there. The young students interviewed the owners of these properties, found out how long they'd been there, why they'd come, and what kind of work went on there.

Next, the students prepared to draw a map of the neighborhood of a century ago. To do so, they visited the local branch of the Federal Archives and a museum of city history, consulting the ordinance surveys and ward lists to find out what had existed on the site at that time. They discovered that a century ago the same land supported newly built, thriving factories, surveys for houses not yet built, and some straggling farms. The names of all those owners survive as the street names in their neighborhood. A century ago there were stables and blacksmiths, new trolley lines extending from the center of town, a densely crowded population, families with many children, cook shops that warmed your dinner when your house had no kitchen.

The children went back in time another hundred years. They found a single farm owned by a man whose family name survives on the ward boundary line. Another hundred years back the children discovered evidence of a river that has long since disappeared under paving stones, a Native American settlement whose name is now used for an amusement park, a meeting place for Native Americans trading among themselves, species of trees not seen in that region for centuries, burial grounds and sacred places. The children can see the history of America from where they sit in class now. They started with themselves—their own multiplicity, their own poverty, their own rich cultural capacities. They found out why they lived where they did. They found out how their school emerged from an industrial society, an agrarian society, a sacred place. History didn't have to be told to them. They told the history themselves. They rummaged in archives, visited digs, and conducted an excavation of their own on the playground. Some of their questions were answered in books, some through interviews, some through maps and plans, diaries and newspapers, some through museum artifacts, some through reconstructions of their own, some through lectures, films, slides, and demonstrations, some through argument, and some through having to write it all down and explain it to someone else. They started with their present-day school, and ended with a history of America. These historians ranged in age from six to twelve.

These are children who, after a year's project studying the history of America through a particular study of a particular place, are conversant with the language of history. They have done a little archaeology, a little economics, a little map reading and map making, a little analytical argument, a little research in libraries, archives, and museums, a little of all of the complex techniques used by real historians doing real history. The children's work was original research of a highly sophisticated kind, dependent on no previous historian's or textbook writer's ideas because none were available on the history of their neighborhood. These children couldn't just copy the encyclopedia article and pass it off as research. And no one told them they were doing "research" or "economics" or "archaeology." The terminology for such activities was of no particular use to them; they were too busy doing them.

Not only are children who engage in doing history like this becoming conversant with the methods of history, they are demonstrating how learning can transform the energy of childhood into a powerful and meaningful creation of culture. Needless to say, their teachers are knowledgeable, visionary, and energetic people as well, for to create circumstances in which children make such powerful contributions to knowledge, teachers must be able to do far more than allow a textbook to carry out the job for them. No textbook is useful in such a process as more than a reference tool, and one of minor importance. A project of this kind marginalizes the textbook instead of marginalizing the teachers and children, who take center stage.

The art of teaching depends on imagination and capacities of an extraordinary order. Not all of our nation's teachers have this ability, but the teachers who created this splendid history lesson certainly did, as did all the teachers who won grants and the many others who carry out similar kinds of approaches to teaching every day without special assistance.

Another elementary art teacher began with the idea of making paper with the children, designing a homemade printing press, and working with classroom teachers to elicit student poetry, drawings, and historical pieces to be printed in books that the children were to publish for the school library, parents, and friends. Along the way, children studied paper, printing, and the story of literacy: how cheap paper and moveable type made it possible for many people to have access to print. China, Egypt, Gutenberg, and the children all connected together in a project that resulted in lovingly made books from the school press. World history made sense, because the children made it so.

Stories like these arise in every school where teachers are trusted to create a curriculum after having learned new things they can't wait to share with their students. In every case, the curricula that work most energetically for the children are those ideas that begin with the children's own cultures and with a concrete particular—not generalized Culture, but *this* school's history; *this* piece of paper, *this* insect, *this* metaphor—and proceed to explore its meaning, its relationship to other particulars of culture, and its connections to a larger world. To begin anywhere else is to begin with preset, pre-known abstractions that leave the children out of the process of making meaning. Teachers who begin with concrete particulars must constantly relate what the children discover to that larger world. It is not enough just to make paper or eat Chinese food. One needs to know how and why paper making evolved, how and why Chinese diets developed, how these technologies and customs related to political or administrative needs or climate or health, how they were used in their place of origin and adopted in other places, who was privileged to use them and who was not—always, always, to tease out the contextual meanings of it all.

I am obviously of the party of particularists. Generalizations are the business of the children, who will draw them after many opportunities to study minutiae, to follow those bits and pieces of cultures wherever they may lead, to trace their meanings from the connections they are able to perceive. I want no talk in school of "poetry" or of "history" or of "science." I want only talk of this poem, this evidence, this object. The specifics—the *what* of the curriculum, need not be selected from on high, but should begin with the objects suggested by the children's cultural contexts. Teachers, working with the matter of the children and the school, are highly capable of finding objects that can lead out from the particular to a larger world. The trick is to be sure they are themselves curious, energetic people, ready to help the children follow out an idea as far as they can using the threads of meaning that can link the particular to the general, across fields and subjects, across cultures, across history, science, math, and imaginative thinking of all kinds, whither it will. This is particularly difficult for high school teachers, limited as they are by the deeply walled corridors of departments and disciplines, of graduation requirements and densely packed textbooks, and of decades of mandates to cover vast acreages of subject matter one millimeter deep. It is far more accessible to elementary teachers whose curricular scope includes all subject areas. Indeed, elementary teachers all over this country are already transforming their classrooms with authentic texts, inquiries, and pedagogies that place students at the center of the work to be done in school. High school teachers have also proven that with support and encouragement, and often with partners from other classrooms, museums, dance companies, archives, and industrial labs, they can begin to identify texts and objects that will stimulate their students' thinking and embark on the journey towards knowledge. That's what I would like to call "teacherly" teaching.

The purpose of such teaching lies in assisting students to discover their own voices. When artists describe their own development, they describe the critical moments, involving first absorption, later confrontation, with the culture of the past or the dissonances that arise when one culture conflicts with another. The artist makes new things out of such conflicts, happily using and transforming whatever materials lie ready to hand to make something new.[15] Artists see themselves as rebellious Promethians, bringing new mythologies into being out of the shards of the old. Many a minority artist in the United States sees this process as peculiar to minority art; in reality, it's peculiar to art as a whole in a Romantic world, where truly new artistic vision is always a minority affair—not because the artist is a person of color, but more interestingly because the Romantic artist sees herself as a lone voice in the wilderness or rebel in a stuffy mansion, a maker of declarations of independence.

An education that dares to go beyond the failed approaches of rote memorization of verities also willingly accepts the risk entailed, that children will reject and refashion the culture. Fear of such refashioning has prevented us from giving full voice to our children in the past. Fear that they will destroy our fondest beliefs holds us back. But we can also trust that they will instead fashion a stronger democracy than any we have yet enjoyed.

Giving voice to students means creating a genuinely multicultural curriculum. Using the arts as a way into school and a method for student creation of culture brings the children directly into contact with the "other." The whole point of reading a poem is to get inside someone else's skin. The whole reason for a picture is to see with someone else's eyes. The whole pleasure in the arts is to smell, taste, feel, experience as someone else has done, and yet paradoxically to recognize this new and different vision as something corresponding with deeply felt, already possessed knowledge of one's own. Why restrict such experiences to American arts or Western arts or Latino arts or any other kind of arts? Artists transcend national and ethnic boundaries precisely because they are rooted in particular cultures. Jamaica Kincaid's West Indian Catholic girlhood is particular, but her portrayal of Annie John, a young girl coming of age, and of her love for her parents, so deep it sometimes seems akin to hatred, is my coming of age, too. Kincaid's heroine is not "other" to me. She is me. She tells me how it is that I am what I am. She gives me ways of knowing I can find nowhere else on earth. And yet I also take pleasure in her particular world—in the way the sun shines on her father's newly caught fish, or the smell of her mother's freshly laundered dress.

Kincaid is a mediator, an interpreter, a translator of her world into mine and mine into hers. She is worth spending time with. The world is full of such writing, of such opportunities to learn through someone else's experience and vision. I hope that writers like Kincaid can enter many classrooms and thereby the lives of young writers still forming their own voices, so they can take on her voice, transform it into their own, and give back to the world something new and valuable.

Teachers must be artists to help this happen, to mediate between the Kincaids, the neighborhood history, the making of paper, and the classroom.[16] Studying the varying successes of minority children in U.S. schools, John Ogbu has observed that black children who fail in school do so because they maintain boundaries against the culture of school, fearing to lose their home culture. To avoid assimilation, they believe, their personal integrity depends on cleaving to the group culture and rejecting anything and everything that appears to have the tang of white culture about it.[17] Ogbu asserts that minority children who succeed, and most do, are those who manage to maintain, negotiate, and use both cultures, each in their appropriate settings.

I would go further. I would seek a schooling that encouraged children to draw on elements of both cultures in school itself, alternately, in combination, in any way appropriate to their finding unique voices for themselves—flexible, plastic voices to use as they see fit. A democratic education, one that prepared students not just for eventual civic participation, but one that modeled civic participation in its very methods, is a schooling for usable, practical ends.[18] A voice is a tool, various for various contexts and purposes. A voice is the sound you hear when you read; it's the vision you see in a picture; it's the reasoning at work in a problem being solved; it's the technique, craft, artistry, method, and discipline at work when someone makes something, acts, or moves. It's the person's style, the flavor and feel of a way of doing that's uniquely his. Each voice grows out of its personal cultural web. But each voice, dependent as it is on primordial relationships, must nevertheless learn to speak to a larger world, reaching out beyond its context to interpret its culture in such a way as to become accessible to others.

In all the multicultural talk we see much discussion of making culture available to children, but nothing about children making their cultures available to others. The old adage about never having to learn something so well as when one is required to teach it to someone else functions here. Students need to tell each other and the world what they know—in order to find out what they know. Through the telling, they will learn. Through the telling they will interpret the world as they see it to the rest of us. A curriculum becomes multicultural when the children, rooted in their cultures, find ways of teaching those cultures to each other and to us. And when they are engaged in doing so, they will be doing the work of the school, whose business is teaching and learning. The artistry of that belongs, ultimately, in the hands of the children.

Bringing School Home
and Leading Children Out

Every child's first experience of school entails a terrifying alienation. When minorities complain that school represents an alien culture, a place where children feel cut off from the supportive comforts of their language, neighborhood, and home, where they are exposed to the demands of a soulless, distant, cold world, they express what all children experience to some extent on leaving home for the institutional world of school. School is the place where the child must leave behind special ties, the loving forgiveness of the family, the warmth, the affection, the world where the child is expected to do nothing she does not wish to do, to enter a place where, for the first time in her life and with none of these home supports available for succor, she is asked to do something at a stranger's bidding.

As a society, we have agreed that children are required to effect this enormous change in their lives no later than the age of six. The fact that school is forbidding, alien, and unloving is not a situation peculiar to minority children. But for them the alienation may include an additional burden, since schools essentially belong to people and ideas that may be very distant from the child's experience. School may use a language the child does not know, and school may expect you to pay attention or sit still or carry out tasks you've never been asked to do before in ways that are foreign to you and your family's culture. Some of this is an alienation special to people of color; some of it is alienating to children regardless of race, class, or sex.

On my own first day of first grade, when we were all told to rise and recite the Lord's Prayer, I rose, but I was in a state of shock and despair. I'd never heard of the Lord's Prayer. I was the only one in the room unable to recite along with the others. They knew something I didn't. They were ahead of me. I was unprepared. I had grown up on a street flanked on one end by the public elementary school and on the other by the church, rectory, convent, and school of an enormous Catholic parish. I was the only child on the block who, when asked the favorite question, "Are you Catholic or Public?" had learned to answer "Public." I arrived in first grade convinced that "Public" was my religion. And yet, I obviously had missed something. All the strange children from other blocks knew that prayer; I alone did not.

School presents children with things to do all day, some of which are fun, some merely odd or puzzling, and most things one has never been asked to do before. That alienation from home has in its essence something right and proper. School is a time and a place that requires work from the child for the first time. The question to be asked is whether the work it requires is either sufficient or meaningful.

Meaningful work should be a major part of the heritage from the Protestant work ethic. The joys of school can only come through work. Gerald Early has put it succinctly: "We must work to make these children *work* for the life of the mind." He adds, "Education must be our self-inflicted, passionate and collective contamination of strange and different wisdom."[19] It is precisely in the contamination with the other, the new, the different—all of which are by definition difficult—that education thrives.

Early's insistence on passion reminds us that the bifurcations that have taken hold of the multicultural debate are false dichotomies. The labor of the mind is a passionate labor. Many educators like to split the "cognitive" from the "affective," new adjectives for "head" and "heart." Indeed, some may want to dismiss my focus on curriculum as merely attending to cognitive growth while ignoring the role of the affective and the social in public schools. I believe, with Gerald Early and many other thoughtful educators, however, that these are misleading distinctions. What separates us from each other is a failure to see that the cognitive and affective realms are inextricably interwoven. The student who writes a passionate poem is making the connection between the labor of the mind and the feeling he has for his little brother. Working with language enables him to express that feeling.

Similarly, the student's private world becomes, through the act of writing and publishing his writing, a public act and a way of inviting public discourse to interact with private feeling. Thomas Bender similarly calls for a new kind of synthesis of history that will link the many and various social histories together with political history. All of the teachers we have witnessed in this book who are struggling with new curricula are striving to make connections between the particulars of their students' personal lives and generic capacities that will enable them to move out powerfully into the world as young adults.

Reconnecting the head and the heart, the private and the public, the social and the political, the particular with the generic is what our schoolrooms can do for all of us. In many ways, schoolrooms are the best and most appropriate places in which these connections can take place, for they consist of the young who are in transition from that most private and feeling world of childhood to the places they will occupy in the social, political, and public world of adult action.

The arts and humanities are peculiarly the school vehicles for reconnecting head and heart because so much of what they have to offer us are ways to articulate and understand the heart and, through public symbols, talk about our otherwise unutterable feelings. The arts and humanities allow us simultaneously to create individual identity and to connect the individual with a larger community. All of school should acknowledge that children's work, whether in mathematics or in poetry, begins with the personal, and through disciplined work, creates public narratives and symbols that all of us can understand.

School will remain an alien place until the children in it make it their own by contributing to it their work. School needs to value work and the creations of the students' hands. And it needs to value that work by increasing, rather than decreasing, the standards for work expected in school. The busywork that has kept students occupied—the worksheets, the fill-in-the-blanks, the answering of questions that teachers and textbooks set and to which there is only one right answer—must be replaced by the real work of doing history and science, mathematics, reading and writing, arts of all kinds, and languages (not just being told about them by somebody else). And it means studying one's own language and the languages of others, as many as possible, rigorously and continuously, by using those languages from the earliest school years on. Language learning is indeed hard work. But it is the surest, fastest, most complete key to otherness. When one finds oneself thinking in someone else's language, one has crossed a border that binds the mind. That's multicultural; and yes, that's work.

The doing begins with the first day of school. It is not postponed to a future neverland that never comes. Knowledge isn't just vocabulary; one learns the names of the things in the course of the doing. Far better that our eighth-grade language skills teacher who worried about similes and metaphors had worked like Terron Kane's teacher did, with the students' own poetry. Terron's metaphors become the subject of the classroom conversation, during which this teacher might provide the term *metaphor* when the real need for such a word arises in the course of classroom discussion of the poem. Vocabulary is certainly helpful, but no substitute for learning. Terron's work presents us all with something of much greater value. The poem itself is a metaphor that allows us as readers to enter into her joy in contemplating her brother—that allows us to join her and "jump leap up and tuch the stars." Terron's poem creates a common place where she and the reader can join together to know and feel something new.

School will always be alien from early childhood, and rightfully so. Students know they are entering an institution that represents at its best the most august purposes, ideals, and principles of the society. To enter the school building is to enter into the grandest civic purposes of the society. There are purposes to be accomplished by asserting the differences between school and home, neighborhood and community. It needn't be forbidding, but the very fact that work is required in school must be quite clear to everyone involved—teachers, students, and parents. The work required must cease to be trivial, however, or disrespectful of the workers themselves, the children who attend. The children who play the game of school, who willingly submit themselves year after year, know full well when their time is being wasted, when tasks assigned are merely ways of satisfying someone else's authority rather than the children's own curiosity. We won't improve that if we substitute a curriculum that seeks to make students feel good instead of stretching them to do good.

Opening American Minds

‿‿‿

As public schooling has developed, its structures, purposes, subjects, text-books and methods have tended toward ever-increasing standardization; President Bush and the governors of the fifty states, along with many citizens of all kinds, pushed toward a national curriculum and national testing for the first time in our education history. At the same time, the most promising experiments in education of the past decade have emphasized locally devised, teacher-generated curricula embedded in the particular cultures of the students they teach. The federal wish is for a way to assure that all Americans learn a certain bedrock curriculum they can hold in common; the multicultural experiments acknowledge the need for teaching the principles of our democracy, but choose to demonstrate these through study of cultural materials not always of the Protestant, Anglo-Saxon heritage. Are these irreconcilable positions? Is one of these approaches to curriculum making better than the other? Can national standards and a national ideology be taught through the use of particulars? Is there, perhaps, some other, quite different alternative?

Traditionalists are not in fact asking that curriculum remain the same as it has been for much of the past forty years, but that it should be reformed to become a more rigorous teaching of the democratic heritage, acknowledging the "contributions" to America of a broader range of people than have hitherto been included in school. Multiculturalists, in their more radical incarnations doubting that a more rigorous, Western-centered education will alter the fundamental assumptions in Western thought that are so alienating for people of color and for the poor, wish to identify for themselves a new story or set of stories to tell about America in school.

Unfortunately, many multiculturalists in their sometimes naive enthusiasm for the holiness of the people end up offering what Guillermo Gómez-Peña has called "a kind of Esperantic Disney World, a *tutti frutti* cocktail of cultures, languages and art forms in which everything becomes everything else."[20] Such multiculturalism hardly improves on the debunked melting-pot myth. Gómez-Peña asserts we must have criteria of value and hard work in order to persuade children that school is a place worth spending time in. From the point of view of many multiculturalists, the culture of America no longer remains a single, sought-after way of being. That is not to say the values of democracy no longer hold—it is only to say that the interpretation of values in cultural acts differs among the many different groups inhabiting the continent. The producers of culture can now be seen to inhabit many places, not just one; and whenever two such cultures interact—and they interact every day for every American—a borderland is created where conversation can take place.[21]

The traditionalist claims there are verities that every American needs to know and believe in order to become American. Many multiculturalists are more interested in the possibility that there are multiple answers to multiple questions that could be raised about who we are, how we came to be this way, what we know and how we know it. These are perhaps the fundamental questions to ask in any subject. How we know what we know is the question that begins with each child's knowledge and proceeds to probe it to help her discover how she knows. It's the "how" that in turn spurs her on to knowing something new. Ironically, many radical multiculturalists are fundamentalists, not wishing to know anything beyond the verities of their own folk, not wishing students to question. Such multiculturalists share an ideological position with the traditionalists who also believe in truths to be told in school. One paradox of Western thought, which occurs in a traditionalist's curriculum as well as in a multicultural reformer's, is that we can know by faith, by reason, or by experience. But we can also know by imagination, which refashions what we know by other means into something new.

The argument between faith and reason ought to be a major subject in school—one that students should explore with passionate work. What kind of work the students do depends on who chooses how they will spend their time in school. Such choices determine the values of the institution. One can choose, as most elementary schools do, to spend children's time reading manufactured prose and filling out worksheets that ask questions about it. Such a choice tells the student that his time is to be valued as the equivalent of the value of the words he is reading. One could, alternatively, spend time in school telling children that they have "contributed" to America, that America has a "story," and that they are a part of it, without ever inviting them into the story as makers of it. In such a curriculum, students learn that value resides primarily in the story, and very little in themselves. Or one could spend time in school asking students to tell part of the story, beginning with themselves and proceeding from their particulars to perceptions of the larger story that school can structure out of the multiple stories the class has to tell. In such a curriculum, the student knows from the inside that her time is as valuable to knowledge-making as that of the various figures of history about whom she is asked to read.

Multiculturalists do not quarrel with some of the basic liberal arts notions about school. They assume we are in the business of teaching democracy, but wish that democracy be part of how we teach as well as what we teach; they assume we will want to go on teaching things called math and science, history, language, and the arts, and that these subjects will structure the school curriculum. Who chooses what we mean by these subjects, however, is where disagreement steps in.

For nearly a decade I have been working with teachers all around the country, in huge city school systems and tiny rural communities alike, to try to give children of the poor access to American and international history, philosophy, literature, reading of all kinds, writing, the other arts, languages, and the infinite possibilities that these subjects can open up for their lives. In each place I have worked, I have asked the schools and their communities to define for themselves how they would ideally spend students' time in school. Teachers' impulses have invariably been to reach beyond the standardized curriculum, the one-size-fits-all mentality that says the curriculum is the equivalent of the textbook even when the textbook says very little and is not a book worth reading.

When asked what they want their children to become, teachers have told me they want readers and writers; young people who exercise their curiosity through school tasks; risk-takers who can engage each other's different perceptions or ideas, not afraid to make mistakes publicly, but to use these as further opportunities for learning; people willing to disagree in order to engage in the joint enterprise of learning.

This is another of the paradoxes of knowledge. It is through disagreement that learning comes. Textbooks aren't just for memorizing, they're for taking issue with; but it's impossible to take issue with a pudding that's so bland that it offers no stimulation to even the most delicate palate. The texts we give our children need to offer real voices, idiosyncratic voices— Madison's, Jefferson's, Jamaica Kincaid's—and the myriad voices of the flesh-and-blood people who have made America as well as those from around the world. As they are now, textbooks seek to offend no one and generally pass, like pudding, benignly through the system without either particularly harming it or offering it anything of substance to help it grow. They allow the least capable of our nation's teachers to get through the school day; they hinder our most capable teachers from helping students to take part in the rigors of thought or action.[22]

As long as nationally produced textbooks continue to substitute the language of leveling, bureaucratic committees for the tougher voices of individuals, we will continue to teach a secondhand or even thirdhand, hand-me-down, curriculum. Students need to get their own hands on language, forceful thought, and idiosyncratic voices, or they will never be able to differ enough from the standard to develop voices of their own. A standard curriculum of standard textbook derivation is a *group* curriculum—one that insists so thoroughly on conformity that individualism never has an opportunity to arise. Traditionalists who wish to emphasize individualism need to insist that textbooks cease to offer language on any subject that lacks individual voice. Ironically, when they do they will find themselves of the same party as the multiculturalists, whose aim is to develop the individual voices of all our children.

A multicultural education, in this sense, is an education whose purpose is to develop individualism. It is one where children encounter the voices of diverse cultures—including their own cultures of origin, each other's, and many others from the world's civilizations—out of which encounters they forge their own individual voices. Paolo Freire has said, "The more the people participate in the process of their own education . . . the more the people participate in the development of their own selves. The more the people become themselves, the better the democracy."[23] In becoming themselves, children need to draw on both the cultures they bring to school with them and the cultures they encounter in school. Neither traditionalists nor multiculturalists can ask the children to choose—to do so would be either to go on shutting twenty to thirty percent of our children out of participation in school or to prevent their access to multiple sources of learning to become themselves.

For all the trumpeting of liberal education by traditionalists or its vilification by multicultural reformers, a truly liberal education is a highly disquieting affair. The humanities do not always provide comfort. They suggest disruption just as often as security. A tolerance for ambiguity some of the time and for disturbances of the mind most of the time is as necessary for learning as a preliminary set of beliefs that enables the student to tolerate those ambiguities and challenges. Fundamentalists worldwide are distressed by this aspect of a liberal education. Disturbances of the mind, they feel, would threaten tradition, the solid ground on which the continuance of the good things in life depends.

I would suggest that we begin to trust our children. Primordial ties, of family, religion, and so on, cannot and will not be taught in school. These foundational beliefs come from elsewhere in a secular democracy. We have to be able to trust to the home, church, and other private institutions to instill or not, as they choose, whatever of tradition children bring to school. Our job in school is to accept those customs and habits as starting places for education, but neither as means nor ends to the kind of learning school will offer. Our trust in the children must depend on their bringing to school with them enough of cultural traditions and beliefs to offer a foundation for education, and we must trust them enough not to discard either what they bring to education or what education has to offer in return. To go to public school in America at all is to accept the belief in American modernity. To reject that given is to wish for a fundamentalism not available in public school, but which can easily be provided in private school, religious school, or at home.

Neither the culture of traditional America nor the culture of any one of its diverse groups is subject to being fixed, known, or finished. Only dead cultures have such characteristics. In a century when massive changes have disrupted whole populations,[24] it is not surprising to find a universal yearning for certainties linked to an earlier, simpler, more territorially centered life. We fear for the continued capacity of the United States to provide a good life for ourselves—as well as for the millions more who wish they, too, could partake. Such fears drive some of us to insist that our future lies in the myths of our past, that all new Americans need to acquire the generalized culture of the country. Minorities fear that generalized culture. It drives them to insist on retrieving or inventing a fixed culture of their own that will link them to the verities of *their* past. Neither group trusts the children to hang on to the beliefs that matter; both groups fear the loss of fundamental beliefs unless children are carefully indoctrinated in school—unless as little as possible is offered there to disturb the mind.

It is time to trust the children. If we put in their hands the raw materials of what the world's many cultures have produced—if we encourage the children to use what seems good to them from the many cultures we offer, their own included—they will make moral decisions on how to use these various materials that will make them and us proud. The only eventuality we genuinely need to fear is that of the ignorance that comes from giving the children no choices to make. Such schooling leaves them as it found them, and leaves our common culture undisturbed—safely and securely dead.

We must trust that the culture will change, and that it is the business of children to change it. Through the changes they enact, moral choice will remain; democracy will remain; value and the critical capacity to recognize value will remain. The question is only one of whether the culture will change because of school or despite it, and of whether we trust our own children to carry out this cultural work.

Morality is implied by every choice we make. To choose to spend children's time reading and writing is a moral choice; to choose to require that they think carefully about their reading and writing is another. To choose to offer them several versions of history is to enact another moral lesson, one which explicitly asks students to interpret those versions both critically and morally. These are moral acts available to the youngest child as well as the oldest if the choices of texts and versions are made carefully and if children clearly see that they are being offered genuine choices. We need not fear students' decisions if we tell them in all honesty that there are endless questions about history and that the purpose of doing history is to go on asking these questions, and to go on revising our answers as fresh perspectives come to light.

Our concern in this pursuit of knowledge is to make sure our students perceive their education as an endless act of becoming, an ever more sophisticated capacity to see new subtleties and patterns in what earlier seemed plain and well known. Such an education sets the standard for knowing, while continuing to want to know more, that is the central moral teaching of school—the act of making critical choices that one may oneself, in the future, come to recognize as wrong and in need of further revision. Such an education has certainties and verities only insofar as it depends on constant, critical, moral choice.

Doing Good

*No illusion is more powerful than that of the inevitability
and propriety of one's own beliefs and judgements.*

BARBARA HERRNSTEIN SMITH,
CONTINGENCIES OF VALUE

In a rural school in South Carolina teachers worked together to create a curriculum based on a craft practiced by many local African-American women. Sweet-grass basket weaving is a tradition handed down through the generations that helps eke out a living for this poor Low Country community. The students were skeptical of the value of studying this material. One young man, incredulous at the suggestion that he might want to investigate the baskets and their history, was heard to say, "You mean that trash my mother makes?" The students nevertheless began to interview mothers, grandmothers—and in this student's case—a great-grandmother, collecting information about the design, lore, and practice of weaving. The high point of the year came during a visit to a museum where Ghanaian basketry was on display. There, our young man saw work with the same patterns as those woven by his family. The link between his family's work and a hitherto unknown African past electrified him. He wrote a thirty-two-page essay on family history, connecting his family outwards to a newly discovered homeland and using that link to gain a larger understanding of his mother's work in the context of international art history. The paper was not only long; it was inspired. A student who had never done well in school and who was not considered adept at reading or writing transcended all expectations, including his own.

Respect for the work of the children in school ought also to extend to respect for work of all kinds. Self-esteem, the capacity to be comfortable with oneself, secure in the knowledge that one is valued by others, comes from knowing one has given value to the world. That comes from the extent to which one has a capacity to work—to become immersed in the pursuit of the task and to judge with a critical capacity the goodness of the results. The task must appear of value to the student if she is to wish to work at it. And that is where multicultural education begins. Teachers, like our friends who assigned the research on sweet-grass baskets, must convince the student to get started. Once a start has been made, the student will take off—will dig, extend, and search out, as the teacher prompts, guides, and suggests new places to look and new possibilities to explore. The students' pride and self-esteem come from the work itself and knowledge of where they stand in the scheme of things as workers. It comes from knowledge that they have worked hard, that they have discovered something worth knowing and doing for themselves, and that they've made something worth the time of others to contemplate, study, and respond to. The student must see himself as a necessary, contributing member of a community of students, out of whose work comes dialogue that furthers his community's knowledge. A continuing dialogue begins anew with each new task, but layers the tasks each undertakes with all the others—before, now, and yet to come.

Are there no facts to learn, no verities to transmit, no absolutes in our society, you wonder? Does every child make her own curriculum? Aren't the *Federalist Papers* of greater value, more worthwhile as the subject of school time, than grandmother's sweet-grass baskets? Shouldn't children at least spend most of their school work on the things (like the *Federalist Papers*) that we all share, rather than on baskets that only a handful of us will ever see?

I want both the baskets and the *Federalist Papers*. But I doubt that the student will ever get to the *Federalist Papers* unless he's given a chance to start with something he can do, and use that to find his way into the school and the society. The question needs to be, how do we get from the basketry research to the *Federalist Papers?* How do we provide this student with a task that enables him to make that connection for himself? I am convinced that, having written a sophisticated piece of history, our student is now in a much better position than ever before in his life to read historical matter of many kinds. The critical question for his teacher is how to go on with him to the steps that will eventuate in his becoming an avid reader and writer, a knower of some of the foundation texts of our democracy. But the student also needs to know that *he* has become a contributor to those texts, that his essay on baskets has a validity in the world all of its own that can be held up alongside other historical texts and not be found wanting.

Value comes from the moral choices we make concerning how we spend children's time in school. But how do we make such choices in the first place, and who is allowed to make them? Principally, the teacher helps the student make choices, but she must so choose in the context of the community's collective decisions. The community, after all, is paying for school and sending its children there. Their collective decisions about why they wish to do so and what should happen once the children graduate must guide the work of teachers and children from start to finish. That community—of parents, laborers, managers, politicians, artists, and educators alike—must rationalize their competing interests in schools, but also rise above mere self-interest to act on behalf of the common weal in deciding how choices should be made and value determined in school.

We have discussed the civic purposes of school, but we also hear a great deal about the economic-success purposes of school—that school must primarily prepare students for the workplace, so the content of school should focus on practical studies that enable young people to earn their living. This argument is most often heard from policy makers and business people who lament young graduates' lack of skills. In the early 1980s it led to pressure on schools to reemphasize the basics—what used to be called the three Rs—at the expense of "the frills," or the smorgasbord schooling of the sixties and seventies. But utilitarian education, interpreted by legislators as "drill for skill," test, and embarrass them into learning, simply hasn't worked. Spending more time on drill and skill means more time spent boring children, failing to reach them, disaffecting them even further from school success and work success. A long time ago W. E. B. DuBois taught us to educate human beings, not workers: "And the final product of our training must be neither a psychologist nor a brickmason, but a man. And to make men, we must have ideals, broad, pure, and inspiring ends of living—not sordid money-getting, not apples of gold." He added that we achieve such ends "only by human strife and longing."[25]

If school were a place that valued work, the students would learn to do valuable work and value it in school, not just after graduation. Schooling for a democracy, of the kind I have been describing, is a schooling for a much broader, more important purpose than merely schooling for an entry-level job. If we can school in such a way as to value the work of children as education's highest value, we will have accomplished the greater goal of the democracy into which the practical lifework of each adult American fits as the lesser goal.

The most precious commodity of school is time. When teachers attempt to do anything out of the ordinary—to teach instead of simply to cover, to explore instead of to drill, to create instead of to parrot—they complain that there's never enough time to pay attention to each child, to read her essays, to coach her, to study a new subject well enough to be able to teach it, to search out and bring new books or poets or lab demonstrations to school, to get the kids to a dig or a salt marsh or a museum. Time and the bell toll a death knell to such teaching and learning every day. And with each day's passing, an irretrievable opportunity for a child to learn is forever lost. However we choose to spend children's time, we are making moral choices—putting value on what we expect them to do. The community has the right to describe in broad outline what kinds of things it wishes to value, but power alone should not determine who gets to make all of those choices. The business community has many opportunities to exercise its power, but should not alone make all moral choices for children. School administrators have exerted great power in interpreting—often foolishly—the dictates of legislators and imposing these interpretations on teachers in the form of standardized curricula, adopted textbooks, or required tests.

In a world that trusted children, we would have to learn to trust teachers as well to act as moral guides with every choice of curriculum they make every day. Teachers are the ones who mediate between what children already know and what we as a community want them to know. Teachers must be profoundly knowledgeable both of children and of the multiple possible choices they could make on the children's behalf. To date, we have never trusted teachers enough to make such choices, preferring to let the textbook industry and committees of legislators and administrators do so instead. None of these people, however, work in classrooms, see the needs of the children, or mediate their development, and none of them are specifically trained to do so. Teachers, presented with other people's choices of curriculum, have been constrained to use what lies at hand rather than to exercise choice; yet when given the opportunity, they range broadly in cultural materials of all kinds to persuade children to read, to write, and to learn.

Choosing one piece of reading rather than another is one of the complex decisions that form the crux of the debate over multicultural education. One group says, let them read the *Federalist Papers,* and another claims that's just more white, European hegemony and we've had enough of that. The first group claims that the *Federalist Papers* are more valuable than other texts because they express the fundamental principles of our democracy and therefore have importance for us all. The second group says that it's nonsense to claim a universal value for a book. To do so is only to say the book agrees with your own group's beliefs, which we don't necessarily share; there are no universals, only dominant groups who claim universality for themselves and impose it on the rest of us.

One professor of English who has thought carefully about the problem, Barbara Herrnstein Smith, points out that canonical books are for the first time being offered to *"noncanonical audiences"* (author's italics) who don't read them the same way they have been read in the past by the group that produced them. New audiences bring with them new contexts for reading that don't necessarily share the beliefs of the traditional culture. New audiences may not value these texts as highly as the traditional audience does, or may have new ways of reading them.[26]

The Western world has for centuries selected and taught "masterworks" because we found in them enduring qualities transcending time and place; we have therefore believed them to possess universal value. If these works fail to affect a reader, says the traditionalist, the fault lies with the reader, not the work. Ultimately, only a few in every society have sufficient taste to choose for the many; they must therefore try to educate the many to cultivate tastes that imitate those of the elite. Alternative tastes are considered deviant and incorrect.[27] The texts chosen by the few for the many are supposed to be timeless, so in teaching them we must suppress or ignore those aspects of them no longer valued by the readers of our day. Another writer suggests that we should all just accept the elitism of education, reminding us that Homer knows more than most of us do. Homer's value in the classroom stretches our minds in ways we have come to value. We do privilege certain kinds of thought—critical consciousness, logical argument, and precision of language, all of which are evident in great writers.[28] A student of classical philosophy, Martha Nussbaum, adds that we shouldn't have to give up Enlightenment universals like justice in order to elevate the "caring" values of the community. She thinks it should be possible to reconcile personal virtues with universal ideals.[29]

Many school reformers, however, wish to remind us that the masterworks leave out the values and opinions of the oppressed—of women, of the conquered, of the daily family and social life that struggles with a different, more personal set of issues. They wish folk art and folk life to merit the same attention in school that elite culture has in the past. Folklore is to popular wisdom as canonical literature is to the justification of the powerful.[30] Many teachers and school systems have eagerly adopted folklore and popular culture for classroom use in an effort to identify materials that represent the new audiences in their student bodies. When the necessity to choose arises—to spend school time on one book at the expense of another—each of us may too easily assume ourselves to be the norm, judging the rest of the world to be more or less normal depending on conformity or deviance from ourselves. An "A" student then becomes one who agrees with me; an "F," one who disagrees.

I would suggest that the question of what to choose should involve both the materials of traditional Western culture and of a great variety of other cultures as well. We need profoundly able teachers to make choices of what students should read in school, and we need plenty of them. We need children to experience the characteristics of choice as made by many different minds. We need students to learn from many teachers precisely because different minds will make different choices. And we even need students to read the same things under the guidance of different teachers, because each reading is different, each new interpretation an opportunity to rediscover an old text in a new light. The difference of choice needs to be part of the conversation in school just as much as the difference of interpretation. Otherwise, we would put our children to school with one teacher and leave them alone for twelve years.

Different choices, moreover, will have different values for the child at different times. The same child bored by *The Scarlet Letter* at age fifteen might come back to it as an adult with a different attitude; the same text as read with different teachers might have different results. Comic books can be good or bad of their kind in some contexts and of great or little value in others. It is impossible to say that *The Scarlet Letter* is absolutely more valuable than a comic book.

The teacher's job is to teach something about reading and something about America—if *The Scarlet Letter* fulfills such purposes, it is a good choice. If it leaves children swearing never to read another word of Hawthorne, it is not so good. The "fault" lies not in Hawthorne, the teacher, or the student, but in the transaction between the three of them. If that transaction ends in bitterness, time has not been well spent and value has been lost. If comic books can teach about reading and America, then time has been well spent. If the child reads only comic books, and if otherwise he would not read at all, the time is still well spent. But if the child can do nothing further and stops there, further choices need to be made.

The child should be expected to do work that has validity for him, for the community of learners in the class, and for the society outside of the school. Every choice the teacher makes, therefore, must reverberate among all of these potential validities. If the child fails to read *The Scarlet Letter,* the time invested is invalid for the child even though there was a potential for it to be valid in the eyes of the society. If the child reads *Spiderman* happily, he has perhaps done valid work for himself but he has not yet done valid work for the society. The teacher must make choices that give each student a chance to move from what she already knows to what she does not yet know. Each choice must move the child further out toward the values of the society at its best. But each choice must also be sure to bring the child along with it in that journey.

Values that decide those choices are the broad ones set by a community that wants its children to be able to participate fully in the society. Those values will demand literacy, quantitative capacities, participation in civic life and the capacity to do so. Parents will want even more for their children, spurring the teacher on to make choices that take the child further than merely a love of reading comic books. But if *The Scarlet Letter* fails, no amount of the *Federalist Papers* is likely to lead to success. We may after all have to allow some time to be spent on *Spiderman.*

Because values are not absolute, but contextual, that does not mean there are no values. There are no values outside of contexts and contingencies, as Barbara Herrnstein Smith has put it, but there are always values.[31] The teachers' job will be to assert their own cultural values in their choices, and to represent among them a variety of values from which the students will make the ultimate choices. Boas and Geertz tell us that we inhabit many shifting and multiple communities, each with its many complex value systems. We owe to family, to friends, to religion, to ethnicity, and to the nation a variety of different kinds of allegiances built on intersecting values, no one of which can dominate entirely the way we value what we learn in school. If the family fears that its traditions will be destroyed by school, school fears that its offerings are undermined by family values it does not share. All of these value systems, however, need to be allowed full play in school so that students are free to choose what will make sense of conflicting values. To leave a child unchanged in *any* beliefs, however, is to leave him uneducated. Fundamental beliefs will be challenged by school. To disagree with such a purpose is to wish for a private education whose purpose can sustain fundamental beliefs.

Ethnicity does not necessitate shared beliefs, only shared circumstances. The "ethnos," or tribe, devises its beliefs in accordance with survival, in response to the conditions it finds itself facing.[32] Such beliefs are an appropriate subject of *study* in school, but not appropriate for inculcation. An ethnic group should not have to defend itself, however, in school. School needs to be a place that is safe enough for all of the children in it to take risks with their beliefs—to evaluate them, encounter new ones, and to learn possibilities that will provide safety in a larger, extratribal world. That is as true for the tribe of European Protestants as for other tribes. No one group's beliefs can be sacred in a democratic school. But the school itself should be a refuge where the tribal can be shaped individually to the child's need to negotiate many intersecting worlds. School ultimately needs to be a place where children learn "worldliness," the capacity to use their personal knowledge to transcend their personal circumstances. This paradox, instead of forming a ground for contention, ought to be the very glory of schooling in a democratic society.

A monolingual child in a school trying to reform itself recently wrote: "Mi madre es importante. La noche pasada venía a la escuela para una conferencia. [*sic*] (My mother is important. Last night she came to school for a meeting.)"[33] The child's pride in her mother is matched by the mother's trust in the school. Parents are invited not just for bake sales, but for conversations with teachers about what they want their children to learn. In such ways, parents, children, and teachers can begin to tease out the intersections of their value systems and make the choices that will help the child learn. Teachers must be conversant with the child's culture and others, or at least willing and able to make connections among the cultures in the class. There is no easy way out: to attempt merely to impose one's own culture on children is to shut them out and fail to reach them. For a dominant group merely to go on imposing culture is to fail to connect; merely to inculcate the culture of the children is to fail equally. But to enlarge the vision—that is to succeed.

We're Doing It for Ourselves

◡〜

I have ever hated all nations, professions, and communities, and all my love is toward individuals: for instance, I hate the tribe of lawyers, but I love Counsellor Such-a-one, and Judge Such-a-one: so with physicians—I will not speak of my own trade—soldiers, English, Scotch, French, and the rest. But principally I hate and detest that animal called man, although I heartily love John, Peter, Thomas, and so forth. I have got materials toward a treatise proving the falsity of that definition animal rationale, *and to show it would be only* rationis capax.

JONATHAN SWIFT

In a democracy there are leaders, but decisions are made by all. The remaking of American education crucially needs to be imagined and carried out by the people for themselves. It is not good enough for a few federal leaders or a few academics or even a few state legislators to do this work. The very nature of the democratic vision requires precisely the kind of grassroots activism we are seeing in local education everywhere in the country today. All of us in positions of power simply need to back off, even or perhaps especially when we think we know better. It's time for the democracy to come of age, and for its people to devise their own education—not to suit the powerful, but to suit themselves, which is a more important and larger goal. Paternalistic education of the poor, which has operated now for one hundred and fifty years, perceives them as of low status and headed for a low-status life.[34] The poor themselves probably have quite a different notion of where their kids should head. If we want not only those kids but all of our children to succeed, we need quite simply to get out of their way. Teachers in cooperation with parents can create the borderland where the real work of the democracy could begin to take shape.

In a penetrating study of the woeful history of liberal reform efforts, Richard H. de Lone has reminded us that in a century of efforts to alleviate the problems of poverty through school reform, we have made no progress at all. The reason is that we confuse equal opportunity to participate in the democracy with equal chances at economic success. These two goals are in inevitable conflict, since the democratic ideal suggests equality whereas the economic ideal suggests inequality. A liberal economy will always leave some of us rich and others poor, a fact that occasionally bothers our otherwise libertarian conscience. As a result, we keep trying to mend matters, primarily by blaming poverty on adults and by trying to solve the poverty of children in school. Like many multiculturalists today, de Lone is convinced that a just society must mend itself in other ways than by reforming children and schools.[35]

If individualism seems to have dropped out of school, it is because school has stood for an economic inequality rather than a democratic egalitarian ideal. True individualism cannot become a part of school or of our democracy as long as economic inequality dominates our purposes for school. The public argument over education today, which pits group solidarity and multicultural education against individualists and traditional education, is less a political, ideological fight than class warfare disguised as ideology. Reformers who continue to pursue the liberal platform are perceived by multiculturalists, therefore, as perpetuating a class dominance that will never allow the poor to rise to *democratic* equality, because the game as played by those in power is an *economic* game.

The multicultural education reformer, therefore, is the one wishing, truly, to change the rules and the game, to make of school a democratic institution. This cannot be done *for* the people. They shall do it themselves. John Dewey in struggling to define democratic education imagined an education that prepared the individual constantly to restructure the environment in an active way. While Dewey cited Hegel on the need to subordinate the individual to the group, he also saw the need to overcome the limitations of the group—whether of class, race, or religion—to see the whole. Equality in democratic education is equal *intellectual* opportunity, not equal economic opportunity. Dewey taught us that too close an association between economic purposes and school purposes results in the perpetuation of class inequalities.[36]

Utilitarian purposes for education are narrow purposes, which perpetuate the hegemony of the powerful. The humanities and sciences therefore are necessary to liberate the mind and heart, but we must revise the way we think of these so as to avoid the subjects themselves becoming the end of education and its territory, and to avoid equally the idea that they should remain the preserve of the privileged, as they have been since ancient times. Dewey said education will never be truly democratic until we overcome Aristotle's separation of practical knowledge from reason, the poor from the privileged: "The problem of education in a democratic society is to do away with the dualism and to construct a course of studies which makes thought a guide of free practice for all and which makes leisure a reward of accepting responsibility for service, rather than a state of exemption from it."[37]

Traditionalists would like to continue to hold on to power, and they fear the shift in power that group activism represents. Yet almost four decades ago Talcott Parsons taught us that power in a democracy is not a zero sum game.[38] When the poor, and the schoolchildren, acquire power, it increases the power of all. Such power can never be given. Those activists seizing power over curriculum in their districts are simply taking it for themselves. That's part of the way democracy works. One can only hope that as they seize power, they will refrain from repeating the old power relationships of school that have served us until now—the relationships that leave the many as powerless as before.

All the presidents and all the governors, all the academics and liberal reformers and radicals, however, can neither make this revolution happen nor prevent it. The real revolution still needs to happen in the classroom where children and teachers work in the context of a community that sanctions the work. The purpose of that education will be to take children beyond what the home and community teach; but it will do so by beginning with what they know. Such an education will incorporate home and community and move far beyond them, with the family's blessing.

The curriculum I am advocating is one built downward from a set of broadly conceived community values—liberty, justice, literacy, and so on—and upward from particular texts and visions of these ideals. Such a curriculum searches out literary, philosophical, artistic, and historical writings that invite reverberations between the student and a transnational understanding of the world. This curriculum draws on poetry and the other arts for twelve years, and it insists on all students becoming powerful and graceful users of English and one additional language. It studies world history for twelve years and sees American history firmly within that international context, but it also invites students to construct narrative arguments that draw on the materials of history to explain causality and change over time. This curriculum also includes a rigorous study of the philosophies of many cultures and the varieties of contemporary philosophy, so that students can better understand and take active part in arguments concerning the values, choices, and conflicts of morality. Students would be provided with the techniques of argument of the humanities disciplines and enabled to use them to extend their understanding. In this curriculum, faith would not be taught but would be taught about; reason would help to discipline thought; experience would be one method of instruction, and imagination another. Heart, head, and hands will all be employed in generating new visions. This curriculum will have as its goal students who ask what we ought to know and how we know what we know, and who will be prepared at all grades to try to discover the answers to such questions. This curriculum will by definition be profoundly multicultural and international and democratic, and ultimately it will be the creation of the children themselves.

NOTES

I. American Revolution (1–31)

1. Larry Hayes, "Building Schools for Tomorrow," *Phi Delta Kappan* (January 1992), 413.

2. John I. Goodlad and Pamela Keating, eds., *Access to Knowledge: An Agenda for Our Nation's Schools* (New York: College Entrance Examination Board, 1990), 45. See also Children's Defense Fund, "An Advocate's Guide to Improving Education," September 1990.

3. See Richard H. de Lone, *Small Futures: Children, Inequality, and the Limits of Liberal Reform* (New York: Harcourt Brace Jovanovich, 1979).

4. Martin Trow, "The Second Transformation of American Secondary Education," in Jerome Karabel and A. H. Halsey, *Power and Ideology in Education* (New York: Oxford Univ. Press, 1977), 106.

5. Ibid., 107 and 109.

6. Debra Viadero, "Dropout Rates for 5 States," *Education Week* (23 September 1992), 24.

7. See Frederick Mosteller and Daniel P. Moynihan, eds., *On Equality of Educational Opportunity: Papers Deriving from the Harvard University Faculty Seminar on the Coleman Report* (New York: Random House, 1972) for analyses of the Coleman report, including Christopher S. Jencks, "The Coleman Report and the Conventional Wisdom," 69.

8. James A. Banks, *Multiethnic Education* (Needham Heights, Mass.: Allyn and Bacon, 1988), 11–12.

9. U.S. Bureau of the Census, *Statistical Abstract of the United States: 1991,* 111th edn., (Washington, D.C., 1991).

10. Lawrence H. Fuchs, *The American Kaleidoscope: Race, Ethnicity, and the Civic Culture* (Hanover, N.H.: University Press of New England, 1990), 278, 283, and 292–93.

11. I am convinced the large differential for Latinos is attributable to new immigrants being included with native-born Americans of Hispanic descent in these figures. See Part IV, "Words Fail Us," for a discussion of how the rate of English acquisition is similarly distorted by proportionately high rates of fresh immigration.

12. Russell Edgerton, "A Long, Deep View of Minority Achievement," *AAHE Bulletin* (April 1991), 3–7 and 30.

13. The Pew Higher Education Research Program, *Policy Perspectives* 4:2:C (Philadelphia: The Pew Charitable Trusts, March 1992).

14. Michael W. Kirst, "The Need to Broaden Our Perspective Concerning America's Educational Attainment," *Phi Delta Kappan* (October 1991), 118–20.

15. The Children's Defense Fund report issued in 1991 gives this statistic, pointing out that the current profile differs from the stereotype. The majority of the poor live outside of central cities; most are not on welfare, most are not black, and two of five live in two-parent households. The persistence of the stereotype, however, imagines the poor as black, welfare-dependent, inner-city dwellers and illegal immigrants. Such

stereotypes inform much of the corresponding school mythologies to be discussed in this book. On the Children's Defense Fund report, see *Education Week*, (12 June 1991), 4.

16. Stanley M. Elam, Lowell C. Rose, and Alec M. Gallup, "The 23rd Annual Gallup Poll of the Public's Attitudes toward the Public Schools," in *Phi Delta Kappan* (September 1991), 47.

17. All statistics in this passage are from David B. Tyack, *The One Best System: A History of American Urban Education* (Cambridge: Harvard Univ. Press, 1974), 57–58, 66, 183, 122–23, and 222.

18. David Nasaw, *Schooled to Order: A Social History of Public Schooling in the United States* (New York: Oxford Univ. Press, 1979), 127.

19. Joel Spring, *The American School 1642–1985: Varieties of Historical Interpretation of the Foundations and Development of American Education* (New York: Longman, 1986), 45.

20. Quoted in Monica Kiefer, *American Children Through Their Books 1700–1835* (Philadelphia: Univ. of Pennsylvania Press, 1948), 132.

21. Much of the above passage is based on Carl F. Kaestle, *The Evolution of an Urban School System: New York City 1750–1850* (Cambridge: Harvard Univ. Press, 1973), 112, 137, 138–39, 154, and 158.

22. David Tyack, "Forming the National Character," *Harvard Educational Review* (Winter 1966), 29–31.

23. Carl F. Kaestle, *Pillars of the Republic: Common Schools and American Society* (New York: Hill and Wang, 1983), x.

24. Ibid., 33.

25. Ibid., 47.

26. Ibid., 55.

27. Ibid., 65 and 69.

II. History Lesson (33–86)

1. David Jenness, *Making Sense of Social Studies* (New York: Macmillan, 1990), 64.

2. Reported to the author in interviews with history teachers in Moscow, Novosibirsk, and Sochi in June 1991.

3. The Bradley Commission on History in Schools, *Building a History Curriculum: Guidelines for Teaching History in Schools* (N.p.: Educational Excellence Network, 1988), 2.

4. Jenness, 157–58.

5. Arthur Woodward and David L. Elliott, "Textbooks: Consensus and Controversy," in Elliott and Woodward's *Textbooks and Schooling in the United States: Eighty-Ninth Yearbook of the National Society for the Study of Education*, Part 1 (Chicago: Univ. of Chicago Press, 1990), 157. The authors report here "that basic subject areas are inadequately presented, that outmoded and inaccurate ideas persist, that higher levels of cognitive functioning are mainly excluded, and that most potentially controversial topics are simply ignored." Despite efforts to reform education, textbooks dominate American teaching even though they have been consistently criticized in such terms for many years.

6. Jenness, 159.

7. Frances Fitzgerald, *America Revised: History Schoolbooks in the Twentieth Century* (New York: Random House, 1979), 19.

8. Richard C. Brown and Herbert J. Bass, *One Flag, One Land*, Vol. 1 (Morristown, N.J.: Silver Burdett Company, 1986), 50–54.

9. Michael R. Olneck and Marvin Lazerson, "Education," in *Harvard Encyclopedia of American Ethnic Groups* (Cambridge: The Belknap Press of Harvard Univ. Press, 1980), 304.

10. John A. Nietz, *The Evolution of American Secondary School Textbooks* (Rutland, Vt.: Charles E. Tuttle Co., 1966), 237.

11. Linda Colley, *Britons: Forging the Nation 1707–1837* (New Haven: Yale Univ. Press, 1992).

12. John A. Nietz, *Evolution*, 8. Elizabeth Flower and Murray G. Murphey, in *A History of Philosophy in America*, Vol. 1 (New York: Capricorn Books and G.P. Putnam's Sons, 1977), 215, also remind us that Scottish philosophical influences on American thought are not sufficiently recognized.

13. Nietz, *Evolution*, 238.

14. Paul K. Conkin, *Puritans and Pragmatists: Eight Eminent American Thinkers* (Bloomington: Indiana Univ. Press, 1968), 10–11 and 18.

15. John A. Nietz, *Old Textbooks: Spelling, Grammar, Reading . . . as Taught in the Common Schools from Colonial Days to 1900* (Pittsburgh: Pittsburgh Univ. Press, 1961), 240–41.

16. Ibid., 245.

17. Ibid., 247.

18. Gary B. Nash, *Red, White, and Black: The Peoples of Early America* (Englewood Cliffs, N.J.: Prentice-Hall, Inc., 1974), 33–34.

19. Simon Pepper, "In Imitation of Castile," *TLS* (5 July 1991), 17.

20. Nietz, *Textbooks*, 247–48.

21. Nietz, *Evolution*, 249.

22. Ibid.

23. Ibid., 250. Nietz provides a chart (p. 22) tracing the decline of space in world history textbooks devoted to India, China, and Japan and consequent rise in space for medieval subjects. Nationalism in Europe remains the single largest topic by far in textbooks throughout the period studied by Nietz (1800–1880).

24. Flower and Murphey, Vol. 1, 206. German Romantic idealism ful-

filled the same American needs as had Scottish Realism, as a basis for morality and religion (p. 427).

25. See ibid., 352, for a discussion of how one American professor of political economy wedded the idea of a nation to moral purposes and to the customs, traditions, and so forth of the people, drawing on both Kant and Hegel as they suited practical aims. The "forty-eighters," victims of the failed European revolutions of 1848, found their way to Milwaukee, where they fused Romantic Fichte with early Hegel to come up with the idea of "a nation as a cultural unity no less than a political one," (Flower and Murphey, Vol. 2, 470). Flower and Murphey go on to say in the same passage that it is the mature Hegel, as tempered by a right-wing backlash, that most strongly influenced twentieth-century thought; but the germ of cultural determinism had been let loose in the land.

26. Flower and Murphey, Vol. 2, 493.

27. Ibid., to which I am indebted for the preceding paragraphs on the St. Louis Hegelians. Flower and Murphey (pp. 495–501) are careful to point out that in Europe as in America, Hegel's work was selectively used to support both left- and right-wing ideas: Marx adopted Hegel's dialectic to support the socialist agenda, while the St. Louis Hegelians, like the German National Socialists, picked up those Hegelian ideas that suggested the state increase its control of individual behavior. They were most comfortable with Hegel's later works—those written when he was a member of the Prussian bureaucracy .

28. Eric Hobsbawm, "Mass-Producing Traditions: Europe 1870–1914," in Eric Hobsbawm and Terence Ranger, eds., *The Invention of Tradition* (New

York: Cambridge Univ. Press, 1983), 280. Throughout this passage I am indebted to Hobsbawm, especially pp. 265 and 268–69.

29. Jenness, 73.

30. Cited in Jenness, 81, among others.

31. Jeannie Oakes, et al., *Educational Matchmaking: Academic and Vocational Tracking in Comprehensive High Schools* (Berkeley: National Center for Research in Vocational Education, 1992).

32. Fitzgerald, 53.

33. Ibid., 55–58.

34. Ibid., 133–35.

35. Quoted in Peter E. Novick, *That Noble Dream: The "Objectivity Question" and the American Historical Profession* (New York: Cambridge Univ. Press, 1988), 199.

36. See Novick, passim.

37. Ruth Miller Elson, *Guardians of Tradition: American Schoolbooks of the Nineteenth Century* (Lincoln: Univ. of Nebraska Press, 1964), 33.

38. Joshua Fishman, *Language and Ethnicity in Minority Sociolinguistic Perspective* (Philadelphia: Multilingual Matters, 1989), 123–24 and 141–42.

39. Pepper, 17.

40. Hillel Black, *The American Schoolbook* (New York: William Morrow and Company, 1967), 99.

41. Morris Vogel, *Cultural Connections: Museums and Libraries of Philadelphia and the Delaware Valley* (Philadelphia: Temple Univ. Press, 1991), 150. The entire discussion here of Williamsburg and Greenfield Village derives from Vogel's work.

42. Ibid., 170.

43. Elson, 25.

44. Ibid., 28.

45. Ibid., 340.

46. Jenness, 173.

47. D. A. Saunders, "Social Ideas in McGuffey Readers," *Public Opinion Quarterly* (Winter 1941), 582.

48. The above passage depends on the work of Richard D. Mosier, *Making the American Mind: Social and Moral Ideas in the McGuffey Readers* (New York: Russell and Russell, 1965), 30, 62, 123, 149, and 168.

49. David L. Elliott and Arthur Woodward, *Textbooks and Schooling in the United States: Eighty-ninth Yearbook of the National Society for the Study of Education,* Part 1 (Chicago: Univ. of Chicago Press, 1990), 8.

50. Elson, 44–45.

51. Ibid., 45–46, 58–60 and 62. See also Frederick M. Bender, *The Age of the Common School, 1830–65* (New York: John Wiley and Sons, 1974), 97, on Americans as chosen people.

52. Quoted in John H. Westerhoff, *McGuffey and His Readers* (Nashville, Tenn.: Abingdon, 1978), 80.

53. See Saunders, 588; Stanley W. Lindberg, *The Annotated McGuffey* (New York: Van Nostrand Reinhold Co., 1976), 147; and Richard L. Venesky, *American Primers: Guide to the Microfiche Collection* (Bethesda, Md.: University Publications of America, 1990), xix–xx.

54. Black, 132 and 136–37.

55. See Mosier.

56. Lindberg, xv.

57. Elson, 101.

58. *The Oxford English Dictionary,* "Race."

59. Eric J. Hobsbawm, *Nations and Nationalism Since 1780: Programme, Myth, Reality* (New York: Cambridge Univ. Press, 1990), 121.

60. Elson, 338.

61. Diane Ravitch, ed., *The American Reader: Words that Moved a Nation* (New York: Harper Collins, 1990), 153–54.

62. See, for example, Charlotte Crabtree in Paul Gagnon, *Historical Literacy: The Case for History in American Education* (New York: Macmillan Publishing Company, 1989), 177–78.

63. Elson, 53.

64. Ibid., 54.

65. Ibid., 76.

66. Ibid., 87.

67. Ibid., 96.

68. Black, 106 and 108; Fitzgerald, 83–84; and Westerhoff, 21.

69. Elson, 297.

70. Edward A. Krug, *The Shaping of the American High School 1880–1920,* Vol. 1 (Madison: Univ. of Wisconsin Press, 1969), 427.

71. Elson, 107–110.

72. Ibid., 143–45.

73. Fitzgerald, 90–101.

74. Joel Spring, *Conflict of Interest: The Politics of American Education* (New York: Longman, 1988), 29.

75. California State Department of Education, *Preliminary History–Social Science Framework for California Public Schools Kindergarten through Grade Twelve* (Sacramento: 1987), 3–6.

76. David L. Kirp, "The Battle of the Books," *San Francisco Examiner: Image* (24 February 1991), 21, 22, and 25.

77. "When Ethnic Studies Are Un-American," in *Social Studies Review: A Bulletin of the American Textbook Council* 5 (Summer 1990), 11–13.

78. Jenness, 287–88.

79. Tom Holt, *Thinking Historically: Narrative, Imagination, and Understanding* (New York: College Entrance Examination Board, 1990), 11.

80. Thomas Bender, "Wholes and Parts: The Need for Synthesis in American History," *Journal of American History* 73.1 (June 1986), 120–36.

81. Jenness, 277.

82. Arthur M. Schlesinger, Jr., *The Disuniting of America* (N.p.: Whittle Direct Books, 1991).

83. National Commission on Social Studies in the Schools, *Charting a Course: Social Studies for the 21st Century* (Washington, D.C., 1989).

84. Jenness, 261–62.

85. Paul Gagnon, *Historical Literacy,* 23–30, 87, 95, 244–45, 177–78, and 216–33.

86. Jenness, 295–96.

87. Louis R. Harlan, "Social Studies Reform and the Historian," *Journal of American History* (December 1990), 806 and 809–10.

88. Cited in Jenness, 170 and 172.

89. Ibid., 159–62 and National Commission on Social Studies in the Schools, *Voices of Teachers: Report of a Survey on Social Studies* (Dubuque, Iowa: Kendall/Hunt Publishing Company, 1991), 7 and 62.

90. Jenness, 192–94 and 196–97.

91. Ibid., 299–300.

92. See the 1991 yearbook on *Global Education: From Thought to Action,* ed. Kenneth A. Tye (Washington, D.C.: ASCD, 1991), which is almost entirely centered in an ahistorical present tense.

93. Jenness, 111–13.

94. Fitzgerald, 112.

95. Nathan Glazer and Ueda Reed, *Ethnic Groups in History Textbooks* (Washington, D.C.: Ethics and Public Policy Center, 1983), 60.

96. Vogel, 172.

97. Council of Europe *Newsletter* (2 and 3, 1990), 4.

98. See Benedict Anderson, *Imagined Communities: Reflections on the Origin and Spread of Nationalism* (London: Verso, 1983).

III. Firing the Canon (87–118)

1. Arthur N. Applebee, *Contexts for Learning to Write: Studies of Secondary*

School Instruction (Norwood, N.J.: ABLEX, 1984); Robert Rothman, "Students Read Little In or Out of School, NAEP Survey Finds," *Education Week* (3 June 1992), 1 and 17.

2. John A. Nietz, *The Evolution of American Secondary School Textbooks*, (Rutland, Vt.: Charles E. Tuttle Co., 1966), 25.

3. Ibid., 27.

4. Paul Lauter, *Canons and Contexts* (New York: Oxford Univ. Press, 1991), 22–47.

5. Nietz, *Evolution*, 155.

6. Walter Jackson Bate, ed., *Criticism: The Major Texts* (New York: Harcourt Brace Jovanovich, [1952]; enlarged edn. 1970), 414.

7. Lawrence A. Cremin, *American Education: The National Experience 1783–1876* (New York: Harper and Row, 1980), 66.

8. United States Department of Education Office of Educational Research and Improvement, *Early American Textbooks 1775–1900: A Catalog of the Titles Held by the Educational Research Library* (Washington, D.C.: USDOE, 1985), 13.

9. As quoted in Hillel Black, *The American Schoolbook* (New York: William Morrow and Company, 1967), 76.

10. Ibid., 80.

11. C. Arnold Anderson and Mary Jean Bowman, "Education and Economic Modernization in Historical Perspective," in Lawrence Stone, ed., *Schooling and Society: Studies in the History of Education* (Baltimore: The Johns Hopkins Univ. Press, 1976), 5.

12. Carl F. Kaestle, " 'The Scylla of Brutal Ignorance and the Charybdis of a Literary Education': Elite Attitudes toward Mass Schooling in Early Industrial England and America," in Stone, ibid., 182–83.

13. People for the American Way survey, as reported in *Education Week* (16 September 1992), 2.

14. Edward A. Krug, *The Shaping of the American High School,* Vol. 1, *1880–1920* (Madison: Univ. of Wisconsin Press, 1969), 5–6.

15. Gerald Graff, *Professing Literature: An Institutional History* (Chicago: Univ. of Chicago Press, 1987), 99.

16. See Ira Katznelson and Margaret Weir, *Schooling for All: Class, Race, and the Decline of the Democratic Ideal* (New York: Basic Books, 1985).

17. Krug, Vol. 1, xii.

18. See Arthur N. Applebee, *A Study of Book-Length Works Taught in High School English Courses* (Albany, N.Y.: Center for the Learning and Teaching of Literature, 1989), 13.

19. This and the preceding passage on Harvard's list are indebted to Krug, Vol. 1, 362–63. In 1894 the College Entrance Examination Board defined the high school exam lists to end the confusion caused by differing college lists.

20. Applebee, *Study*, passim. Similarly, Phyllis Franklin, Bettina J. Huber, and David Lawrence state in "Continuity and Change in the Study of Literature," *Change* (January/February 1992), 42–52, that most college English teachers adhere to a core list of texts with only a few alterations over time.

21. Sandra Stotsky, "Whose Literature? America's!" *Educational Leadership* (December 1991/January 1992), 54.

22. The discussion that follows is deeply indebted to Graff, *Professing*.

23. Ibid., 19.

24. Ibid., 37–38.

25. Cremin, *The National Experience*, 67–69.

26. Ibid., 311–18, 488–90, and 509.

27. Nietz, *Evolution*, 231 and 233.

28. Ruth Miller Elson, *Guardians of Tradition: American Schoolbooks of the Nineteenth Century* (Lincoln: Univ. of Nebraska Press, 1964), 4 and 6.

29. Nietz, *Evolution*.

30. Ibid., 41–42.

31. Brian McCrea, *Addison and Steele Are Dead: The English Department, Its Canon, and the Professionalization of Literary Criticism* (Cranbury, N.J.: Associated University Presses, 1990), 160. McCrea is a special pleader, however, insisting on a canon that separates public writers such as Addison and Steele out of the academy.

32. Richard L. Venezky, "From the Indian Primer to Dick and Jane," in *American Primers: Guide to the Microfiche Collection* (Bethesda, Md.: University Publications of America, 1990), xxiii–xxiv.

33. Richard Hofstadter, *Anti-Intellectualism in American Life* (New York: Alfred A. Knopf, 1963), 305.

34. Ibid., 55–56, 87, and 104–05.

35. Marshall Graney, "Role Models in Children's Readers," *School Review* (February 1977), 248–49 and 262.

36. Allan D. Bloom, *The Closing of the American Mind: How Higher Education Has Failed Democracy and Impoverished the Souls of Today's Students* (New York: Simon and Schuster, 1987), 33–34, 37, 59–61, 66, and 82.

37. Gerald Graff and Michael Warner, *The Origins of Literary Studies in America: A Documentary Anthology* (New York: Routledge, 1989), 5.

38. Ibid., 8.

39. Ibid., 11.

40. Irving Howe, "The Value of the Canon," *The New Republic* (18 February 1991), 40–47.

41. Ibid., 43.

42. Henry Louis Gates, Jr., "Introduction: 'Tell Me, Sir, . . . What *Is* "Black" Literature?' " *PMLA* (January 1990), 13.

43. Ibid., 13–14.

44. Henry Louis Gates, Jr., *Loose Canons: Notes on the Culture Wars* (New York: Oxford Univ. Press, 1992), 17–42.

45. Susan Ohanian, "Classroom Structures that Really Count," *Education Week* (2 December 1992), 18–20.

46. Roberto Fernandez Retamar, *Caliban and Other Essays* (Minneapolis: Univ. of Minnesota Press, 1989), 4.

47. Ibid., 63 and 65.

48. Quoted in Stanley W. Lindberg, *The Annotated McGuffey* (New York: Van Nostrand Reinhold Co., 1976), xviii.

IV. Words Fail Us (119–168)

1. William Labov, *Language in the Inner City: Studies in the Black English Vernacular* (Philadelphia: Univ. of Pennsylvania Press, 1972), 201 and 213.

2. Shirley Brice Heath, *Ways with Words: Language, Life and Work in Communities and Classrooms* (Cambridge: Cambridge Univ. Press, 1983).

3. Ibid., 109, 131, and 142.

4. Robert L. Cooper, *Language Planning and Social Change* (New York: Cambridge Univ. Press, 1989), 147–48.

5. Dennis Baron, *The English-Only Question: An Official Language for Americans?* (New Haven: Yale Univ. Press, 1990), 43.

6. Ibid., 112.

7. Charles A. Ferguson, Shirley Brice Heath, and David Hwang, eds., *Language in the U.S.A.* (Cambridge: Cambridge Univ. Press, 1981), 11.

8. Quoted in Ferguson, Heath, and Hwang, 9.

9. Joshua Fishman, *Language and Ethnicity in Minority Sociolinguistic Perspective* (Philadelphia: Multilingual Matters, 1989), 274–76.

10. Ruth Miller Elson, *Guardians of Tradition: American Schoolbooks of the Nineteenth Century* (Lincoln: Univ. of Nebraska Press, 1964), 1–2.

11. Carl F. Kaestle, *Pillars of the Republic: Common Schools and American Society* (New York: Hill and Wang, 1983), 99.

12. Ibid., 7.

13. Gerald Graff, *Professing Literature: An Institutional History* (Chicago: Univ. of Chicago Press, 1987), 30.

14. Fishman, 282–83.

15. Ibid., 300 and 572–73.

16. Ibid., 447–49.

17. Christina Brett Paulston, "Bilingualism and Education," in Ferguson, Heath, and Hwang, 478–79.

18. Charles F. Gallagher, "North African Problems and Prospects: Language and Identity," in Joshua A. Fishman, Charles A. Ferguson, Jyotirindra Das Guptas, eds., *Language Problems of Developing Nations* (New York: John Wiley and Sons, 1968), 129–50.

19. Suzanne Romaine, "The More Monoglot the Better," *TLS* (31 May 1991), 8.

20. Arturo Madrid, "Official English: A False Policy Issue," in *English Plus: Issues in Bilingual Education*, Vol. 508, *The Annals of the American Academy of Political and Social Science* (March 1990), 63.

21. Pastora San Juan Cafferty and Carmen Rivera-Martinez, *The Politics of Language: The Dilemma of Bilingual Education for Puerto Ricans* (Boulder, Colo.: Westview Press, 1981), 2.

22. Baron, *English Only*, 88.

23. James Crawford, *Bilingual Education: History, Politics, Theory and Practice* (Trenton, N.J.: Crane Publishing Company, 1989), 19.

24. John A. Nietz, *The Evolution of American Secondary School Textbooks* (Rutland, Vt.: Charles E. Tuttle, 1966), 222–23.

25. Diego Castellanos, *The Best of Two Worlds: Bilingual-Bicultural Education in the U.S.* (Trenton, N.J.: Department of Education, 1983), 9.

26. Ibid., 15.

27. Nietz, *Evolution*, 155–56, 203, and 220.

28. Castellanos, 19 and 23–24.

29. Ibid., pp. 18–20.

30. Stanley W. Lindberg, *The Annotated McGuffey* (New York: Van Nostrand Reinhold Co., 1976), 227 and 229.

31. Baron, 12.

32. Ibid., 14.

33. Castellanos, 22.

34. Joel Perlman, "Historical Legacies: 1840–1920," in Madrid, ed., 32–33.

35. Edward A. Krug, *The Shaping of the American High School 1880–1920*, Vol. 1 (Madison: Univ. of Wisconsin Press, 1969), xii.

36. Perlman, 35 and 37.

37. Castellanos, 25.

38. Ibid., 30.

39. Ibid., 42–43.

40. Ibid., 44 and 48.

41. June K. Phillips, "Language and Instruction in the United States: Policy and Planning," in Diane W. Birckbichler, ed., *New Perspectives and New Directions in Foreign Language Education* (Lindenwood, Ill.: National Textbook Company, 1990), 47.

42. Ferguson, Heath, and Hwang, 17.

43. Castellanos, 38.

44. Colman Brez Stein, Jr., *Sink or Swim: The Politics of Bilingual Education* (New York: Praeger Publishers, 1986), 3.

45. Krug, Vol. 1, 410–11 and 417–18.

46. Castellanos, 39.

47. Ferguson, Heath, and Hwang, 17.

48. Jack Citrin, Beth Reingold, and Evelyn Walters, "The 'Official English' Movement and the Symbolic Politics of Language in the United States," in *The Western Political Quarterly* (September 1990), 537.

49. Stein, 12.

50. Ibid., 23–24.

51. Audrey L. Heining-Boynton, "Using FLES History to Plan for the Present and Future," *Foreign Language Annals* (December 1990), 504.

52. Thomas Weyr, *Hispanic U.S.A., Breaking the Melting Pot* (New York: Harper and Row, 1988), 54.

53. See Weyr, 55, and Alba N. Ambert and Sarah E. Melendez, *Bilingual Education: A Sourcebook* (New York: Teachers College Press, 1985), 5.

54. Castellanos, 81.

55. Ibid., 81 and 86–87.

56. Crawford, 33–35.

57. Castellanos, 95–96.

58. Cafferty and Rivera-Martinez, 18–19.

59. Weyr, 58.

60. Suzanne Romaine, *Bilingualism* (New York: Basil Blackwell, 1989), 224.

61. Joshua A. Fishman, "Language Policy: Past, Present and Future," in Ferguson, Heath, and Hwang, 517–18.

62. Fishman, *Language and Ethnicity,* 204.

63. Richard H. de Lone, *Small Futures: Children, Inequality, and the Limits of Liberal Reform* (New York: Harcourt Brace Jovanovich, 1979), 101.

64. Fishman, *Language and Ethnicity,* 678.

65. Stein, 407, citing Joseph Califano, *Governing America* (New York: Simon and Schuster, 1981), 313.

66. Castellanos, 187–88.

67. Weyr, 61–63.

68. Stein, 71–72.

69. Phillips, 61.

70. Citrin, Reingold, and Walters, 538 and 62.

71. Nancy H. Hornberger, "Bilingual Education and English-Only: A Language-Planning Framework," in Madrid, ed., 15.

72. Citrin, 62.

73. Martha M. McCarthy, "The Changing Federal Role in Bilingual Education," *Journal of Educational Equity and Leadership* (Spring 1986), 76.

74. Weyr, 71–72.

75. Fishman, *Language and Ethnicity,* 632 and 643–45.

76. Baron, *English-Only,* 31–32.

77. Fishman, *Language and Ethnicity,* 7.

78. Ibid., 213 and 218.

79. Ibid., 460.

80. Ibid., 467.

81. Ibid., 266.

82. Ibid., 408–09.

83. Paulston, 44.

84. Eric J. Hobsbawm, *Nations and Nationalism Since 1780: Programme, Myth, Reality* (New York: Cambridge Univ. Press, 1990), 54.

85. Ibid., 59–61.

86. Ibid., 91–92, 95, and 110.

87. Ibid., 99–103.

88. Ibid., 108, 113, and 117.

89. Citrin, 539.

90. Ibid.

91. Mildred K. Rudolph, Priscilla P. Waynant, and Rosemary G. Wilson, *Step Up,* Level E, Teacher's Edition (London: Charles E. Merrill Publishing Co., 1986 [1966]), T-12. Note that this teacher's manual for a schoolbook doesn't even paginate like a normal book.

92. Mildred K. Rudolph and Rosemary G. Wilson, *I Can,* Level A, Teacher's Edition (London: Charles E. Merrill Publishing Co., 1986 [1966]), T-19.

93. Harriet Tyson-Bernstein, *A Conspiracy of Good Intentions: America's Textbook Fiasco* (Washington, D.C.: The Council for Basic Education, 1988), 19–21.

94. Margaret Early, et al., *Stairways*, Teacher's Edition, Part 1, Level 7 (Orlando: Harcourt Brace Jovanovich, 1987), T-32.

95. Heining-Boynton, 504–05.

96. See U.S. Department of Education, *The Condition of Bilingual Education in the Nation* (Washington, D.C.: Office of the Secretary, 1992), 74, and Romaine, *Bilingualism*, 225. See also Robert L. Cooper, *Language Planning and Social Change* (New York: Cambridge Univ. Press, 1989), 52–53.

97. Stein, 60 and 154–56.

98. Baron, *English Only*, 195.

99. Stein, 61.

100. Castellanos, 79.

101. Dale L. Lange, "The Language Teaching Curriculum and A National Agenda," in Richard D. Lambert, ed., *Foreign Language Instruction: A National Agenda*, Vol. 490, *The Annals of the American Academy of Political and Social Science* (March 1987), 71 and 76.

102. Theodore Anderson, *Foreign Language in the Elementary School: A Struggle Against Mediocrity* (Austin: Univ. of Texas Press, 1969), 7.

103. Castellanos, 63–67 and 135–39.

104. Romaine, *Bilingualism*, 222.

105. Baron, *English Only*, 151.

106. Ibid., 164–67.

107. Ibid., 154–55.

108. Discussed in Dennis E. Baron, *Grammar and Good Taste: Reforming the American Language* (New Haven: Yale Univ. Press, 1982), 173.

109. Frank Smith, "Learning to Read: The Never-Ending Debate," *Phi Delta Kappan* (February 1992), 435 and 438.

110. Cynthia Greenleaf, *An Evaluation of the Impact of the HERALD Project* (San Francisco: San Francisco Education Fund, 1992), 47.

111. Romaine, *Bilingualism*, 244–47.

112. Ibid., 248.

113. Ibid., 247 and 250.

114. See, for example, Weyr, 65.

115. Fishman, *Language and Ethnicity*, 632 and 647.

116. Romaine, *Bilingualism*, 217–18.

117. Cooper, 136.

118. Stein, 13–15.

119. Ibid., 17.

120. Rosalie Pedalino Porter, *Forked Tongue: The Politics of Bilingual Education* (New York: Basic Books, 1990), 32.

121. Rosalie Pedalino Porter, "The False Alarm over Early English Acquisition," 36.

122. Lily Wong Filmore, "A Question for Early Childhood Programs: English First or Families First?" *Education Week* (19 June 1991), 32.

123. University Art Museum, *The Go-Betweens: The Lives of Immigrant Children*, (Minneapolis: University of Minnesota, 1986), 8.

124. Ibid., 10.

125. Ferguson, Heath, and Hwang, 137–41.

126. Baron, *The English-Only Question*, 7–9.

127. Ibid., 28.

128. Fishman, *Language and Ethnicity*, 404.

129. Miles Horton and Paulo Freire, in *We Make the Road By Walking: Conversations on Education and Social Change*, Brenda Bill, et al., eds., (Philadelphia: Temple Univ. Press, 1990), 145.

130. Baron, *English-Only*, 178.

131. Romaine, *Bilingualism*, 39.

132. Richard D. Lambert, "The Improvement of Foreign Language

Competency in the United States," in Lambert, 10.

133. Rexford G. Brown, *Schools of Thought: How the Politics of Literacy Shape Thinking in the Classroom* (San Francisco: Jossey-Bass Publishers, 1991), 79.

134. I am indebted to Brown, *Schools of Thought,* and to various speeches and conversations with Joseph Featherstone in this passage.

135. Baron, *English-Only,* 180.

136. Peter West, "Law Encourages Schools to Use Indian Languages," *Education Week* (7 November 1990), 20.

137. Baron, *English-Only,* 182–85.

138. Anthony Grafton, "A Lost Latin World: New Maps for the Terra Incognita of the English Renaissance," *TLS* (8 March, 1991), 3–4.

139. Joshua A. Fishman, "Nationality-Nationalism and Nation-Nationalism," in Fishman, Ferguson, and Guptas, 39–51.

140. Ali A. Mazrui, *The Political Sociology of the English Language: An African Perspective* (The Hague: Mouton and Co., 1975), 204.

141. James J. Lyons, "The Past and Future Directions of Federal Bilingual-Education Policy," in Madrid, ed., 79. See also Russell N. Campbell and Susan Schnell, "Language Conversation," in the same volume, 178–82.

142. Lyons, 78, and publications of the U.S. Department of Education on its "America 2000" initiative. The omission was later corrected after protests from the foreign language education community.

143. Lyons, 78; see also Campbell and Schnell, 183–84.

144. U.S. Department of Education newsletters, "America 2000," published from September 1, 1991 through April 1993, at which time the title changed to *Community Update* on what was then renamed the "Goals 2000, Educate America" program of the Clinton Administration. See also Dennis Baron, *English-Only,* 12–14.

145. Baron, *English-Only,* 16.

146. Council of Europe, "Czechoslovakia: Education and Political Change," *Newsletter* (December 1989), 9–10.

147. Ferguson, Heath, and Hwang, 524–25.

148. "Our Voices Our Vision: American Indians Speak Out for Educational Excellence" (The College Board and American Indian Science and Engineering Society, 1989), 6 and passim.

149. Hobsbawm, *Nations,* 160–61.

150. Ibid., 163–69.

151. Romaine, *Bilingualism,* 254.

V. Mapping Culture (163–200

1. Philip Gleason, "American Identity and Americanization," *Harvard Encyclopedia of American Ethnic Groups* (Cambridge: The Belknap Press of Harvard Univ. Press, 1980), 31–33.

2. Meyer Weinberg, *A Chance to Learn: The History of Race and Education in the United States* (New York: Cambridge Univ. Press, 1977), 2–6 and 362–63.

3. Michael R. Olneck and Marvin Lazerson, "Education," *Harvard Encyclopedia of American Ethnic Groups,* 306–07.

4. Ibid., 309–11.

5. Ibid., 311.

6. Ibid., 312–14.

7. Ibid., 315.

8. Ibid., 317.

9. Ibid., 318.

10. Michael R. Olneck, "The Recurring Dream: Symbolism and Ideology in Intercultural and Multicultural Education," *American Journal of Education* 98:2 (February 1990), 149–58.

11. Olneck and Lazerson, 319.

12. The metaphor of story and plot is James Banks's, quoted in Debra Viadero, "Battle Over Multicultural Education Rises in Intensity," *Education Week* X:13 (28 November 1990), 11.

13. State Commissioner of New York Thomas Sobol, quoted in Viadero, ibid.

14. Ronald Takaki, *Strangers from a Different Shore* (New York: Penguin, 1989), 3–18.

15. See, for example, Renato Rosaldo in "Opening Academia Without Closing It Down," *New York Times* (9 December 1990), E5.

16. Professors Molefi Kete Asante, Asa Hilliard, and Leonard Jeffries have all used this designation in conferences, meetings, and conversations with the author.

17. Andrew Sullivan, "Racism 101," *The New Republic* (26 November 1990), 18–21.

18. Quoted in Innerst, "Multiethnic Education Aims for History's Untold Stories," *Washington Times* (13 November 1990), A10. I suspect the teacher is referring to Amenhotep, via folk etymology. A similar penchant for folk etymology was displayed in a photograph of a blackboard in the *New York Times* (30 December 1990), showing an elementary Latin teacher incorrectly deriving "company" from the Latin for "bread."

19. Albert Shanker has been a strong supporter of the democratic story as the basis for common culture and continues to advocate the list idea inherent in E. D. Hirsch, Jr.'s *Cultural Literacy*. See Albert Shanker, "Where We Stand," *New York Times* (1 October 1989), E7. William Bennett in his role as Chairman of the National Endowment for the Humanities brought *The Federalist Papers* into schoolrooms, and when the baton passed to Lynne Cheney, she took up that work as well. Diane Ravitch, who frequently cites her involvement with the state-mandated *California History–Social Studies Framework*, advocates "a civic culture" ("Multiculturalism Yes, Particularism, No," *Chronicle of Higher Education* 24 [October 1990], A44), "our common political culture" ("Multiculturalism in the Curriculum," *Network News and Views*, Vanderbilt University Institute for Public Policy Studies: The Educational Excellence Network, IX.3 [March 1990], 1), and "the democratic political condition" ("Diversity and Democracy: Multicultural Education in America," *American Educator* [Spring 1990], 48).

20. Quoted in Takaki, 16.

21. Sullivan.

22. Jennifer Wong, "Conservative Scholars See 'Multiculturalism' as a Plague," *Chronicle of Higher Education* (19 September 1990).

23. Diane Ravitch, "Multiculturalism Yes."

24. Carol Innerst, "'Racist' History Assailed," *Washington Times* (13 November 1990), A1.

25. Gilbert T. Sewall, "California: The Story Continues," *Social Studies Review: A Bulletin of the American Textbook Council* 6 (Fall 1990), 11.

26. John Taylor, "Are You Politically Correct?" *New York* (21 January 1991), 35. See also *The New Republic*, "A Special Issue: Race on Campus" (18 February 1991), 6; and Innerst.

27. Asa G. Hilliard III, "Why We Must Pluralize the Curriculum," *Educational Leadership* (December 1991/January 1992), 13.

28. See for example Donald Leake and Brenda Leake, "African-American Immersion Schools in Milwaukee: A

View from Inside," *Phi Delta Kappan* (June 1992), 783–85.

29. Larry Cuban, "Four Stories about National Goals for American Education," *Phi Delta Kappan* (December 1990), 268.

30. See, for example, Ravitch, "Diversity and Democracy," 18; Lynne V. Cheney, *Humanities in America: A Report to the President, the Congress, and the American People* (Washington, D.C.: The National Endowment for the Humanities, 1988), 12. Her last report as chairman is entitled, "Telling the Truth." See also *Tyrannical Machines: A Report on Educational Practices Gone Wrong and Our Best Hopes for Setting Them Right* (Washington, D.C.: The National Endowment for the Humanities, 1990), 35; Chester A. Finn, Jr., "Why Can't Colleges Convey Our Diverse Culture's Unifying Themes?" *Chronicle of Higher Education* (13 June 1990), A40.

31. Ruth Miller Elson, *Guardians of Tradition: American Schoolbooks of the Nineteenth Century,* (Lincoln: Univ. of Nebraska Press, 1964), passim.

32. Eric J. Hobsbawm, *Nations and Nationalism Since 1780: Programme, Myth, Reality* (New York: Cambridge Univ. Press, 1990), 67–68.

33. Irving Kristol, "Taking Political Things Personally," *TLS* (1 March 1991), 5.

34. *Social Studies Review: A Bulletin of the American Textbook Council* (Summer 1991), 2. This journal generally takes a position strongly *against* Afrocentric belief; their call here for reinstating the study of religion as a historical force in American history would serve, if freely carried out, to unpack the religiosity of many of the beliefs the journal editor stands for.

35. See Oswyn Murray, "Sovereignty for All?" *TLS* (25 October 1991), 8.

36. Quoted in Gojendra K. Verma, *Education for All: A Landmark in Pluralism* (London: The Falmer Press, 1989), 138–39.

37. Joan Strouse, "Continuing Themes in Assimilation Through Education," *Equity and Excellence* 22:1–2 (Spring 1987), 112.

38. Reprinted as "A Talk to Teachers" in Rick Simonson and Scott Walker, eds., *The Graywolf Annual Five: Multicultural Literacy* (Saint Paul, Minn.: Graywolf Press, 1988), 3–12. This essay originally appeared as "The Negro Child—His Self-Image."

39. "A Journey into Speech," in Simonson and Walker, 57–62.

40. "How I Started to Write," in Simonson and Walker, 83–111.

41. See also Guillermo Gómez-Peña, "Documented/Undocumented," in Simonson and Walker, 127–34.

42. David Mura, "Strangers in the Village," in Simonson and Walker, 150.

43. For extended descriptions of some of these experiments see Paul G. LeMahieu and Richard Sterling, *CHARTing Educational Reform: An Interim Report of Evaluations of The Collaboratives for Humanities and Arts Teaching* ([Philadelphia: CHART,] 1991), and Randolph Jennings, ed., *Fire in the Eyes of Youth: The Humanities in American Education* (St. Paul, Minn.: Occasional Press, 1993).

44. Frank B. Murray and Daniel Fallon, "The Reform of Teacher Education for the 21st Century: Project 30 Year One Report," (N.p.: University of Delaware, n.d.), 22.

45. See Amy Gutman, *Democratic Education* (Princeton: Princeton Univ. Press, 1987), 290, and Thomas Short, " 'Diversity,' and 'Breaking the Disciplines': Two New Assaults on the Curriculum," *Academic Questions*, (Summer 1988), 14.

46. Neil Burtonwood, *The Culture Concept in Educational Studies* (Philadelphia: NFER-NELSON, 1986), 21.

VI. Life on the Border (201–248)

1. See Fouad Ajami, "Islam and the West: A Cultural Duel," in *TLS* (8 February 1991), 8, on Mazrui's *Cultural Forces in World Politics* (Portsmouth, N.H.: Heinemann, 1990).

2. See for example, Thomas Short, " 'Diversity' and 'Breaking the Disciplines': Two New Assaults on the Curriculum," *Academic Questions* I:3 (Summer 1988), 21–17.

3. See Brian Rotman, "The Grand Hotel and the Shopping Mall," *TLS*, (6–12 April 1990), 379, on Jim Collins's *Uncommon Cultures: Popular Culture and Post-Modernism* (New York: Routledge, 1989).

4. See Mark Halstead, *Education, Justice and Cultural Diversity: An Examination of the Honeyford Affair 1984–85* (London: The Falmer Press, 1988), 162 and passim, for a thorough and reasoned discussion of the injustices that remain in schools after legal remedies have been enacted. See Molefi Kete Asante, "Multiculturalism: An Exchange," *American Scholar* (Spring 1991), 270, on society and culture.

5. See Amy Gutman, *Democratic Education* (Princeton: Princeton Univ. Press, 1987); John I. Goodlad and Pamela Keating, eds., *Access to Knowledge: An Agenda for Our Nation's Schools* (New York: College Entrance Examination Board, 1990); and Richard Dagger, "Education, Autonomy and Civic Virtue," *The Civic Arts Review* 3:4 (Fall 1990), 11–16.

6. Annette Weiner, President of the American Anthropological Association, in an article on "Anthropology's Lessons for Cultural Diversity," *Chronicle of Higher Education* (22 July 1992), B1–B2.

7. This and the entire passage to follow on culture are derived from Clifford Geertz, *The Interpretation of Cultures: Selected Essays* (New York: Basic Books, 1973). The quoted words can be found on p. 6.

8. Ibid., 13–15.

9. Ibid., 22–23, 24 35, 37, and 43–44.

10. Ibid., 47–49, 51, and 52.

11. Ibid., 242–43 and 252.

12. Ibid., 258–59.

13. James Clifford, "The Transit Lounge of Culture," *TLS* (3 May 1991), 7–8. Author's italics.

14. Maxine Greene, "Texts and Margins," *Harvard Educational Review* 61:1 (February 1991), 27–29.

15. See the autobiographies of diverse writers in Rick Simonson and Scott Walker, eds., *The Graywolf Annual Five: Multicultural Literacy* (Saint Paul, Minn.: Graywolf Press, 1988), and Guillermo Gómez-Peña, "The Multicultural Paradigm: An Open Letter to the National Arts Community," *High Performance* (Fall 1989), 20.

16. See Gutman, 76; and Ellen Pechman, "The Child As Meaning Maker" in Marsha Levine, ed., *Professional Practice Schools: Building a Model*, Vol. 2 (American Federation of Teachers: Centers for Restructuring, June 1990), 1–88.

17. See Ogbu variously in Goodlad and Keating; "Minority Education in Comparative Perspective," *Journal of Negro Education* 59:1 (Winter 1990), 45–57; and *Minority Education and Caste* (New York: Academic Press, 1978).

18. See Gutman; and Lauren B. Resnick, "The 1987 Presidential Address: Learning In School and Out," *Educational Researcher* 16:9, 19.

19. Gerald Early, "Education, Then Multicultural Education: Black Minds Are Not Being Destroyed by Whiteness, But By Neglect," *St. Louis Post Dispatch* (6 October 1991), 14.

20. Gómez-Peña, 26.

21. Ibid., 20–21.

22. David L. Elliott and Arthur Woodward, "Textbooks, Curriculum, and School Improvement," in their *Textbooks and Schooling in the United States: Eighty-Ninth Yearbook of The National Society for the Study of Education*, Part 1 (Chicago: Univ. of Chicago Press, 1990), 226.

23. Miles Horton, Paolo Freire, et al., *We Make the Road by Walking: Conversations on Education and Social Change* (Philadelphia: Temple Univ. Press, 1990), 145.

24. By November of 1991 *The New York Times* (17 November 1991, 4E) was reporting 18.3 million worldwide refugees, prior to the Somalian and Yugoslav disasters..

25. W. E. Burghardt DuBois, *The Souls of Black Folk: Essays and Sketches* (Greenwich, Conn.: Fawcett Publications, 1961), 72.

26. Barbara Herrnstein Smith, *Contingencies of Value: Alternative Perspectives for Critical Theory* (Cambridge: Harvard Univ. Press, 1988), 25 and 35–36.

27. Ibid., 37–41.

28. John Pfordresher, "Better and Different Literature in Our Time," in *Perspective* (Council for Basic Education: Summer 1992), 10–11.

29. Martha Nussbaum, "Virtue Revived: Habit, Passion, Reflection in the Aristotelian Tradition," *TLS* (3 July 1992), 9–11.

30. Herrnstein Smith, 51–52.

31. Ibid., 101–02.

32. Ibid, 169.

33. Quoted in Mary Nordhouse, *Let There Be Change in Schools and Let It Begin With Me: A Report on the 1990 New Mexico Academy for School Leaders* (University of New Mexico Bureau of Educational Planning and Development: March 1991), 33.

34. William Julius Wilson, *The Truly Disadvantaged: The Inner City, the Underclass, and Public Policy* (Chicago: Univ. of Chicago Press, 1987), 103.

35. Richard H. de Lone, *Small Futures: Children, Inequality, and the Limits of Liberal Reform* (New York: Harcourt Brace Jovanovich, 1979), ix–xiv.

36. John Dewey, *Democracy and Education: An Introduction to the Philosophy of Education* (New York: The Macmillan Company, 1916), 67–81, 89, 101–02, and 140.

37. Ibid., 226 and 305.

38. Talcott Parsons, "The Distribution of Power in American Society," *World Politics* (October 1957), 123–43.

BIBLIOGRAPHY

Ajami, Fouad. "Islam and the West: A Cultural Duel." Review of *Cultural Forces in World Politics*, by Ali Mazrui. *TLS*, 8 February 1991: 8.

Ambert, Alba N., and Sarah E. Melendez. *Bilingual Education: A Sourcebook*. New York: Teachers College Press, 1985.

American Federation of Teachers Convention. Convention "Resolutions." Unpublished Convention Adoptions 1990: 3–5.

Anderson, Benedict. *Imagined Communities: Reflections on the Origin and Spread of Nationalism*. London: Verso, 1983.

Anderson, James A. "Cognitive Styles and Multicultural Populations." *Journal of Teacher Education* 39.1 (January/February 1988): 2–8.

Anderson, Theodore. *Foreign Languages in the Elementary School: A Struggle Against Mediocrity*. Austin: Univ. of Texas Press, 1969.

Applebee, Arthur N. *Contexts for Learning to Write: Studies of Secondary School Instruction*. Norwood, N.J.: ABLEX, 1984.

———. *A Study of Book-Length Works Taught in High School English Courses*. Albany, N.Y.: Center for the Learning and Teaching of Literature, 1989.

Aronowitz, Stanley, and Henry Giroux. *Education Under Siege: The Conservative, Liberal, and Radical Debate Over Schooling*. South Hadley, Mass.: Bergin and Garvey Publishers, 1985.

Asante, Molefi Kete. "Afrocentric Curriculum." *Educational Leadership* 49.4 (December 1991/January 1992): 28–31.

———. *The Afrocentric Idea*. Philadelphia: Temple Univ. Press, 1987.

———. "Multiculturalism: An Exchange." *American Scholar* 60 (Spring 1991): 267–76.

Ascher, Carol. "School Programs for African-American Males . . . and Females." *Phi Delta Kappan* 73.10 (June 1992): 777–82.

Bailyn, Bernard. *Education in the Forming of American Society: Needs and Opportunities for Study*. New York: Vintage Books, 1960.

Baker, Houston A., Jr. *The Journey Back: Issues in Black Literature and Criticism*. Chicago: Univ. of Chicago Press, 1980.

Baker, Houston A., Jr., ed. *Three American Literatures: Essays in Chicano, Native American, and Asian-American Literature for Teachers of American Literature*. New York: Modern Language Association, 1982.

Banks, James A. *Education in the 80's: Multiethnic Education*. Washington, D.C.: National Education Association, 1981.

———. "Multicultural Education: For Freedom's Sake." *Educational Leadership* 49.4 (December 1991/January 1992): 32–36.

———. *Multiethnic Education*. Needham Heights, Mass.: Allyn and Bacon, 1988.

Banks, James A., and Cherry A. McGee Banks, eds. *Multicultural Education: Issues and Perspectives.* Boston: Allyn and Bacon, 1989.

Banks, James A., and James Lynch. *Multicultural Education in Western Societies.* Westport, Conn.: Praeger Publishers, 1986.

Baptiste, H. Prentice, Jr. "Multicultural Education and Urban Schools from a Sociohistorical Perspective: Internalizing Multiculturalism." *Journal of Educational Equity and Leadership* 6.4 (Winter 1986): 295–312.

Baratz, Stephen S., and Joan C. Baratz. "Early Childhood Intervention: The Social Science Base of Institutional Racism." *Harvard Educational Review* 40.1 (Winter 1970): 29–50.

Baron, Dennis. *The English-Only Question: An Official Language for Americans?* New Haven: Yale Univ. Press, 1990.

———. *Grammar and Good Taste: Reforming the American Language.* New Haven: Yale Univ. Press, 1982.

Bartlett, Richard A., and Claire W. Keller. *Freedom's Trail.* Boston: Houghton Mifflin Company, 1981.

Barzun, Jacques. "Thinking About Education." *Education Week,* 24 October 1990: 27.

Bate, Walter Jackson, ed. *Criticism: The Major Texts.* Enl. ed. New York: Harcourt Brace Jovanovich [1952], 1970.

Bauman, Zygmunt. "The Banality of the Good." *TLS,* 14 June 1991: 13.

Beaulieu, David. "The State of the Art: Indian Education in Minnesota." *Change* 23.2 (1991): 31–35.

Beller, Steven. Review of *Die hellen und die finstern Zeiten,* by Hilde Spiel. *TLS,* 30 March–5 April 1990: 340.

Bender, Thomas. "Wholes and Parts: The Need for Synthesis in American History." *Journal of American History* 73.1 (June 1986): 120–36.

Bennett, William J. "Why Western Civilization?" *National Forum: The Phi Kappa Phi Journal* 69.3 (Summer 1989): 3–6.

Bernal, Martin. *Black Athena: The Afroasiatic Roots of Classical Civilization.* Vol. 1, *The Fabrication of Greece 1785–1985.* New Brunswick, N.J.: Rutgers Univ. Press, 1987.

Bernstein, Basil. *Towards a Theory of Educational Transmissions.* Vol. 3, *Class, Codes and Control.* Boston: Routledge and Kegan Paul, 1975.

Bernstein, Richard. "The Rising Hegemony of the Politically Correct." *New York Times,* 28 October 1990.

Binder, Frederick M. *The Age of the Common School, 1830–65.* New York: John Wiley and Sons, 1974.

Billington, Ray Allen. *The Protestant Crusade 1800–1860: A Study of the Origins of American Nativism.* [1938]. Chicago: Quadrangle Books, 1964.

Black, Hillel. *The American Schoolbook.* New York: William Morrow and Company, 1967.

Blassingame, John W. *The Slave Community: Plantation Life in the Antebellum South.* New York: Oxford Univ. Press, 1979.

Bloom, Allan D. *The Closing of the American Mind: How Higher Education Has Failed Democracy and Impoverished the Souls of Today's Students.* New York: Simon and Schuster, 1987.

Bloom, Harold, and David Rosenberg. *The Book of J.* New York: Grove Weidenfeld, 1990.

Bohning, Gerry. "The McGuffey Eclectic Readers: 1836–1986." *The Reading Teacher* 40 (December 1986): 263–69.

Bond, Ruth. "Back to Africa." *City Paper*, Washington, D.C., 29 March 1991: 16–25.

Bowles, Samuel, and Herbert Gintis. *Schooling in Capitalist America: Educational Reform and the Contradictions of Economic Life*. New York: Basic Books, 1976.

Bradley, Ann. "L.A. Board Adopts Guidelines on School-Based Management." *Education Week*, 4 April 1990: 5.

Bradley Commission on History in Schools. *Building a History Curriculum: Guidelines for Teaching History in Schools*. N.p.: Educational Excellence Network, 1988.

Brembeck, Cole S., and Walker H. Hill. *Cultural Challenges to Education: The Influence of Cultural Factors in School Learning*. Lexington, Mass.: Lexington Books, 1973.

Brown, Rexford G. *Schools of Thought: How the Politics of Literacy Shape Thinking in the Classroom*. San Francisco: Jossey-Bass Publishers, 1991.

Brown, Richard C., and Herbert J. Bass. *One Flag, One Land*. Vol 1. Morristown, N.J.: Silver Burdett Company, 1986.

Bruner, Jerome S. *The Process of Education*. Cambridge: Harvard Univ. Press, 1961.

Burtonwood, Neil. *The Culture Concept in Educational Studies*. Philadelphia: NFER-NELSON, 1986.

Butts, R. Freeman, and Lawrence A. Cremin. *A History of Education in American Culture*. New York: Henry Holt and Company, 1953.

Cafferty, Pastora San Juan, and Carmen Rivera-Martinez. *The Politics of Language: The Dilemma of Bilingual Education for Puerto Ricans*. Boulder, Colo.: Westview Press, 1981.

California State Department of Education. History–Social Science Curriculum Framework and Criteria Committee. *Preliminary History–Social Science Framework for California Public Schools Kindergarten through Grade Twelve*. Sacramento: California State Department of Education, 1987.

Carnoy, Martin. *Education as Cultural Imperialism*. New York: David McKay Company, 1974.

Carpenter, Charles. *History of American Schoolbooks*. Philadelphia: Univ. of Pennsylvania Press, 1963.

Castellanos, Diego. *The Best of Two Worlds: Bilingual-Bicultural Education in the U.S.* Trenton: New Jersey Department of Education, 1983.

Chanan, Gabriel, and Linda Gilchrist. *What School Is For*. New York: Praeger Publishers, 1974.

Charnofsky, Stanley. *Educating the Powerless*. Belmont, Calif.: Wadsworth Publishing Company, 1971.

Chavez, Linda. "The Real Aim of the Promotors of Cultural Diversity is to Exclude Certain People and to Foreclose Debate." *Chronicle of Higher Education*, 18 July 1990: B1–2.

Cheney, Lynne V. *Humanities in America: A Report to the President, the Congress, and the American People*. Washington, D.C.: The National Endowment for the Humanities, 1988.

———. *Tyrannical Machines: A Report on Educational Practices Gone Wrong and Our Best Hopes for Setting Them Right*. Washington, D.C.: The National Endowment for the Humanities, 1990.

Children's Defense Fund. "An Advocate's Guide to Improving Education." September 1990.

Citrin, Jack, Beth Reingold, and Evelyn Walters. "The 'Official English' Movement and the Symbolic Politics of Language in the United States."

The Western Political Quarterly 43 (September 1990): 535–60.

Clifford, James. "The Transit Lounge of Culture." *TLS*, 3 May 1991: 7–8.

Cohan, Susannah. Unpublished notes from the *Second National Conference on The Infusion of African and African-American Content in the School Curriculum.* Atlanta, Ga.: October/November 1990.

Coleman, James S. *Equality of Educational Opportunity.* Washington, D.C.: National Center for Educational Statistics, 1966.

Collins, Jim. *Uncommon Cultures: Popular Culture and Post-Modernism.* New York: Routledge, 1989.

Conkin, Paul K. *Puritans and Pragmatists: Eight Eminent American Thinkers.* Bloomington: Indiana Univ. Press, 1968.

Cooper, Robert L. *Language Planning and Social Change.* New York: Cambridge Univ. Press, 1989.

Cornuelle, Richard. "New York for Invisible Hands." *TLS*, 5 April 1991: 5–6.

Cortés, Carlos E. "Multicultural Education: A Curricular Basic for our Multiethnic Future." *Doubts and Certainties* 4.7 (March/April 1990): 1–5.

Cosin, Ben, and Margaret Hales. *Education, Policy and Society: Theoretical Perspectives.* London: Routledge and Kegan Paul, 1983.

Cottrol, Robert J. "America the Multicultural." *American Educator* 14.4 (Winter 1990): 18–39.

Council of Europe. "Czechoslovakia: Education and Political Change." *Newsletter.* Documentation Centre for Education in Europe: no. 5 (December 1989): 9–10.

———. *Education Newsletter* 2 and 3/1990.

Crane, Theodore Rawson, ed. *The Dimensions of American Education.* Reading, Mass.: Addison-Wesley Publishing Company, 1974.

Crawford, James. *Bilingual Education: History, Politics, Theory and Practice.* Trenton, N.J.: Crane Publishing Company, 1989.

Cremin, Lawrence A. *American Education: The Colonial Experience 1607–1783.* New York: Harper and Row, 1970.

———. *American Education: The National Experience 1783–1876.* New York: Harper and Row, 1980.

Crossette, Barbara. "Campaign to Oust English is Revived in India." *New York Times*, 27 May 1990.

Cuban, Larry. "Four Stories About National Goals for American Education." *Phi Delta Kappan* 72.4 (December 1990): 265–71.

———. *How Teachers Taught: Constancy and Change in American Classrooms 1890–1980.* New York: Longman, 1984.

Cubrillos, Enrique M. "The Bilingual Education Act: 1988 Legislation." *Focus.* The National Clearinghouse for Bilingual Education Occasional Papers in Bilingual Education. Washington, D.C.: Fall 1988.

Culler, A. Dwight, ed. *Poetry and Criticism of Matthew Arnold.* Boston: Houghton Mifflin Company, 1961.

Cummins, Jim. "Empowering Minority Students: A Framework for Intervention." [*Harvard Educational Review*, 56.1 (February 1986)] in *Empowering Teachers and Students.* Harvard Educational Review, 1989: 1–18.

Dagger, Richard. "Education, Autonomy and Civic Virtue." *The Civic Arts Review* 3.4 (Fall 1990): 11–16.

Daley, Suzanne. "Inspirational Black History Draws Academic Fire." *New York Times*, 10 October 1990: A1.

de Lone, Richard H. *Small Futures: Children, Inequality, and the Limits of Liberal Reform*. New York: Harcourt Brace Jovanovich, 1979.

Delpit, Lisa D. "The Silenced Dialogue: Power and Pedagogy in Educating Other People's Children." In *Empowering Teachers and Students*. *Harvard Educational Review*, 1989: 280–98.

de Montellano, Bernard Ortiz. "Chariots of the [Black?] Gods." Available from Erich Martel, Washington, D.C. public schools.

DeMott, Benjamin. *The Imperial Middle: Why Americans Can't Think Straight About Class*. New York: William Morrow and Company, 1990.

Dewey, John. *Democracy and Education: An Introduction to the Philosophy of Education*. New York: Macmillan Company, 1916.

Diop, Cheikh Anta. *The African Origin of Civilization: Myth or Reality*. Trans. Mercer Cook. Chicago: Lawrence Hill and Company, 1974.

Dorn, Edwin. "Racism in America: A Conversation with Edwin Dorn." *The Civic Arts Review* 2.4 (Fall 1989): 4–8.

DuBois, W. E. Burghardt. *The Souls of Black Folk: Essays and Sketches*. Greenwich, Conn.: Fawcett Publications, 1961.

Early, Gerald. "Education, Then Multicultural Education: Black Minds Are Not Being Destroyed by Whiteness But by Neglect." *St. Louis Post-Dispatch*, 6 October 1991: 14.

———. *Tuxedo Junction: Essays on American Culture*. New York: The Ecco Press, 1989.

Edgerton, Russell. "A Long, Deep View of Minority Achievement." *AAHE Bulletin* (April 1991): 3–7.

"Education." *New York Times*, 30 December 1990: A17.

Education for Democracy: A Statement of Principles, Guidelines for Strengthening the Teaching of Democratic Values. Washington D.C.: American Federation of Teachers Education for Democracy Project, 1987.

Educational Leadership 48.2 (October 1990).

Edwards, A. D. *Language in Culture and Class: The Sociology of Language and Education*. London: Heinemann Educational Books, 1976.

Eisner, Elliot W. *The Educational Imagination: On the Design and Evaluation of School Programs*. New York: Macmillan Publishing Company, 1979.

Elam, Stanley M. "The 22nd Annual Gallup Poll of the Public's Attitudes Toward the Public Schools." *Phi Delta Kappan* 72.1 (September 1990): 41–55.

Elam, Stanley M., Lowell C. Rose, and Alec M. Gallup. "The 23rd Annual Gallup Poll of the Public's Attitudes Toward the Public Schools." *Phi Delta Kappan* 73.1 (September 1991): 41–56.

Eliot, George. *The Mill on the Floss*. Gordon S. Haight, ed. Boston: Houghton Mifflin Company, The Riverside Press, 1961.

Elliott, David L., and Arthur Woodward. *Textbooks and Schooling in the United States: Eighty-ninth Yearbook of the National Society for the Study of Education*. Part 1. Chicago: Univ. of Chicago Press, 1990.

Elliott, Emory. "The Politics of Literary History." *American Literature* 59 (May 1987): 268–76.

Elmore, Richard F., and Milbrey Wallin McLaughlin. *Steady Work: Policy, Practice, and the Reform of American*

Education. Santa Monica: RAND Corporation, 1988.

Elson, Ruth Miller. *Guardians of Tradition: American Schoolbooks of the Nineteenth Century*. Lincoln: Univ. of Nebraska Press, 1964.

Engle, Shirley H., and Anna S. Ochoa. *Education for Democratic Citizenship: Decision Making in the Social Studies*. New York: Teachers College Press, 1988.

Fass, Paula S. *Outside In: Minorities and the Transformation of American Education*. New York: Oxford Univ. Press, 1989.

Featherstone, Joseph. "A Note on Liberal Learning." *Colloquy* 2.1 (Fall 1988): 1–8.

———. "The Politics of Education." *New York Times*, 18 June 1978.

Feder, Kenneth L. *Frauds, Myths, and Mysteries: Science and Pseudoscience in Archeology*. Mountain View, Calif.: Mayfield Publishing Company, 1990.

Ferdman, Bernardo M. "Literary and Cultural Identity." *Harvard Educational Review* 60 (1990): 181–204.

Ferguson, Charles A., Shirley Brice Heath, and David Hwang, eds. *Language in the U.S.A.*. Cambridge: Cambridge Univ. Press, 1981.

Fillmore, Lily Wong. "A Question for Early Childhood Programs: English First or Families First?" *Education Week*, 19 June 1991: 32–35.

Finn, Chester E., Jr. "The Biggest Reform of All." *Phi Delta Kappan* 71.8 (April 1990): 584–92.

———. "A Truce in the Curricular Wars?" *National Forum: The Phi Kappa Phi Journal* 69.3 (Summer 1989): 16–18.

———. *We Must Take Charge: Our Schools and Our Future*. New York: The Free Press, 1991.

———. "Why Can't Colleges Convey Our Diverse Culture's Unifying Themes?" *Chronicle of Higher Education*, 13 June 1990: A40.

Fishman, Joshua A. *Language and Ethnicity in Minority Sociolinguistic Perspective*. Philadelphia: Multilingual Matters, 1989.

Fishman, Joshua A., Charles A. Ferguson, and Jyotirindra Das Guptas, eds. *Language Problems of Developing Nations*. New York: John Wiley and Sons, 1968.

Fitzgerald, Frances. *America Revised: History Schoolbooks in the Twentieth Century*. New York: Random House, 1979.

Flesch, Rudolph. *Why Johnny Still Can't Read: A New Look at the Scandal of Our Schools*. New York: Harper and Row, 1981.

Flower, Elizabeth, and Murray G. Murphey. *A History of Philosophy in America*, Vols. 1 and 2. New York: Capricorn Books and G. P. Putnam's Sons, 1977.

Franklin, Phyllis, Bettina J. Huber, and David Lawrence. "Continuity and Change in the Study of Literature." *Change* 24.1 (January/February 1992): 42–52.

Franklin, Phyllis. "English Studies: The World of Scholarship in 1883." *PMLA* 99 (May 1984): 356–70.

Fuchs, Lawrence H. *The American Kaleidoscope: Race, Ethnicity, and the Civic Culture*. Hanover, N.H.: University Press of New England, 1990.

Fuchs, Lucy. "Images of Hispanics in 4 American Reading Series." *The Reading Teacher* 40 (1987): 848–54.

Fulbrook, Mary. *A Concise History of Germany*. Cambridge: Cambridge Univ. Press, 1990.

Gagnon, Paul. *Democracy's Half-Told Story: What American History*

Textbooks Should Add. Washington, D.C.: American Federation of Teachers Education for Democracy Project, 1989.

———. *Democracy's Untold Story: What World History Textbooks Neglect.* American Federation of Teachers Education for Democracy Project, 1987.

———. *Historical Literacy: The Case for History in American Education.* New York: Macmillan Publishing Company, 1989.

Garcia, Jesus, and Viola Florez-Tighe. "The Portrayal of Blacks, Hispanics, and Native Americans in Recent Basal Reading Series." *Equity and Excellence* 22.4–6 (Summer 1986): 72–76.

Gates, Henry Louis, Jr. "Introduction: 'Tell Me, Sir, . . . What is "Black" Literature?'" *PMLA* 105 (January 1990): 11–22.

———. *Loose Canons: Notes on the Culture Wars.* New York: Oxford Univ. Press, 1992.

Gay, Geneva. "Achieving Educational Equality Through Curriculum Desegregation." *Phi Delta Kappan* 72.1 (September 1990): 56–62.

Geertz, Clifford. *The Interpretation of Cultures: Selected Essays.* New York: Basic Books, 1973.

Gill, Brendan. "The Sky Line: Battery Park City." *The New Yorker*, 20 August 1990: 69–78.

Glazer, Nathan, and Daniel Patrick Moynihan. *Beyond the Melting Pot: The Negroes, Puerto Ricans, Jews, Italians, and Irish of New York City.* Second edn. Cambridge, Mass.: The M.I.T. Press, 1970.

Glazer, Nathan, and Ueda Reed. *Ethnic Groups in History Textbooks.* Washington D.C.: Ethics and Public Policy Center, 1983.

Gleason, Philip. "American Identity and Americanization." *Harvard Encyclopedia of American Ethnic Groups.* Cambridge: The Belknap Press of Harvard Univ. Press, 1980: 31–58.

Goetzmann, William H., ed. *The American Hegelians: An Intellectual Episode in the History of Western America.* New York: Alfred A. Knopf, 1973.

Gollnick, Donna M., and Philip C. Chinn. *Multicultural Education in a Pluralist Society.* Columbus, Ohio: Charles E. Merrill Publishing Company, 1986.

———, guest co-eds. "Multiculturalism in Contemporary Education." *Journal of the School of Education*, Indiana Univ., 56.1 (Winter 1980).

Gómez-Peña, Guillermo. "The Multicultural Paradigm: An Open Letter to the National Arts Community." *High Performance* 12.3 (Fall 1989): 18–27.

Goodlad, John I., and Pamela Keating, eds. *Access to Knowledge: An Agenda for Our Nation's Schools.* New York: College Entrance Examination Board, 1990.

Gould, Stephen Jay. *The Mismeasure of Man.* New York: W. W. Norton and Company, 1981.

"Governors Pushing Education Issue." *New York Times*, 29 July 1990: 22.

Graff, Gerald. *Beyond the Culture Wars: How Teaching the Conflicts Can Revitalize American Education.* New York: W. W. Norton and Company, 1992.

———. *Professing Literature: An Institutional History.* Chicago: Univ. of Chicago Press, 1987.

Graff, Gerald, and Michael Warner. *The Origins of Literary Studies in America: A Documentary Anthology.* New York: Routledge, 1989.

Grafton, Anthony. "A Lost Latin World: New Maps for the Terra Incognita of the English Renaissance." *TLS*, 8 March 1991: 3–4.

Graney, Marshall. "Role Models in Children's Readers." *School Review* 85 (February 1977): 247–63.

Grant, Carl A. "Desegregation, Racial Attitudes, and Intergroup Contact: A Discussion of Change." *Phi Delta Kappan* 72.1 (September 1990): 25–32.

Greene, Maxine. "Texts and Margins." *Harvard Educational Review* 61.1 (February 1991): 27–39.

Greenleaf, Cynthia. *An Evaluation of the Impact of the HERALD Project.* San Francisco: San Francisco Education Fund, 1992.

Griffin, Jasper. "Who Are These Coming to the Sacrifice?" *New York Review of Books* 36 (15 June 1989): 25.

Gutman, Amy. *Democratic Education.* Princeton: Princeton Univ. Press, 1987.

Halstead, Mark. *Education, Justice and Cultural Diversity: An Examination of the Honeyford Affair, 1984–85.* London: The Falmer Press, 1988.

Harlan, Louis R. "Social Studies Reform and the Historian." *Journal of American History* 77 (December 1990): 801–11.

Hartnett, Anthony, and Michael Naish. "Multicultural Education: Paregoric or Panacea?" *Journal of Curriculum Studies* 19.4 (July 1987): 361–69.

Hayes, Floyd W, III. "Politics and Education in America's Multicultural Society: An African-American Studies' Response to Allan Bloom." *The Journal of Ethnic Studies* 17.2 (Summer 1989): 71–88.

Hayes, Larry. "Building Schools for Tomorrow." *Phi Delta Kappan* 73.5 (January 1992): 412–13.

Heath, Shirley Brice. *Ways with Words: Language, Life, and Work in Communities and Classrooms.* Cambridge: Cambridge Univ. Press, 1983.

Heining-Boynton, Audrey L. "Using FLES History to Plan for the Present and Future." *Foreign Language Annals* 23.6 (December 1990): 503–09.

Heller, Scott. "Colleges Becoming Havens of 'Political Correctness,' Some Scholars Say." *Chronicle of Higher Education*, 21 November 1990: A1.

Hidalgo, Nitza M., Ceasar L. McDowell, and Emilie V. Siddle. *Facing Racism in Education.* Cambridge: Harvard Educational Review, 1990.

Hilliard, Asa G., III. "Why We Must Pluralize the Curriculum." *Educational Leadership* 49.4 (December 1991/January 1992): 12–16.

Himmelfarb, Gertrude. "Telling It As You Like It: Post Modernist History and the Flight from Fact." *TLS*, 16 October 1992: 12–15.

Hirsch, E. D., Jr. *Cultural Literacy: What Every American Needs to Know.* Boston: Houghton Mifflin Company, 1987.

Hobsbawm, Eric J. *Nations and Nationalism Since 1780: Programme, Myth, Reality.* New York: Cambridge Univ. Press, 1990.

Hobsbawm, Eric, and Terence Ranger, eds. *The Invention of Tradition.* New York: Cambridge Univ. Press, 1983.

Hodgkinson, Harold. "Reform Versus Reality." *Phi Delta Kappan* 73.1 (September 1991): 9–13.

Hofstadter, Richard. *Anti-Intellectualism in American Life.* New York: Alfred A. Knopf, 1963.

Holt, Tom. *Thinking Historically: Narrative, Imagination, and Understanding.* New York: College Entrance Examination Board, 1990.

Horton, Miles, and Paulo Freire. *We Make the Road by Walking: Conversations on Education and Social Change*. Eds. Brenda Bill, John Gaventa, and John Peters. Philadelphia: Temple Univ. Press, 1990.

Howe, Irving. "The Value of the Canon." *The New Republic*, 18 February 1991: 40–47.

Hunter, James Davison. *Culture Wars: The Struggle to Define America*. New York: Basic Books, 1991.

Illich, Ivan. *Deschooling Society*. New York: Harper and Row, 1970.

Illich, Ivan, et al. *After Deschooling, What?* Eds. Alan Gartner, Colin Greer, and Frank Riesman. New York: Harper and Row, 1973.

Inglis, Fred. *The Management of Ignorance: A Political Theory of the Curriculum*. Oxford: Basil Blackwell, 1985.

Innerst, Carol. "Multiethnic Education Aims for History's Untold Stories." *Washington Times*, 13 November 1990: A10.

———. " 'Racist' History Assailed." *Washington Times*, 13 November 1990: A1.

Jackson, Philip W. *Life in Classrooms*. New York: Holt, Rinehart and Winston, 1968.

Jenness, David. *Making Sense of Social Studies: A Publication of the National Commission on Social Studies in the Schools*. New York: Macmillan, 1990.

———. "When Does a Nation Start Teaching Its History?" *OAH Magazine of History* 6.1 (Summer 1991): 12–17.

Jennings, Randolph, ed. *Fire in the Eyes of Youth: The Humanities in American Education*. St. Paul, Minn.: Occasional Press, 1993.

Johnson, Dirk. "Milwaukee Creating 2 Schools Just for Black Boys." *New York Times*, 30 September 1990: 1.

Johnson, Samuel. *A Dictionary of the English Language: In Which the Words Are Deduced from Their Originals, and Illustrated in Their Different Significations by Examples from the Best Writers. To Which Are Prefixed, a History of the Language, and an English Grammar*. 1755. New York: AMS Press, 1967.

Jordan, William Chester. "Segregation Won't Work." *New York Times*, 21 October 1990: E19.

The Journal of Ethnic Studies 17:2 (Summer 1989).

Judt, Tony. "Whose Common Culture?" *TLS*, 14–20 September 1990: 967–68.

Kaestle, Carl F. *The Evolution of an Urban School System: New York City 1750–1850*. Cambridge: Harvard Univ. Press, 1973.

———. *Pillars of the Republic: Common Schools and American Society*. New York: Hill and Wang, 1983.

Kamm, Henry. "One Sign of Our Times: World's Refugee Flood." *New York Times*, 12 August 1990: 16.

Karabel, Jerome, and A. H. Halsey. *Power and Ideology in Education*. New York: Oxford Univ. Press, 1977.

Katz, Michael B. *Class, Bureaucracy, and Schools: The Illusion of Educational Change in America*. New York: Praeger Publishers, 1971.

Katznelson, Ira, and Margaret Weir. *Schooling for All: Class, Race, and the Decline of the Democratic Ideal*. New York: Basic Books, 1985.

Kaufman, Jonathan. *Broken Alliance: The Turbulent Times Between Blacks and Jews in America*. New York: Charles Scribner's Sons, 1988.

Keating, Pamela, and Jeannie Oakes. *Access to Knowledge: Breaking Down School Barriers to Learning*. Denver: Education Commission of the States, 1988.

Kelly, David H. "Egyptians and Ethiopians: Color, Race, and Racism." *The Classical Outlook* 68.3 (Spring 1991): 77–82.

Kiefer, Monica. *American Children through Their Books 1700–1835.* Philadelphia: Univ. of Pennsylvania Press, 1948.

Kirp, David L. "The Battle of the Books." *San Francisco Examiner: Image,* 24 February 1991: 17–25.

Kirst, Michael W. "The Need to Broaden Our Perspective Concerning America's Educational Attainment." *Phi Delta Kappan* 73.2 (October 1991): 118–20.

Klawans, Stuart. "American Notes." *TLS,* 20–26 July 1990: 774.

Kliebard, Herbert M. *The Struggle for the American Curriculum 1893–1958.* Boston: Routledge and Kegan Paul, 1986.

Knapp, Michael S., and Patrick M. Shields. "Reconceiving Academic Instruction for the Children of Poverty." *Phi Delta Kappan* 71.9 (June 1990): 753–58.

Kohn, Hans. *The Idea of Nationalism: A Study in Its Origins and Background.* New York: Collier Books, 1944.

Kraemer, Dagmar, and Manfred Stassen. *Europe in U.S. Social Studies: Textbooks and Teaching Materials. A Study for the German Marshall Fund of the United States.* Fall 1991.

Kramer, Jane. "Letter from Europe." *The New Yorker,* 12 March 1990: 74–90.

———. "Letter from Europe." *The New Yorker,* 14 January 1991: 60–75.

Kristof, Nicholas D. "Where Gengis Khan Is In." *New York Times Magazine,* 27 May 1990: 21.

Kristol, Irving. "Taking Political Things Personally." *TLS,* 1 March 1991: 5.

Krug, Edward A. *The Shaping of the American High School 1880–1920,* Vol. 1. Madison: Univ. of Wisconsin Press, 1969.

———. *The Shaping of the American High School 1920–1941,* Vol. 2. Madison: Univ. of Wisconsin Press., 1972.

Labov, William. *Language in the Inner City: Studies in the Black English Vernacular.* Philadelphia: Univ. of Pennsylvania Press, 1972.

Lambert, Richard D., ed. *Foreign Language Instruction: A National Agenda.* The Annals of the American Academy of Political and Social Science , Vol. 490, March 1987.

Lauter, Paul. *Canons and Contexts.* New York: Oxford Univ. Press, 1991.

Lawton, Millicent. "2 Schools Aimed for Black Males. Set in Milwaukee: Critics Raise Moral and Legal Questions." *Education Week,* 10 October 1990: 1.

Leake, Donald, and Brenda Leake. "African-American Immersion Schools in Milwaukee: A View from Inside." *Phi Delta Kappan* 73.9 (June 1992): 783–85.

Leathes, Stanley. *The Teaching of English at the Universities.* Pamphlet 26. London: The English Association, 1913.

LeMahieu, Paul G. and Richard Sterling. *CHARTing Educational Reform: An Interim Report of Evaluations of the Collaboratives for Humanities and Arts Teaching.* Philadelphia: CHART, 1991.

LeMahieu, Paul G., and Richard C. Wallace. "Up Against the Wall: Psychometrics Meets Praxis." *Educational Measurement: Issues and Practice* 5.1 (Spring 1986): 12–16.

Leo, John. "A Fringe History of the World." *U.S. News and World Report,* 12 November 1990: 25.

Levine, Arthur. "A Time to Act." *Change* (January/February, 1992): 4–5.

Levine, Marsha, ed. *Professional Practice Schools: Building a Model.* Vol. 2. American Federation of Teachers: Centers for Restructuring, June, 1990.

Lindberg, Stanley W. *The Annotated McGuffey.* New York: Van Nostrand Reinhold, 1976.

The Literacies Institute: Its Mission, Activities and Perspective on Literacy. Technical Report No. 1. Newton, Mass.: Education Development Center, September, 1989.

Lynch, James. *The Multicultural Curriculum.* London: Batsford Academic and Educational, 1983.

McCarthy, Martha M. "The Changing Federal Role in Bilingual Education." *Journal of Educational Equity and Leadership* 6.1 (Spring 1986): 73–79.

McCrea, Brian. *Addison and Steele Are Dead: The English Department, Its Canon, and the Professionalization of Literary Criticism.* Cranbury, N.J.: Associated University Presses, 1990.

McGuffey, William Holmes. *The Eclectic Fourth Reader.* Cincinnati: Truman and Smith, 1838.

———. *Rhetorical Guide; or Fifth Reader of the Ecletic Series.* Cincinnati: Sargent, Wilson and Hinkle, 1853.

———. *McGuffey's New Third Eclectic Reader.* Cincinnati: Wilson, Hinkle and Company, 1865.

———. *McGuffey's Third Eclectic Reader.* Cincinnati: American Book Company, 1879.

———. *McGuffey's Fourth Eclectic Reader.* Cincinnati: Van Antwerp and Company, 1879.

———. *McGuffey's Alternate Second Reader.* Cincinnati: American Book Company, 1889.

———. *The New McGuffey Second Reader.* Cincinnati: American Book Company, 1901.

———. *The New McGuffey Third Reader.* Cincinnati: American Book Company, 1901.

———. *The New McGuffey Fourth Reader.* Cincinnati: American Book Company, 1901.

———. *McGuffey's Fourth Eclectic Reader.* Cincinnati: American Book Company, 1920.

———. *McGuffey's Fifth Eclectic Reader.* Cincinnati: American Book Company, 1920.

———. *McGuffey's Sixth Eclectic Reader.* Cincinnati: American Book Company, 1921.

McNeil, William H. "Colleges Must Revitalize the Teaching and Study of World History." *Chronicle of Higher Education,* 8 August 1990: A36.

Madrid, Arturo, ed. *English Plus: Issues in Bilingual Education.* Vol. 508. *The Annals of the American Academy of Political and Social Science* (March 1990).

Magner, Denise K. "Minority Update." *Chronicle of Higher Education,* 19 December 1990: A26.

Marcus, George E., and Michael M. J. Fischer. *Anthropology as Cultural Critique: An Experimental Moment in the Human Sciences.* Chicago: Univ. of Chicago Press, 1986.

Martel, Erich. "How Valid Are The Portland Baseline Essays?" *Educational Leadership* 49.4 (December 1991/January 1992): 20–23.

Mazrui, Ali. *Cultural Forces in World Politics.* Portsmouth, N.H.: Heinemann, 1990.

Mazrui, Ali A. *The Political Sociology of the English Language: An African Perspective.* The Hague: Mouton and Company, 1975.

Mazrui, Ali A., and Pio Zirinu. "Church, State and Marketplace in the Spread of Kiswahili: Comparative

Educational Implications." In *Case Studies in Bilingual Education*. Eds. Bernard Spolsky and Robert L. Cooper. Rowley, Mass.: Newbury House Publishers, 1978: 427–53.

Menand, Louis. "Illiberalisms." *The New Yorker*, 20 May 1991: 101–07.

Merriam, Allen H. "Literature as Window: Developing Interracial Understanding through Fiction." *Journal of Black Studies* 19.1 (September 1988): 61–69.

Meyer, Adolphe E. *An Educational History of the American People*. New York: McGraw-Hill Book Company, 1957.

Minnich, Harvey C. *William Holmes McGuffey and the Peerless Pioneer McGuffey Readers*. Miami University Bulletin Series XXVI.11 (July 1928).

Mitchell, Henry H. *Black Preaching*. Philadelphia: J.B. Lippincott Company, 1970.

Modern Language Association. Executive Council. *Statement on the Curriculum Debate*. New York: Modern Language Association, May 1991.

Mosier, Richard D. *The American Temper: Patterns of Our Intellectual Heritage*. Berkeley: Univ. of California Press, 1952.

———. *Making the American Mind: Social and Moral Ideas in the McGuffey Readers*. New York: Russell and Russell, 1965.

Mosteller, Frederick, and Daniel P. Moynihan, eds. *On Equality of Educational Opportunity: Papers Deriving from the Harvard University Faculty Seminar on the Coleman Report*. New York: Random House, 1972.

Muhly, James D. "Black Athena Versus Traditional Scholarship." *Journal of Mediterranean Archeology* 3/1 (March 1990): 83–110.

———. "Preface." *Journal of Mediterranean Archeology* 3/1 (March 1990): 53–55.

Murchland, Bernard. *The Mind of Mamardashvili*. Dayton: The Kettering Foundation, 1991.

Murphy, Anna Marie, and Cullen Murphy. "Onward, Upward with McGuffey and Those Readers." *Smithsonian* 15 (November 1984): 182–208.

Murray, Frank B., and Daniel Fallon. *The Reform of Teacher Education for the 21st Century: Project 30 Year One Report*. N.p.: Univ. of Delaware, n.d., [1990].

Murray, Oswyn. "Sovereignty for All?" *TLS*, 25 October 1991: 8.

Nasaw, David. *Schooled to Order: A Social History of Public Schooling in the United States*. New York: Oxford Univ. Press, 1979.

Nash, Gary B. *Red, White, and Black: The Peoples of Early America*. Englewood Cliffs, N.J.: Prentice-Hall, 1974.

National Association of Scholars. "Is the Curriculum Biased? A Statement of the National Association of Scholars." *The New Republic*, 14 May 1990: 31.

———. "The Wrong Way to Reduce Campus Tensions." *Chronicle of Higher Education*, 24 April 1991: A15.

National Commission on Social Studies in the Schools. *Charting a Course: Social Studies for the 21st Century*. Washington, D.C., 1989.

———. *Voices of Teachers: Report of a Survey on Social Studies*. Dubuque: Kendall/Hunt Publishing Company, 1991.

National Council for the Social Studies. Task Force on Ethnic Studies. *Curriculum Guidelines for Multicultural*

Education. Washington, D.C.:
National Council for the Social
Studies, 1992.

Newmann, Fred. *Linking Restructuring
to Authentic Student Achievement.*
Indiana University Annual Education Conference, Bloomington, 11
April 1990.

New Mexico State Board of Education.
*Consolidating Initiatives for
Tomorrow's Education (CITE) Plan.*
Santa Fe: New Mexico State Board of
Education, September 1990.

New Republic, The. "A Special Issue:
Race on Campus." 18 February
1991.

Nietz, John A. *Old Textbooks: Spelling,
Grammar, Reading, Arithmetic,
Geography, American History, Civil
Government, Physiology, Penman-
ship, Art, Music as Taught in the
Common Schools from Colonial Days
to 1900.* Pittsburgh: Pittsburgh Univ.
Press, 1961.

————. *The Evolution of American Secondary School Textbooks.* Rutland,
Vt.: Charles E. Tuttle Company,
1966.

Nordhouse, Mary. "Let There Be
Change in Schools and Let It Begin
With Me: A Report on the 1990 New
Mexico Academy for School
Leaders." N.p.: University of New
Mexico Bureau of Educational Plan-
ning and Development, March 1991.

Novick, Peter. *That Noble Dream: The
"Objectivity Question" and the Amer-
ican Historical Profession.* New York:
Cambridge Univ. Press, 1988.

Nussbaum, Martha. "Virtue Revived:
Habit, Passion, Reflection in the
Aristotelian Tradition." *TLS,* 3 July
1992: 9–11.

Oakes, Jeannie, and Martin Lipton.
Making the Best of Schools. New
Haven: Yale Univ. Press, 1990.

Oakes, Jeannie, Mollie Selvin, Lynn
Karoly, and Gretchen Guiton. *Educational Matchmaking: Academic
and Vocational Tracking in Comprehensive High Schools.* Berkeley:
National Center for Research in
Vocational Education, 1992.

————. *Keeping Track: How Schools
Structure Inequality.* New Haven:
Yale Univ. Press, 1985.

Ogbu, John U. "Cultural Diversity and
School Experience." In *Literacy as
Praxis: Culture, Language, and Pedagogy.* Ed. Catherine E. Walsh. Norwood, N.J.: ABLEX, 1991.

————. *Minority Education and Caste:
The American System in Cross-
Cultural Perspective.* New York: Aca-
demic Press, 1978.

————. "Minority Education in Comparative Perspective." *Journal of Negro
Education* 59.1 (Winter 1990): 45–57.

————. "Minority Status and Literacy
in Comparative Perspective." *Daed-
alus* 119.2 (Spring 1990): 141–68.

Ohanian, Susan. "Classroom Structures
That Really Count." *Education Week,*
2 December 1992: 18–20.

Olneck, Michael R. "Americanization
and the Education of Immigrants,
1990–1925: An Analysis of Symbolic
Action." *American Journal of Education* 97.8 (August 1989): 398–423.

————. "The Recurring Dream: Symbolism and Ideology in Intercultural
and Multicultural Education."
American Journal of Education 98.2
(February 1990): 147–74.

Olneck, Michael R., and Marvin Lazerson. "Education." *Harvard Encyclopedia of American Ethnic Groups.*
Cambridge: The Belknap Press of
Harvard Univ. Press, 1980.

"Opening Academia Without Closing It
Down." *New York Times,* 9 December
1990: E5.

Organization of American Historians. "Historians State Position on Educational Changes." (February 1991).

Our Voices Our Vision: American Indians Speak Out for Educational Excellence. The College Board and American Indian Science and Engineering Society, 1989.

Parsons, Talcott. "The Distribution of Power in American Society." *World Politics* X.1 (October 1957): 123–43.

Paz, Octavio. "In Search of the Present." Trans. Anthony Stanton. *TLS,* 21–27 December 1990: 1374.

———. *The Labyrinth of Solitude.* Trans. Lysander Kemp, Yara Milos, and Rachel Phillips Belash. New York: Grove Press, 1985.

Pepper, Simon. "In Imitation of Castile." *TLS,* 5 July 1991: 17.

Pew Higher Education Research Program. *Policy Perspectives* 4.2.C (Philadelphia: The Pew Charitable Trusts, March 1992).

Pfaff, William. "Reflections: The Absence of Empire." *The New Yorker,* 10 August 1992: 59–69.

Pfordresher, John. "Better and Different Literature in Our Time." *Perspective* 3.2 (Summer 1991): 1–16.

Phillips, June K. "Language and Instruction in the United States: Policy and Planning." In *New Perspectives and New Directions.* Ed. Diane W. Birckbichler. Lindenwood, Ill.: National Textbook Company, 1990: 45–75.

Pine, Gerald J., and Asa G. Hilliard III. "Rx for Racism: Imperatives for America's Schools." *Phi Delta Kappan* 71.8 (April 1990): 593–600.

Porter, Rosalie Pedalino. "The False Alarm Over Early English Acquisition." *Education Week,* 5 June 1991: 36.

———. *Forked Tongue: The Politics of Bilingual Education.* New York: Basic Books, 1990.

President's Commission on Foreign Language and International Studies. *Strength Through Wisdom, a Critique of U.S. Capability.* Washington, D.C.: USGPO, 1979.

Pressman, Harvey, and Alan Gartner. "The New Racism in Education." *Social Policy* 17.1 (Summer 1986): 11–15.

Quay, James, and James Veninza. *Making Connections: The Humanities, Culture and Community.* American Council of Learned Societies, Occasional Paper, No. 11, 1990.

QEM Network. "Multicultural Education." *Background, Issues, and Action Paper.* I.2 (4 March 1991).

Ravitch, Diane. "Diversity and Democracy: Multicultural Education in America." *American Educator* 26.2 (Spring 1990): 16–20, 46–48.

———. "Multiculturalism in the Curriculum." *Network News and Views.* Vanderbilt University Institute for Public Policy Studies: The Educational Excellence Network, IX.3 (March 1990): 1–11.

———. "Multiculturalism Redux." *Network News and Views.* Vanderbilt University Institute for Public Policy Studies: The Educational Excellence Network, IX.10 (October 1990): 77–81.

———. "Multiculturalism Yes, Particularism No." *Chronicle of Higher Education,* 24 October 1990: A44.

———. *The Troubled Crusade: American Education, 1945–1980.* New York: Basic Books, 1983.

———, ed. *The American Reader: Words That Moved a Nation.* New York: Harper Collins, 1990.

Raymond, Chris. "Global Migration Will Have Widespread Impact on Society, Scholars Say." *Chronicle of Higher Education,* September 1990: A1.

"Religion in America." *Education Week,* 24 April 1991: 3.

Rényi, Judith. *First Seminar on Education for a Diverse Society.* Philadelphia: CHART, 7–8 January 1991.

Rényi, Judith, ed. *A Greater Voice for Africa in the Schools: A Report Prepared for the Rockefeller Foundation.* Philadelphia: CHART, July 1990.

"Reports of Attempted Censorship Reach 10-Year High, Survey Finds." *Education Week,* 16 September 1992: 2.

Resnick, Lauren B. "The 1987 Presidential Address: Learning in School and Out." *Educational Researcher* 16.9 (December 1987): 13–20.

Retamar, Roberto Fernandez. *Caliban and Other Essays.* Minneapolis: Univ. of Minnesota Press, 1989.

Ricoeur, Paul. *Time and Narrative.* Vol. 3. Trans. Kathleen Blamey and David Pellauer. Chicago: Univ. of Chicago Press, 1988.

Romaine, Suzanne. *Bilingualism.* New York: Basil Blackwell, 1989.

———. "The More Monoglot the Better." *TLS,* 31 May 1991: 8.

Rosaldo, Renato. "We don't want to throw out the Great Books, though William Bennett seems to think we do." *Chronicle of Higher Education,* 5 September 1990: B7.

Rose, Mike. *Lives on the Boundary: The Struggles and Achievements of America's Underprepared.* New York: The Free Press, 1989.

Rothman, Robert. "Group to Promote Multicultural Science Education." *Education Week,* 18 April 1990: 5.

———. "Students Read Little In or Out of School, NAEP Survey Finds." *Education Week,* 3 June 1992: 1.

Rotman, Brian. "The Grand Hotel and the Shopping Mall." Review of *Uncommon Cultures: Popular Culture and Post-Modernism,* by Jim Collins. *TLS,* 6–12 April 1990: 379.

Said, Edward W. "Empire of Sand." *The Guardian Weekend,* 12–13 January 1991: 4–7.

———. "The Politics of Knowledge." *Raritan XI* (Summer 1991): 17–31.

———. "Representing the Colonized: Anthropology's Interlocutors." *Critical Inquiry* 15 (Winter 1989): 205–25.

Salemi, Joseph S. "The Imaginary Canon." *Social Studies Review: A Bulletin of the American Textbook Council* 6 (Fall 1990): 12–14.

Samuda, Ronald J., John W. Berry, and Michael Laferriere. *Multiculturalism in Canada.* Toronto: Allyn and Bacon, 1984.

Saunders, D. A. "Social Ideas in McGuffey Readers." *Public Opinion Quarterly* 5 (Winter 1941): 579–89.

Schlesinger, Arthur M., Jr. *The Disuniting of America.* N.p.: Whittle Direct Books, 1991.

"Schools Report Progress in Assessing Limited-English-Proficient Students." *Education Week,* 18 April 1990: 1.

Schubert, William H. *Curriculum: Perspective, Paradigm, and Possibility.* New York: Macmillan Publishing Company, 1986.

Scruton, Roger. "The Myth of Cultural Relativism." In *Anti-Racism: An Assault on Education and Value.* Ed. Frank Palmer. London: The Sherwood Press, 1986.

SEF News. Southern Education Foundation, April 1990.

Seton-Watson, Hugh. *Nations and States: An Enquiry into the Origins of Nations and the Politics of Nationalism.* Boulder, Colo.: Westview Press, 1977.

Sewall, Gilbert T. "California: The Story Continues." *Social Studies Review: A*

Bulletin of the American Textbook Council 6 (Fall 1990): 10–12.

Shanker, Albert. "Where We Stand: Afrocentric Education." *New York Times,* 31 March 1991: E9.

———. "Where We Stand: America, the Multicultural." *New York Times,* 17 February 1991: E7.

———. "Where We Stand: Literacy Requires Learning the Culture." *New York Times,* 4 August 1985: E7.

———. "Where We Stand: Multicultural and Global Education: Value Free?" *New York Times,* 6 January 1991: E7.

———. "Where We Stand: Textbooks Tell America's Story . . . Half Right." *New York Times,* 1 October 1989: E7.

Shapiro, Bruce. "Rad-Baiting Comes to Brookline." *The Nation,* 21 May 1990: 706–09.

Short, Thomas. " 'Diversity' and 'Breaking the Disciplines': Two New Assaults on the Curriculum." *Academic Questions* 1.3 (Summer 1988): 6–29.

Sigel, Roberta S., and Marilyn Hoskin, eds. *Education for Democratic Citizenship: A Challenge for Multi-Ethnic Societies.* Hillsdale, N.J.: Lawrence Erlbaum Associates, 1991.

Simonson, Rick, and Scott Walker, eds. *The Graywolf Annual Five: Multicultural Literacy.* Saint Paul, Minn.: Graywolf Press, 1988.

Skutnabb-Kangas, T., and J. Cummins, eds. *Minority Education: From Shame to Struggles.* Clevedon and Philadelphia: Multilingual Matters, 1988.

Sleeter, Christine E. "Staff Development for Desegregated Schooling." *Phi Delta Kappan* 72.1 (September 1990): 33–40.

Sleeter, Christine E., and Carl A. Grant. "An Analysis of Multicultural Education in the United States." *Harvard Educational Review* 57.4 (November 1987): 421–44.

Smith, Barbara Herrnstein. *Contingencies of Value: Alternative Perspectives for Critical Theory.* Cambridge: Harvard Univ. Press, 1988.

Smith, Frank. "Learning to Read: The Never-Ending Debate." *Phi Delta Kappan* 74.6 (February 1992): 432–41.

Smith, Timothy L. "Protestant Schooling and American Nationality, 1800–1850." *Journal of American History* 53.4 (March 1967): 679–95.

Snowden, Frank M., Jr. "Bernal's 'Blacks,' Herodotus, and Other Classical Evidence." *Arethusa* (Fall 1989): 83–93.

Social Studies Review: A Bulletin of the American Textbook Council 5 (Summer 1990).

Social Studies Review: A Bulletin of the American Textbook Council 7 (Winter 1991).

Social Studies Review: A Bulletin of the American Textbook Council 9 (Summer 1991).

Social Studies Review: A Bulletin of the American Textbook Council 10 (Fall 1991).

Spengemen, William C. "American Things/Literary Things: The Problem of American Literary History." *American Literature* 57.3 (October 1985): 456–81.

Spolsky, Bernard, and Robert L. Coopers, eds. *Case Studies in Bilingual Education.* Rowley, Mass.: Newbury House Publishers, 1978.

Spring, Joel. *American Education: An Introduction to Social and Political Aspects.* New York: Longman, 1978.

———. *Conflict of Interest: The Politics of American Education.* New York: Longman, 1988.

———. *The American School 1642–1985: Varieties of Historical Interpretation of the Foundations and Development of American Education.* New York: Longman, 1986.

Stankiewicz, Mary Ann. "Beauty in Design and Pictures: Idealism and Aesthetic Education." *The Journal of Aesthetic Education* 21.4 (Winter 1987): 63–76.

———. " 'The Eye is a Nobler Organ': Ruskin and American Art Education." *The Journal of Aesthetic Education* 18.2 (Summer 1984): 51–64.

Steele, Shelby. *The Content of Our Character: A New Vision of Race in America.* New York: St. Martin's Press, 1990.

Stein, Colman Brez, Jr. *Sink or Swim: The Politics of Bilingual Education.* New York: Praeger Publishers, 1986.

Stewner-Manzanares, Gloria. "The Bilingual Education Act: Twenty Years Later." *Focus.* Washington, D.C.: The National Clearinghouse for Bilingual Education Occasional Papers in Bilingual Education, Fall 1988.

Stone, Lawrence, ed. *Schooling and Society: Studies in the History of Education.* Baltimore: Johns Hopkins Univ. Press, 1976.

Stotsky, Sandra. "Whose Literature? America's!" *Educational Leadership* 49.4 (December 1991/January 1992): 53–56.

Strouse, Joan. "Continuing Themes in Assimilation Through Education." *Equity and Excellence* 22.1–2 (Spring 1987): 105–13.

Sullivan, Andrew. "Racism 101." *The New Republic,* 26 November 1990: 18–21.

Summary of SB 539 (Act 76) "English Fluency in Higher Education Act." Pennsylvania State Senate. 9 July 1990.

Takaki, Ronald. *Strangers from a Different Shore.* New York: Penguin, 1989.

Taylor, John. "Are You Politically Correct?" *New York,* 21 January 1991: 32–40.

Teitelbaum, Herbert, et. al. *Changing Schools: The Language Minority Student in the Eighties.* Washington D.C.: Center for Applied Linguistics, 1982.

"This is Your Life, Generally Speaking: A Statistical Portrait of the 'Typical' American." *New York Times,* 26 July 1992: E5.

Thompson, Paul. "Learning and the Fear of Learning." Review of *Literacy and Popular Culture: England 1750–1914,* by David Vincent. *TLS,* 16 March 1990: 294.

Tölölyan, Khachig. "The Nation-State and Its Others: In Lieu of a Preface." *Diaspora: A Journal of Transnational Studies* (Spring 1991): 3–7.

Troyna, Barry. "Beyond Multiculturalism: Towards the Enactment of Anti-Racist Education in Policy, Provision and Pedagogy." *Oxford Review of Education* 13.3 (1987): 307–20.

Tumin, Melvin M., and Walter Plotch. *Pluralism in a Democratic Society.* Praeger Special Studies in U.S. Economic, Social, and Political Issues. New York: Praeger Publishers, 1977.

Tyack, David. "Forming the National Character." *Harvard Educational Review* 36.1 (Winter 1966): 29–41.

———. *The One Best System: A History of American Urban Education.* Cambridge: Harvard Univ. Press, 1974.

———. ed. *Turning Points in American Educational History.* Lexington, Mass.: Xerox College Publishing, 1967.

Tye, Kenneth A. *Global Education: From Thought to Action.* N.p.: Association for Supervision and Curriculum Development, 1991.

Tyson-Bernstein, Harriet. *A Conspiracy of Good Intentions: America's Textbook Fiasco.* Washington, D.C.: The Council for Basic Education, 1988.

United States Department of Education. *America 2000.* Washington, D.C.: 1 September 1991–. *Community Update.* April 1993–.

———. *The Condition of Bilingual Education in the Nation: A Report to the Congress and the President.* Washington, D.C.: Office of the Secretary, June 1991.

———. *The Condition of Bilingual Education in the Nation: A Report to the Congress and the President.* Washington, D.C.: Office of the Secretary, June 1992.

———. Office of Educational Research and Improvement. *Early American Textbooks 1775–1900: A Catalog of the Titles Held by the Educational Research Library.* Washington, D.C.: USDOE, 1985.

The University Art Museum. *The Go-Betweens: The Lives of Immigrant Children.* Minneapolis: Univ. of Minnesota, 1986.

"Urban Schools' Group Adopts Six National Goals." *Education Week,* 28 March 1990: 5.

Van Alstyne, R. W. *The Rising American Empire.* New York: Oxford Univ. Press, 1960.

Venezky, Richard L. "From the Indian Primer to Dick and Jane." Introduction to *American Primers: Guide to the Microfiche Collection.* Bethesda, Md.: University Publications of America, 1990.

Verma, Gojendra K. *Education for All: A Landmark in Pluralism.* London: The Falmer Press, 1989.

Viadero, Debra. "Afro-Centric Study Boosts Performance by Black Students, Researcher Finds." *Education Week,* 14 November 1990: 6.

———. "Battle Over Multicultural Education Rises in Intensity." *Education Week,* 28 November 1990: 1.

———. "Dropout Rates for 5 States." *Education Week,* 23 September 1992: 24.

———. "In Two Years Since California Adoption, Record Mixed for Firm's History Texts." *Education Week,* 4 November 1992: 16.

———. "N.Y. Regents Weigh Report on 'Multicultural' Curiculum." *Education Week,* 31 July 1991: 35.

———. "Notion of 'Literary Canon' in Schools not Valid, Report Says." *Education Week,* 5 December 1990: 5.

———. "Over Protests California Board Adopts History Textbooks." *Education Week,* 24 October 1990: 18.

———. "Researcher Sees Reason for Optimism in Social-Studies Texts." *Education Week,* 18 March 1992: 6–7.

Vogel, Morris. *Cultural Connections: Museums and Libraries of Philadelphia and the Delaware Valley.* Philadelphia: Temple Univ. Press, 1991.

Walker, Galal. "Gaining Place: The Less Commonly Taught Languages in American Schools." *Foreign Language Annals* 24.2 (April 1991): 131–50.

Walker, Reagan. "School Built by Mississippi Indian Tribe 'Breaks New Ground.'" *Education Week,* 24 October 1990: 11.

Weber, Eugen. "Imagined Communities." *TLS,* 26 October–1 November 1990: 1149.

Weinberg, Meyer. *A Chance to Learn: The History of Race and Education in the United States.* New York: Cambridge Univ. Press, 1977.

Weiner, Annette B. "Anthropology's Lessons for Cultural Diversity." *Chronicle of Higher Education*, 22 July 1992: B1–2.

Wellesley College Center for Research on Women. *How Schools Shortchange Girls: A Study of Major Findings on Girls and Education.* Washington, D.C.: AAUW Educational Foundation and National Education Association, 1992.

Welter, Rush. *Popular Education and Democratic Thought in America.* New York: Columbia Univ. Press, 1962.

Wescott, Siobhan Maureen. "Educate to Americanize: Captain Pratt and Early Indian Education." *Change* 23.2 (March/April 1991): 45–46.

West, Cornel. "Learning to Talk of Race." *New York Times Magazine*, 2 August 1992: 26.

———. *Prophetic Fragments.* Grand Rapids, Mich.: William B. Eerdmans Publishing Company, 1988.

West, Peter. "Federal Officials See a 'Ray of Hope' for Indian Education." *Education Week*, 24 October 1990: 11.

———. "Law Encourages Schools to Use Indian Languages." *Education Week*, 7 November 1990: 20.

———. "Proposal to Restructure B.I.A. Draws Cool Response from Indian Leaders." *Education Week*, 5 December 1990: 20.

Westerhoff, John H. *McGuffey and His Readers.* Nashville: Abingdon, 1978.

Weyr, Thomas. *Hispanic U.S.A., Breaking the Melting Pot.* New York: Harper and Row, 1988.

Whitfield, Stephen J. "A Question of Character." *American Quarterly* 41.4 (December 1989): 724–28.

Wilson, William Julius. *The Truly Disadvantaged: The Inner City, the Underclass, and Public Policy.* Chicago: Univ. of Chicago Press, 1987.

Winkler, Karen J. "Proponents of 'Multicultural' Humanities Research Call for a Critical Look at Its Achievements." *Chronicle of Higher Education*, 28 November 1990: A5.

Wolf, Dennis Palmer, and Nancy Pistone. "Performances of Thought: The Work Towards Excellence in the Arts."

Wolf, Eric R. *Europe and the People Without History.* Berkeley: Univ. of California Press, 1982.

Wong, Jennifer. "Conservative Scholars See 'Multiculturalism' as a Plague." *Chronicle of Higher Education*, 19 September 1990: A40.

Woodson, Carter Godwin. *The Miseducation of the Negro.* Washington, D.C.: The Associated Publishers, 1933.

Yeakey, Carol Camp, and Clifford T. Bennett. "Race, Schooling, and Class in American Society." *Journal of Negro Education* 59.1 (Winter 1990): 3–18.

Yurco, Frank J. "An Evaluation of the Portland Social Studies Baseline Essay." In *News and Views.* Washington, D.C.: Education Excellence Network, n.d.: 21–26.

———. Review of *Kemet, Afrocentricity and Knowledge*, by Molefi Asante. 1990.

Zimet, Sara Goodman. *What Children Read in School: Critical Analysis of Primary Reading Texts.* New York: Grune Stratton, 1972.

INDEX

Perot, H. Ross, 73

Philadelphia National Gazette, 100

Philip II (king), 49

Phillips Exeter Academy, 132, 176

Pilgrim's Progress (Bunyan), 47, 48

Pine, Gerald, 180

Plessy v. *Ferguson,* 175

Poland, 186

Politics (Aristotle), 114

Pope, Alexander, 96, 104, 219

Popper, Karl, 200

Prayer, school, 97, 227–28

Presbyterians, 48, 50, 66, 111, 175

President's Commission on Foreign Language and International Studies, 141, 163

Protestantism, 19, 25–27, 43–55 *passim,* 66–68, 103, 144, 175, 190, 231, 242; and Afrocentrism, 183; and anti-Catholicism, 71; and the Bible, 47, 48, 92–99 *passim,* 117; and Britain, 47–49; and the common-school movement, 44–45; ethic of, 175; and martyrs, 95, 99; and nationalism, 55, 97, 115, 204–5; and the "school canon," 105. *See also* Reformation

Public Education Funds, 206–7

Puerto Rico, 105, 138, 156, 158

Puritans, 47–50, 63, 66, 92, 94, 97, 105; as "benevolent founders," 49; in *Silas Marner,* 103

Quakers, 194

Queen of Spain, 35, 40

Raleigh, Walter, 49

Ravitch, Diane, 70, 180, 185, 260*n*19, 261*n*30

Reagan, Ronald, 141, 142

Reformation, 19, 53, 71, 112; Counter-, 94; democratizing influence of, 208; printing centers since, 125; study of, and the Bradley group, 79

Renaissance, 19, 36–37, 43, 51–53, 92; England during, 49; language exper-

imentation during, 125; study of, and the Bradley group, 79

Richelieu (cardinal), 126

Rockefeller, John D., 63

Romanticism, 21, 47, 63, 116, 129, 145; and Afrocentrism, 186; and art, 224–25; and the "cult of the people," 77–78, 145; and heroism, 70, 73; and a Manichaean view of history, 84; and nationalism, 47, 53–56, 92, 97, 125, 126, 175; and racial theories, 21–22, 55–56, 69, 84, 92

Roman tradition, 36, 40, 79, 94, 106, 175, 183; and the "Fall of Rome", 43, 47; and "honorary Englishmen," 51–53; and serfdom, 55–56. *See also* Holy Roman Empire

Roosevelt, Theodore, 142, 176

Roots (Haley), 74

Royal and Pontifical University, 41

Russia, 55. *See also* Soviet Union

Sabbath, 98

St. Jerome, 51

St. Paul, 188

San Marcos University, 41

Scarlet Letter, The (Hawthorne), 104, 242, 243

Schiller, Friedrich von, 97, 107

Schlegel brothers, 54, 97

Schlesinger, Arthur, Jr., 77–78, 79

Scholastic Aptitude Test (SAT), 16, 104, 178

Schurz, Carl, 33

Second Eclectic Reader, 68

Segregation, 13–14, 175–77, 184

Sewall, Gilbert, 185

Shakespeare, William, 20, 54, 90, 96, 97, 102–3, 107, 164, 196

Shanker, Albert, 260*n*19

Silas Marner (Eliot), 103, 104

Simon, Paul, 166

Skinner, B. F., 151

Slave Community, The (Blassingame), 181

Smith, Barbara Herrnstein, 237, 240–41, 242